Directory Services

Directory Services

Design, Implementation, and Management

Nancy Cox
Editor

Digital Press
An imprint of Butterworth-Heinemann

Boston • Oxford • Auckland • Johannesburg • Melbourne • New Delhi

Copyright © 2002 Butterworth–Heinemann

 A member of the Reed Elsevier group

∞ Recognizing the importance of preserving what has been written, Butterworth–Heinemann
prints its books on acid-free paper whenever possible.

Library of Congress Cataloging-in-Publication Data

Directory services : design, implementation, and management / Nancy Cox, editor.
    p. cm.
    Includes index.
    ISBN 1-55558-262-1 (pbk. : alk paper)
      1. Directory services (Computer network technology) I. Cox, Nancy, 1950–

    TK5105.595 .D57 2002
    005.7'1376—dc21   2001052954

British Library Cataloguing-in-Publication Data

A catalogue record for this book is available from the British Library.

The publisher offers special discounts on bulk orders of this book.
For information, please contact:

Manager of Special Sales
Butterworth–Heinemann
225 Wildwood Avenue
Woburn, MA 01801-2041
Tel: 781-904-2500
Fax: 781-904-2620

For information on all Butterworth–Heinemann publications available, contact our
World Wide Web home page at: http://www.bh.com.

Printed and bound in the United Kingdom
Transferred to Digital Printing, 2011

Dedications

Nancy Cox—To my sons, Jason and Chris.

Jan De Clercq—To my wife, Katrien, and my son, Johannes.

Micky Balladelli—To my dear children, Alexandre and Manon.

Mark W. Foust—To those who would seek to learn from others' experiences.

Curtis M. Sawyer—To my wife, Cheryl, for always being there.

Bob Johnson—To my wife; yes, dear, those last few pages are *finally* finished.

Alexis Bor—To the love of my life, my wife Cheraya, who has always been supportive in all of my excitement, late nights on the computer, and frequent travels in pursuit of my passion for directory—even though to this day she still can't explain to our friends what I really do for a living. And, of course, to our children, Sarah, Seth, Olga, Nadya, Valyentyna, Sveta, Masha, Ekateryna, and Krestyna, who have brought such immense joy into our lives.

Contents

Foreword

Electronic directories have been the cornerstone and the curse of IT departments for longer than most of us can remember. In the early 1980s, most company directories were based on the mainframe and life was straightforward. With the proliferation of local area networks during the late 1980s, each new messaging system and network operating system came with its own custom-built address book or registry. The standards bodies that were working to create the X.400 series of standards for electronic mail soon realized that a set of standards for the underlying directory infrastructure was also required, and the X.500 series was born.

If the vision of X.500, as envisaged more than ten years ago, had been flawless and timeless, it *might* have been universally adopted by now and we would have a mix of service providers and major businesses supporting a global directory service for e-mail, security services, and other popular directory-based applications. The reasons why X.500 did not become pervasive were reflected in two trends that originated in the mid-1990s:

- LDAP was widely adopted as both an access mechanism for clients and an API for developers, primarily because it is relatively easy to implement and simple to deploy; and

- Metadirectory concepts were developed to address the core issues that were lacking in the existing standards; notably, how information about people and resources is managed across multiple, diverse directory and database systems found in most medium-to-large businesses.

Despite their initial popularity, both LDAP and metadirectory have taken much longer than expected to gain critical mass. But in the last two years, "killer" applications and services have emerged, making the justification for directory deployments much easier than before.

- *Security*—The explosion of portals and web applications mandate authentication and authorization requests, which in turn require an identity and resource infrastructure, typically supplied by a directory service, to facilitate various access mechanisms;

- *Provisioning*—Companies have long recognized the value of more efficiently creating accounts and access rights for new users across a company's applications, mail systems, and hardware platforms. Once an employee leaves a company, those privileges have to be removed. Referred to as "hire and fire," there are a number of vendors now offering provisioning tools to solve these scenarios, which again use the directory for storing identity and access information.

Looking at the industry landscape today, it almost appears as if the wheel has turned full circle. Although the vision of a global, distributed X.500 infrastructure has faded, it is rapidly being replaced with one based on a new set of requirements driven by the very dynamic forces of e-business. The efforts of all those involved in directory services over the last ten to fifteen years are finally bearing fruit.

David Goodman
CMO, Metamerge
www.metamerge.com

Preface

What makes this book different?

Directory Services provides practical technical, operational, and business advice on how to design, build, and manage today's key enabling technology within a large, global enterprise. Written by authors who are consultants and considered experts in their fields, for the first time, under one cover, this comprehensive book:

- Covers all major directories

- Provides critical information for the design, management, and migration of multiple directory platforms and metadirectory services

- Provides case studies and guidelines for deployment and integration issues

- Explores directory's historical perspective and makes predictions on future trends and emerging directory technology

Directory Services is an all-encompassing and practical guide that provides organizations and consultants with a road map to create the directory-enabled global enterprise. I found the information contained in this book fundamentally relevant in my work with a Fortune 100 organization where I managed the implementation of a metadirectory service linking five different directories to provide account provisioning for over 55,000 employees. To optimally design a directory service, the reader is privy to an in-depth review of current state-of-the-art products, including Novell's NDS eDirectory; Microsoft's Active Directory; UNIX directories; and products by iPlanet, NEXOR, Siemens, Critical Path, Radiant Logic, eTrust, and others. Directory design fundamentals and products are then woven into case studies of large enterprise deployments written by users and consultants with current field experience. Pivotal components of any directory implementation, such as replication, security, migration, and legacy system integration and interoperability, are thoroughly explored. Business issues, such as how to cost-justify, plan, budget, and manage a directory project are also included. The book culminates in a visionary discussion of future trends and emerging directory technologies, including what's being developed in labs, strategic directions of the top directory products, the impact of wireless technology on directory-enabled applications, and using directories to customize content delivery.

Who should read this book?

Directory Services is a comprehensive, consultant-in-a-book approach to building directory solutions and should be used by information system architects, managers, developers, and analysts in large organizations, as well as consultants who focus on emerging technologies, applications, and services. The book is also useful for computer network designers and messaging systems professionals. *Directory Services* is a practical guide as supplementary reading material in college and university courses on computer and information system design and development, computer system operations, and network management.

How can this book be used?

Directory Services can be used to formulate a strategy for implementing and managing a particular directory platform or for consolidating multiple directory instances under the umbrella of a metadirectory service. The first three chapters explore all the major directories currently enjoying market share (Active Directory, NDS, iPlanet, Radiant Logic, Critical Path, NEXOR, etc.). After a careful review of the competitive features and functionality of these products, the reader will have enough pertinent information to devise the technical specifications portion of a Request for Information intended for the major directory vendors reviewed in the book. Chapter 4 is a handy reference guide for the more tactical issues of migrating to a new directory platform, including several case studies of large enterprise implementations. The material assists with migrations by highlighting typical pitfalls and thorny design issues such as replication strategy or naming conventions and suggesting optimal and proven solutions. In any strategic planning for the implementation and leveraging of a directory service, Chapter 5 would then be used as the final decision-making tool for an analysis of the past and current state of directory and for a look into emerging directory trends.

Acknowledgments

Nancy Cox—I extend my heartfelt thanks to Theron Shreve, publisher at Digital Press, for believing in the need for this book and for supporting and guiding me through the publication of it. I would like to thank all of the individual contributors to this book. Without their unparalleled industry expertise and superb writing ability, this work would not have been possible. Several directory industry gurus, to whom I am also grateful, offered advice on topics or suggested potential contributors: Roger Mizumori, Ed Harrington, Ian Clark, and David Zimmer.

Micky Balladelli—I would like to thank Andreas Luther from Microsoft for all the help he has provided. Also many thanks to Dung Hoang Khac, Pierre Bijaoui, and Tony Redmond, from Compaq.

Mark W. Foust—Thanks to Paul Reiner, Jeff Johnson, and experience, my best teachers!

Curtis M. Sawyer—Many thanks to my clients, too numerous to mention all by name; it was their projects that contributed to my understanding of and experience with directories. Also, a very special thanks to Jack L. Finley of the General Services Administration, who started it all.

Bob Johnson—I would like to acknowledge all those who have invested untold effort toward the evolution of X.500 and LDAP directory services. They left a huge trail of cookie crumbs (technical documents, white papers, Internet RFCs, etc.) for those of us who want to follow the path they blazed.

Alexis Bor—My thanks go out to numerous employers along the way who helped me pursue my dreams and interests, especially Digital Equipment, Hughes Aircraft, and, most of all, the Boeing Company. The encouragement at Boeing came from many places and many people. My communications technology group headed up by Les Kerr was supportive at both the best and worst of times and kept me going and helped me achieve my vision for this technology.

Special thanks have to go out to Doug Julien, who constantly helped me put reality to my often visionary statements—from our first LDAP client called the BLUES (Boeing Look-Up Everything System), to building a Web to directory server (when most people had never even heard of the Web), to helping me bring ActiveLDAP to reality.

The support from my many friends and associates on the industry and standards committees has given me the encouragement and insight into moving technology from a laboratory to global deployment.

Introduction

Global competition frenetically drives the need to locate anyone or anything from anywhere at anytime using any device. A reliable and robust yet cost-effective global directory service storing relevant information on people, devices, objects, and applications is a core enabling technology of the Information Age. This new infrastructure must be fully accessible with a high level of trust and up-to-the-nanosecond accuracy. The electronic foundation must permit people and computer applications to transparently and quickly search, locate and access information in order for leaders to make effective decisions wickedly fast.

In the embryonic days, directories were developed specifically for and joined at the hip to an individual application. The directory, an integral component of any system, typically contained information on authorized system users, their passwords, machine addresses, and application specific items such as permission levels. And, as the number of applications grew exponentially, so did the number of program-locked directories. Managing all those disparate directories became ever more labor and cost intensive. Administrators were constantly adding, deleting, modifying users and addresses and other assorted fields, updating, replicating and refreshing the directory. And, it was no picnic for the users either since they had to remember different log on names and passwords for each of the programs they used. For example, in a large organization with literally hundreds of directories, a user, John Smith, would be known as Smith III, John Allen in the Human Resources system, as JASmith in the e-mail address book, as JAS32 in NDS, as JSmith7 in the Remote Access System, John A. Smith in Building 27 in the telephone directory, and so on and on. There were just too many directories housing too much redundant and inaccurate information. It's a wonder people ever found themselves much less anyone else.

Figure I.1
*Embryonic
directory state:
applicaton specific
directories.*

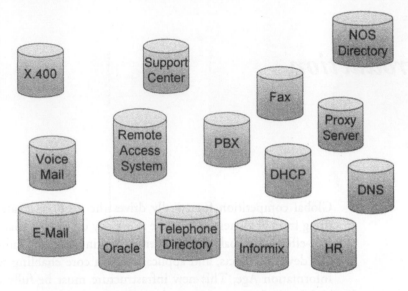

Then, in the 1980s sheer brilliance struck the world of directories when the X.500 standard for distributed directories was formulated and adopted by the international standards bodies. They reasoned that if the entire cosmos of electronic mail was going to be open via the X.400 standard, then the directories for the messaging systems should likewise be open. This standard enabled directories for the first time to be ready and willing to send and receive queries from other like-minded directories regardless of the application to which they were tied. The foundational work done in these committees led to the market driven development of the Lightweight Directory Access Protocol (LDAP) that, like SMTP and VHS, gave the electronic world a simple and low cost alternative.

The unprecedented growth sparked by e-mail and the Internet, as well as in LDAP enabled applications, crystallized in the minds of information technology visionaries the concept of an Enterprise Directory Service tying together all these disparate application directories. In the late 1990s, recognizing the need to provide a service layer linking connected directories, The Burton Group coined the term "metadirectory." Metadirectories provide services that enable a particular directory to synchronize and exchange information with other directories or repositories of information.

Initially, metadirectories were primarily used as synchronization tools to map user accounts, distribution lists, and mailboxes between different e-mail systems during migrations. For example, a tool such as Zoomit's Via (now known as Microsoft's Meta Services [MMS]) would be implemented

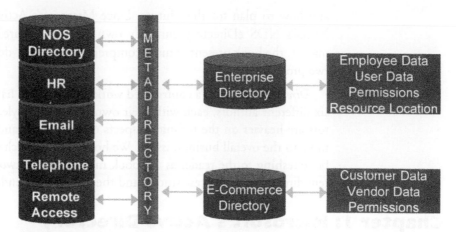

Figure I.2
*Enterprise
Directory Services
vision.*

to facilitate the migration of the cc:Mail e-mail system to Lotus Notes or Microsoft Exchange. Metadirectories, as a by-product, also created one fully populated entry for each resource (user, machine, application) composed of information gleaned from each connected directory. This "e-persona", as it later became known, would then be shared by each connected directory and used in the development of new applications, thus eliminating the need to continually create individual program-specific directories. New applications would be developed using the Enterprise Directory from the beginning, thus saving time and eliminating redundant administrative expense. Metadirectories will also be used extensively in the near future to migrate legacy system directories to the new Enterprise Directory.

Additional benefits of an Enterprise Directory Service include more rapid application development, account provisioning, providing the necessary foundation for a Public Key Infrastructure and a Privilege Management Infrastructure, the capability of single sign-on, facilitation of role-based workflow services, the delivery of customized content to users of Enterprise Portals, and expansion outside of the enterprise to include e-business with customers, suppliers, and the government. The optimized administration and management permits the eventual reduction in the number of separate directories and more accurate and current data about each resource known to the Enterprise Directory.

Realizing this Enterprise Directory Services vision is what this book is all about. Written by internationally recognized directory industry experts, *Directory Services* presents a thorough exploration of the most current capabilities of all of the major directory products on the market today, how to design, implement and manage them, how to upgrade and migrate them

and how to plan for their future. Since Microsoft's Active Directory and
Novell's NDS eDirectory currently own the lion's share of the directory
market, the book presents a more comprehensive and in-depth look at these
two products.

Directory Services is a contributed work and, as such, has been written by
six different authors, each with their own inimitable style. Some contributors are heavier on the technical aspects of their topic and others gravitate
more to the overall business issues. We hope that these changes in style will
be refreshing to the reader as the book moves from network operating system directories to the case studies and then to future trends.

Chapter 1: Microsoft's Active Directory

Jan De Clercq and Micky Balladelli take the reader through the tough yet
fundamental architectural issues such as whether to have single or multiple
forests, schema design, how to configure name spaces, conventions and
contexts, and how to establish trust relationships and groups. Also treated
in-depth are the roles of DNS (Domain Name System), DHCP and WINS
and their integration with the new Active Directory infrastructure. Since
Active Directory typically is fully distributed over multiple corporate sites in
a large enterprise, the chapter completely describes replication basics, design
and operations as well as database sizing and the extensive storage engine.
Securing the Active Directory is a primary concern, and as such, is treated
with an in-depth look at authentication, access control, management, and
Public Key Infrastructure. To facilitate migration and integration, the chapter also includes how to prepare, detailing the pros and cons of several
different upgrade strategies. The chapter closes by proposing several commonly used and effective migration, administrative and management tools.

Chapter 2: Novell NDS eDirectory

What sets eDirectory apart from its nearest competitor, Active Directory, is
operating system independence. After a brief overview of all the prior NDS
releases, Mark Foust comprehensively describes the new eDirectory including the basics, terminology, design recommendations, security, tools and
utilities, tuning and optimization recommendations. His treatment of
directory synchronization and replication goes down to the code level. The
directory security model discusses object, property, and default rights, and
makes a careful design recommendation. The tools required to expand,

maintain, troubleshoot and repair the directory are presented in exacting detail.

Chapter 3: Standards-Based Directory Services

In this chapter, Bob Johnson offers a concise history and explanation of the premier directory standards of X.500, LDAP (Lightweight Directory Access Protocol) and DNS and an overview of how distributed directories operate and provide security. After thoroughly grounding the reader in the standards and why they are so important to the open directory vision, Bob then undertakes the daunting mission of detailing 11 front-running directories including X.500-based eTrust, Injoin and DC-Directory, and LDAP-based iPlanet, SecureWay, and RadiantOne. Each directory is thoroughly evaluated for inherent strengths and weaknesses and the features and functionality that set the product apart from the competition.

Chapter 4: Migrations, Upgrades, Metadirectories and Case Studies

Curt Sawyer and Bob Johnson render in exquisite detail the business and management aspects of implementing a large directory service. Beginning with the basic design question of "One directory service or many?" the chapter explores deployment and legacy system integration strategies. In this chapter, implementation issues such as the political, technical, business, security, and operational ramifications are closely viewed. The chapter proposes recommendations for the design, migration, and population of a metadirectory. The business case for a directory service is presented including a thorough cost/benefit analysis, risk analysis, and total cost of ownership. Case studies of directory implementations at large customer sites as well as the efforts of industry user groups are presented.

Chapter 5: Trends and Emerging Directory Technologies

Alexis Bor presents a comprehensive overview of the history of directory technologies and services including the initial directory strategic vision and the impact of LDAP. Using this historical perspective, he cites current directory developments, directory deficiencies such as interoperability, and the components for a future directory. The chapter then explores prevailing directory trends such as data mining and makes predictions to facilitate strategic planning for the next generation of directory services.

Nancy Cox
Orlando, Florida
October 2001

Microsoft's Active Directory

by Jan De Clercq and Micky Balladelli

1.1   Introduction

Windows 2000 is a complete redesign of the operating system that aims to meet the requirements of enterprise deployments. Active Directory (AD), a scalable and robust directory service (DS) for Windows 2000 servers, is deeply embedded in the operating system. Many other components of Windows 2000 depend on data held in the directory. These facts mean that careful thought must be given to the deployment of the AD before any implementation of Windows 2000 can begin.

Essentially, a DS is a way to look up and retrieve information from anywhere within a distributed environment. A DS provides storage for data, a schema for defining what the data are, methods for accessing these data, and the ability to organize these data hierarchically. The AD provides the storage, the access methods, and the security for the OS and applications that use its services. It is extensible and shareable, and it provides the scalability and manageability required by large enterprises.

Many different objects can be stored in the AD:

- All the objects necessary for running a Windows 2000–based infrastructure, such as the following:

    - Users and groups;
    - Security credentials such as certificates;
    - System resources, such as computers (or servers) and resources;
    - Replication components and settings, which are themselves objects in the AD;
    - COM components, which in previous versions of Windows NT Server 4.0 were required to store information about their location in the registry but which are now stored in the AD's Class Store;
    - Rules and policies to control the working environment.

Figure 1.1
The AD.

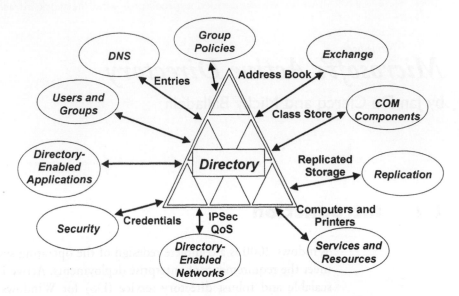

- AD-enabled applications, which can extend the schema of the AD to define their own objects. The release of Microsoft Exchange Server 2000 is the first AD-enabled application. This version of Exchange uses the AD to store information about servers, mailboxes, recipients, and distribution lists in the AD.

- Directory-enabled networks (DEN), which use the AD to retrieve security rules and user and computer settings to set the networking environment. Quality of Service (QoS) will be among the first areas to use DEN and AD. QoS allows applications to reserve bandwidth on the network.

- The Domain Naming System (DNS), which can take advantage of the AD's replication features as well as its secure dynamic updates.

  Figure 1.1 illustrates the AD.

1.2   AD namespaces

Windows NT Server 4.0 uses a flat namespace, meaning that the names of domains do not reflect a hierarchical naming structure that represents the geographical or business organization of the company. The names of domains in Windows NT Server 4.0 are based on the NetBIOS convention and can be up to 15 alphanumeric characters long. Windows NT Server 4.0 uses Windows Naming Service (WINS) to resolve NetBIOS names into

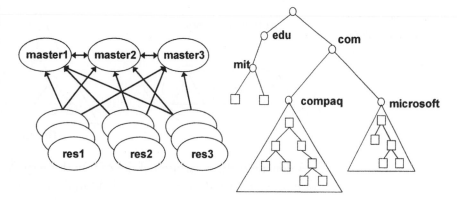

Figure 1.2
Namespaces.

Internet Protocol (IP) addresses. NetBIOS names can also be used to refer to services on the network, such as directory shares or printer shares.

While WINS is the primary name resolution service in Windows NT Server 4.0, DNS is used to resolve IP-based host names for applications such as File Transfer Protocol (FTP) or Telnet software.

DNS today is configured via static files containing information about server or host computers. Administrators are required to create or update details manually about the hosts in the domain they manage. WINS, on the other hand, is updated automatically at system boot. WINS requires only that the NetBIOS name requested by the system be unique on the network.

The Windows 2000 namespace is hierarchical. This fact has a tremendous impact on the roles of services such as DNS and WINS. DNS becomes the primary name service for Windows 2000, which implements a new version of DNS called Dynamic DNS, or DDNS, to overcome the management limitations of classic DNS. DDNS also takes advantage of a new feature, SRV records (discussed later in this book), which allows Windows 2000 to resolve the names of services and locate computers that provide those services. Figure 1.2 illustrates namespaces.

While DNS is used to find servers and services in the AD, the Lightweight Directory Access Protocol (LDAP) is also used to access objects in the Directory.

1.3 Domains

Similar to a Windows NT Server 4.0 domain, a Windows 2000 domain is a security boundary. This means that a domain boundary limits the scope of access control and policy rules implemented within the domain.

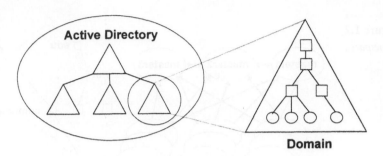

Figure 1.3
*Windows 2000
domain.*

A domain is also a partition of the AD. In this respect, a domain is a partition of the data and the namespace held in the AD. In fact, the AD is the sum of all domains within an enterprise. In other words, the AD is composed of one or more domains linked together. As the namespace within the AD is hierarchical, the domain structure in Windows 2000 is made up of a series of parent-child relationships between the different domains. This is very different from the trust relationships that connected domains in earlier versions of Windows NT Server 4.0. Figure 1.3 illustrates a Windows 2000 domain.

Windows NT 4.0 uses a single master replication model in which all changes are made at a single primary domain controller (DC), then replicated out to the backup DCs. The AD allows Windows 2000 to use a multimaster replication model, which means that an administrator can use any DC in a Windows 2000 domain to manage resources. The need to connect to the primary DC is therefore eliminated. The Windows NT SAM database (DB) is limited to a size of approximately 60 MB, which in turn limits the size of a domain to the number of accounts that can be stored in the SAM. By comparison, the AD can grow to store millions of objects, so Windows 2000 domains can contain millions of accounts. Theoretically, the AD can host 2^{32}, or some 4 billion, objects.

1.4   Organizational units and objects

The AD is built from a collection of organizational units (OUs) and containers, which forms the base of the hierarchical representation of objects within a domain. An OU is a generic object container. It can contain any object in the domain, including other OUs.

OUs can be used to delegate administration control to a particular group of users without allowing them to have administrative permissions for other objects in the domain. Delegation of administration must not, however, be

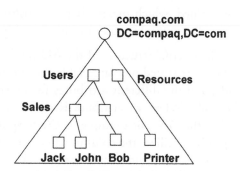

Figure 1.4
Distinguished names.

CN=Jack, OU=Sales, OU=Users, DC=compaq, DC=com

confused with access control. OUs are not groups and must not be used to control access to resources within the domain.

AD objects include users, groups, computers, and printers to name but a few. Objects can be organized hierarchically using organizational units. Every object in the AD has a unique name referenced by an LDAP distinguished name (DN). Distinguished names are the fully qualified LDAP representation of an object and are composed of a sequence of relative DNs (RDNs). RDNs are a portion of a DN identifying all the ancestors or containers of the object and the object itself.

Figure 1.4 illustrates a domain composed of a number of organizational units. The user Jack is referenced by the RDN CN = Jack. User Jack belongs to a tree of organizational units. Each OU is identified by its own RDN in the hierarchical order in which it was created. The OUs belong to the com-paq.com domain, which is referenced by the domain DC RDN. The full representation of the DN is the sum of all the RDNs composing it, which results in CN = JACK; OU = SALES; OU = USERS; DC = COMPAQ; DC = COM. To retrieve the full description of DNs, refer to RFC 2247.

1.5   AD schema

The schema contains the definition of all the objects in the AD. Every object has its own class and a set of attributes (also called properties) associated with it. A class is the unit of storage in the AD. This means that for an object to be stored in the AD, it must first have a class, which defines how it is stored and what attributes it may have. Attributes hold the value of a particular property in the object. Attributes are typed, which means that their value is stored as a string, octet, numeric, and so on. Attributes may be multivalued, which means that an attribute may be stored using multiple values. For example, a user can have multiple telephone numbers.

The internal structure of the AD can be compared with a relational DB. Objects are stored in a large table. Each object is stored in a row within the table, and the different attributes for objects are stored in the columns in the table. When an attribute is not used, it does not occupy any space within the DB. For example, if the telephone number attribute for a user object is not filled, the column will be empty, and no space will be allocated to store the attribute inside the DB. This feature is necessary because the number of attributes associated with an object may be considerable. For example, the class user went from a few attributes in Windows NT 4.0 to more than 100 in Windows 2000.

Attributes may be associated with multiple classes, which means that they are created independently of classes. Attributes have their own IDs and their own characteristics. The AD schema is object oriented. This means that classes can derive from other classes to inherit their characteristics. For example, the class user, which, as its name implies, describes the user object, is associated with a number of attributes related to the user account, such as principalName, logonHours, groupMembership, and many more.

The class user derives from the class organizationalPerson. The class organizationalPerson defines a person with such attributes as homePostalAddress, homeNumber, mobile, EmployeeID, and more.

Now, organizationalPerson derives from person, which simply defines five attributes: cn, seeAlso, sn, userPassword, and telephone-Number.

The class contact also inherits its parent classes (superclasses in object-oriented terms) from the characteristics of organizationalPerson and person, which means that the instance of a contact may also have any of the attributes associated with organizationalPerson and person. A contact is a lightweight object containing information about a person. It is generally used to store a mail recipient in the AD. Looking carefully at the person class, we can see that cn, which stands for common name, is a mandatory attribute.

There are two types of attributes: mandatory and optional. Mandatory attributes must be provided with a value to allow the object to be created. Given that cn is the only mandatory attribute of class user and its parents, to create an object of class user we must define its common name, or cn.

Optional attributes may be filled after the object has been created and are not required to create the object.

Classes and attributes have a unique ID, as mentioned previously. This ID is called, wrongly, the Object ID (OID)—wrongly because in object-oriented terms an object is the instance of a class, so the Object ID should really have been Class ID. Given that OID comes from the X.500 world and can be found in other DS implementations, such as Exchange, Microsoft decided to use the same term in the AD.

There may be multiple instances of the class user: users Joe and Jack may be those instances. The OID identifies the class user, whereas the Globally Unique Identifier (GUID) identifies the instances of the objects. GUIDs are generated by the operating system when the object is created. They are 128-bit numbers computed to be unique. Various "issuing authorities," such as the International Organization for Standardization (ISO), issue OIDs; enterprises can then extend them to add their own class extensions.

Objects are identified by their GUID, not by their names. This allows objects to always be referenced when they are moved or are renamed. This behavior is an improvement over how Exchange Server 5.5 references the objects it manages. Exchange uses a DN for every object—not the object GUID. This implies that when an object has to be moved in Exchange, it must first be deleted and then be recreated. Using GUIDs, objects can not only be moved anywhere in the domain, but anywhere within the forest.

The schema itself is stored in the AD as a partition and is replicated to all DCs in the AD. This is very important, because it allows AD-enabled applications to browse the directory programmatically, learn how objects (or classes) are defined, and adapt a user interface accordingly. These schema-driven applications automatically adapt to meet the requirements of different companies and are able to view and manage AD objects that have been implemented in different ways at different companies. For example, a company may require a particular set of attributes to identify the organization in which users belong. At Compaq, we use user badge numbers and cost centers. Another company may have a totally different identification system based on other business rules. A schema-driven application could browse the directory for the definition of a user. When the application needs to display a UI for a user, it does it following the schema definition, and, in our example, the cost center and badge number would be part of the list of displayed attributes.

Applications can extend the AD with their own class definitions or extend the definition of an existing class. For example, Microsoft Exchange Server extends the user object to allow it to store information about mailboxes on an Exchange server. One of the most important features introduced in Windows 2000 is that different levels of access control can be defined to allow users to view different portions of an object. For example, we might want to have different levels of administrative access to user objects. We can define a set of administrators who are allowed to modify user passwords and modify logon hours. We can then define a different set of administrators, which might come from the Human Resources (HR) department, who can manage sensitive user information, such as home addresses, personal telephone numbers, and so on. The goal is to permit different views of information held in a common directory, allowing administrators to access the information they need to do their jobs, while restricting access to data that should not be generally available.

1.6   Trust relationships

Windows NT 4.0 links domains together through trust relationships. The collection of Windows NT 4.0 domains that are linked together form the enterprise Windows NT 4.0 infrastructure. Domains can also be linked together in Windows 2000, in this case to form the enterprise namespace. The link set by a trust relationship in Windows NT 4.0, however, establishes a very loose connection between the participating domains. Connecting Windows 2000 domains together within an enterprise namespace forms a far more coherent and well-connected infrastructure.

Trust relationships link Windows NT 4.0 domains together. Trusts allow users in trusted domains to access resources in the trusting domain. In Windows NT 4.0 trust relationships must be explicitly defined. There are a number of limitations that must be considered when setting up trust relationships in large enterprise deployments.

Trust relationships also exist in Windows 2000, but the trusts take on a very different nature because they are based on Kerberos and can be transitive. Trust relationships are transitive and use Kerberos within the same forest only. Administrators can also create explicit trusts within a forest. These trusts are called shortcut and are transitive. Trusts created between Windows 2000 forests are not transitive, since they are based on the NTLM protocol; however, trusts created with non-Windows 2000 Kerberos realms can be transitive.

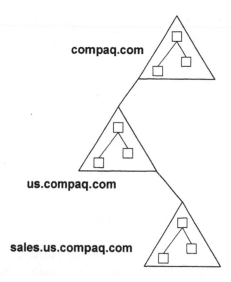

Figure 1.5
A tree of domains.

compaq.com

us.compaq.com

sales.us.compaq.com

1.6.1　Trees

Trees are hierarchies of domains linked by trust relationships. Each tree shares a contiguous namespace. Figure 1.5 illustrates a tree formed by the Compaq, U.S., and Sales domains. The names of the three domains are compaq, us.Compaq, and sales.us.compaq. The names are contiguous, because the child domains inherit from the names of the parent domains. Hence, the U.S. domain inherits part of its name from its parent, the Compaq domain, and in turn provides the root of the name for its child, the Sales domain. When generating the tree, you must start with its root. You cannot create a domain and later decide to create the parent of this domain. The parent domain must be there before any child domain can be created.

New subtrees can be created within a tree. For example, we could create a new subtree, Europe, under the compaq domain. This new subtree would then be called europe.compaq. The europe portion of the name is contiguous with the compaq name but is disjointed from the us name. This is why we have two separate subtrees, the europe subtree and the us subtree.

1.6.2　Forests

A forest is a set of trees linked together via trust relationships. The trees that are joined together at the top level of the forest do not necessarily have to share the same namespace. Figure 1.6 illustrates a forest formed by two

Figure 1.6
A forest.

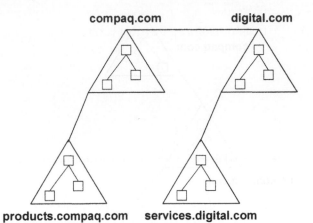

compaq.com   **digital.com**

products.compaq.com   **services.digital.com**

trees. The trees are formed from domains called compaq and digital. After the forest is formed, each domain remains unchanged, and each domain remains at the head of its own tree. A forest is sometimes referred to as the AD. Earlier we defined a domain to be a portion of the AD, and we defined the AD as the sum of all the domains that are connected together. A forest is exactly this: the sum of all trees, which are composed of domains connected together via transitive Kerberos trusts. A forest and the AD are the same thing.

The trees within the same forest share the following characteristics:

■ *A common configuration.* The topology of the domains within the forest is known by all domains and is replicated immediately whenever a new domain joins the forest. The topology includes objects, such as connection objects, sites, IP subnets, site links, site link bridges, and so on. These objects are discussed later.

■ *A common schema.* The schema defines all the objects in the forest and is composed of classes and attributes.

■ *A common Global Catalog (GC).* Global catalogs are discussed later in this section.

1.6.3   Flexible single-master operation roles

Windows 2000 supports multimaster replication of directory data. This means that any DC in the domain can be used to modify the values of an object. Replication then occurs between DCs to update all the DCs with the latest data for the object. Inevitably, some potential for update conflicts exists in a multimaster replication model. The replication process is covered in more detail later on, but for now it is enough to say that when a replication conflict occurs, the time stamps of each modification are evaluated, and the last writer wins.

Some objects in the directory, such as the schema itself, cannot be resolved with such methods, because two versions of the schema may generate instances of objects using different properties. It would be hard to resolve such conflicts without losing data. To avoid schema conflicts, a single-master replication mechanism is performed by a special DC called the "Schema Master." This is one of five flexible, single-master operation (FSMO, pronounced "fizmo") roles, also known as "Operation Masters," implemented in a single-master replication model:

1. *The Schema Master.* The Schema Master is unique in the entire forest. New classes or attributes can only be created by the Schema Master. Updates are then replicated to all domains in the forest. Note: A Schema Master must also be set to allow schema updates before the schema can actually be modified.

2. *Domain Naming Master.* The Domain Naming Master manages the names of every domain in the forest. It is unique in the forest. Only the Domain Naming Master can add and remove domains in the tree or forest to avoid having naming conflicts occur. In future releases, the Domain Naming Master will allow domain moves within the forest.

3. *Primary DC (PDC) Emulator.* The PDC Emulator is unique in the domain and provides backward compatibility to down-level clients and servers in the following ways:

    - Provides down-level clients support for password updates;

    - Performs replication to down-level Backup DCs (BDCs) (NT 4.0);

    - Acts as the Master Domain Browser, if the Windows NT 4.0 browser service is enabled;

    - Verifies password uniqueness (Windows 2000 DCs attempt to replicate password changes to the PDC first—each time a DC fails to authenticate a password, it contacts the PDC to see whether the password can be authenticated there, perhaps as a result of a change that has not yet been replicated down to the particular DC);

- Synchronizes time (the PDC Emulator synchronizes time for the computers in the domain. The PDC Emulator of the first domain in the forest [the root domain] also synchronizes time with the PDC Emulators of the other domains in the forest).

4. *RID Master.* The RID Master is unique in the domain. When a security principal (e.g., user, group) is created, it receives a domain-wide Security ID (SID) and a domain-wide unique Relative ID (RID). Every Windows 2000 DC receives a pool of RIDs it can use. The RID Master ensures that these IDs remain unique on every DC by assigning different pools.

5. *Infrastructure Master.* The Infrastructure Master is unique in the domain. When an object from another domain is referenced, this reference contains the GUID, the SID, and the DN of that object. If the referenced object moves, the following happens:

    - The object GUID does not change (it is issued when the object is created and never changes).

    - The object SID changes if the move is across domains (when it will receive an SID from the new domain).

    - The object DN always changes.

A DC holding the infrastructure master role in a domain is responsible for updating the SIDs and DNs in cross-domain object references in that domain. An example of such objects is groups. Groups can contain members from other domains and the Infrastructure Master is responsible for updating and maintaining the reference.

1.7   Naming contexts

Naming contexts (NCs) are portions of the AD that follow different replication rules—they are boundaries for AD replication. The domain NC contains all the data within a domain. The schema NC contains all the classes and attributes and is replicated throughout the forest. The configuration NC contains the topology of the forest and is replicated throughout the forest. The three NCs are replicated to the global catalog either entirely or partially. All NCs have a location in the directory. The root of a domain namespace is its DNS name, and all objects within the domain are children of this root. When the first domain is created, the first DC in the domain generates the configuration NC. This NC is then replicated to all DCs joining the forest.

1.8   Global catalog

The GC is a special type of DC. As a DC it contains all the objects and attributes of its own domain. It is a full replica of the other DCs in the same domain. However, in addition to the objects of its own domain, a GC contains a subset of the attributes of all the other domain NC objects in the forest as well as the schema NC and the configuration NC. The GC contains all the objects in the AD. The role of the GC is to provide the AD with a search engine. By containing an indexed partial replica of all the objects in the forest, GCs become extremely fast search engines. The subset of the attributes is defined and modifiable in the schema and contains by default the attributes most commonly searched, such as name, e-mail address, and phone number for a user.

Any DC can be configured to become a GC. A GC incurs more overhead than a DC because it performs more replication and requires more disk space for its DB; however, because users and applications connect to the GC to search for objects in the AD, it is recommended to deploy enough GCs to ensure that clients can make a high-quality connection. Normally, this implies a Local Area Network (LAN)–quality connection established by locating a GC close to each major user community.

In order to understand how a search works against a GC, let us imagine that we are looking for a color printer located on the same floor in a building. We only know a subset of the characteristics of the printer we wish to use. We know that it supports color and we have a rough idea of its location, but we do not know its network name, so we cannot connect to it and print our documents. We can use LDAP to search the indexes maintained by the GC for all matching printer objects using the known characteristics. The search will return all matching objects, hopefully including the printer we want to use. Without the GC, we would have to conduct a search against a DC and drill down through the entire forest. Such a search would take too much time, and the response time would be unacceptable.

In order to provide the ability to perform GC queries, at least one GC must be defined in a domain. That GC will accept LDAP requests to both port 389 and port 3268. The Domain Naming Master role must be hosted on a GC. By containing all the objects of the AD, including the accounts for the domains in the forest, GCs provide the necessary visibility to allow the Domain Naming Master to know if a domain name is currently in use.

It is not recommended, however, to place the Infrastructure Master on GCs owing to phantom records. These records are created on DCs when a referenced object does not exist in the same domain. For example, a user object may reference another user residing in another domain using an attribute, such as manager. The role of the Infrastructure Master in this case is to update the phantom object if the remote object is removed or deleted. The Infrastructure Master would not be able to perform this operation on a GC. GCs do not create phantom records because they have a copy of the real object.

1.9 Groups

Windows NT 4.0 supports groups, a convenient way to bring one or more users together under a common heading. Windows 2000 introduces two types of general-purpose groups: security groups and distribution lists. Security groups contain security principals and are used for access control. Conceptually, they are similar in use and function to Windows NT 4.0 groups. Distribution lists are similar to the distribution lists currently in use by Exchange Server. Windows 2000 also introduces four group scopes with special behavior: universal groups, global groups, domain local groups, and local groups.

1.9.1 Universal groups

Universal groups are available throughout the forest. They may contain other universal or global groups or users from the current domain or any trusted domain. Because this type of group may contain objects located anywhere in the forest, they are expensive to use in terms of performance when used in Access Control Lists (ACLs). Authorization still requires authentication performed by the domain in which the user belongs.

Universal groups are published in GCs; however, when used as distribution lists, replicating them locally to users via GCs provides applications such as Exchange with a convenient, powerful, and simple way to implement global address list.

The implication of publishing universal groups in GCs affects the authentication process. During the authentication process a DC will contact a GC to verify the membership of the users in the universal groups. This means that DCs require GCs to add the SID of universal groups in the token or ticket of the authenticating security principal.

Placement of GCs is usually desired in remote sites in order to improve performance in user logon time, searches, and other actions requiring communication with GCs, as well as reducing Wireless Area Network (WAN) traffic. However, in some instances, it may be desirable not to locate a GC at a remote site to reduce administrative intervention, hardware requirements, and replication overhead—in short, to avoid duplicating the functions of the BDC in the Windows NT 4.0 environment.

It is possible to remove the need to involve GCs during the authentication process; however, careful consideration must be applied, because this may introduce a security breach. Administrators can use regedit to modify a key for the LSA process that allows it to ignore GCs during the authentication process. The key is \\HKLM\System\CurrentControlSet\Control\ Lsa\IgnoreGCFailures. If this key is set, administrators must not use universal groups to deny access to resources. The key will prevent the authentication process from adding the SIDs of the universal groups to the user's token; therefore, the access control cannot verify that the user is denied access to the resource. Use this key very cautiously.

1.9.2   Global groups

Global groups are available throughout the forest. They can contain other global groups, computers, and users from the same domain, but they cannot contain security principals from other domains.

1.9.3   Domain local groups

Domain local groups cannot be exported to other domains. They can be applied only to resources in the domain in which they are created. Domain local groups may contain references to universal groups; global groups; computers, and users from any domain; as well as domain local groups, computers, and users from its own domain.

1.9.4   Local groups

Local groups are available only on the local computer but may contain objects from anywhere in the forest, just as they may in Windows NT 4.0.

1.10   Domain modes

There are two domain modes: mixed mode and native mode. Mixed mode is the default mode and is used when a new domain is created or when a Windows NT 4.0 PDC is upgraded to Windows 2000. Mixed mode implies that there are NT 4.0 backup DCs in the domain. One of the Windows 2000 DCs takes the FSMO role of PDC Emulator and acts as a

Windows 2000 PDC in the eyes of the down-level clients and BDCs. This is quite important, because it allows Windows NT 4.0 operations to be maintained while the domain is migrated to Windows 2000. It is important to remember that in a mixed-mode environment there may be down-level BDCs. In an effort to reduce domains and consolidate resources, these BDCs use a SAM DB with the same limitation as a Windows NT 4.0—its 65-MB size.

The groups in the domain use Windows NT 4.0 behavior when operating in mixed mode, which means that groups cannot be nested. In addition, security universal groups are not available in mixed mode. When all the down-level clients and BDCs have been upgraded to Windows 2000, the domain can be switched over to native mode. This is a one-shot operation, which cannot be undone. Once in native mode, the groups can be nested, and universal groups are available. In native mode it is also possible to have Windows NT 4.0 member servers; however, Windows NT 4.0 BDCs are no longer accepted in the domain. It is worth noting that once in native mode, the PDC Emulator is still available. It performs other unique tasks in the domain, such as ensuring that passwords remain unique and synchronizing time.

1.11 Sites

A site is a collection of IP subnets that share LAN-type connectivity. In fact, the best way to think of a site is to compare it to a LAN. Sites reflect locality—all the systems that belong to the same site are close to each other and benefit from good bandwidth. Sites play a major role in replication of data.

When a Windows 2000 server creates a new domain, the AD creates the site Default-First-Site-Name and stores the DC there. All the DCs joining the domain are added to the default site. Systems continue to be added to the default site until a new site is explicitly created. A domain may span multiple sites (see Figure 1.7); however, multiple domains may belong to the same site. Sites are independent from the domains they belong to.

Sites are used for the following two roles:

1.   During workstation logon to determine the closest DC. We will get into how workstations discover the closest DC in the next section.

2.   During AD data replication to optimize the route and transport of replicated data depending on the DC sites.

Figure 1.7
*Steps for finding
the closest site.*

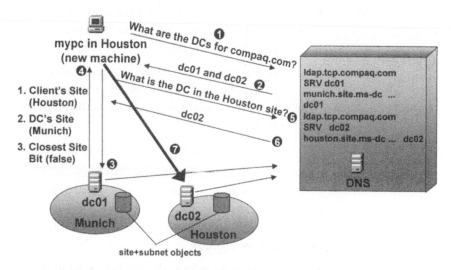

1. Client's Site
   (Houston)

2. DC's Site
   (Munich)

3. Closest Site
   Bit (false)

In order to achieve these two roles, all DCs in the forest know about all
the sites, which are stored in the configuration NC. Finding the closest DC
at boot time or, more precisely, when the net logon service starts, DCs publish information about the domain and site they belong to in DNS using
SRV records. As previously mentioned, they cache information about all
sites locally. When a workstation boots, it either receives its IP address from
a Dynamic Host Configuration Protocol (DHCP) server or the network
administrator statically has assigned this address to it. DHCP may also provide the DNS server address, unless this information was entered manually.

During the logon process, the workstation attempts to locate the closest
DC to improve logon performance. The workstation does not have information about sites so it must perform five steps to receive it (see Figure 1.7):

1. The workstation asks DNS for DCs in the domain it is trying to
    log onto. In our example of the domain compaq.com, DNS
    returns two names: DC01 and DC02.

2. The workstation then performs the logon on for the DC01 DC.
    When the workstation receives multiple servers in response to a
    DNS query, it will use an internal algorithm to choose a DC.
    This allows for spreading the load when multiple clients are per-
    forming the same operation. DC01 accepts the logon and returns
    information about the site the workstation belongs to. This is
    possible since the workstation provided its own IP address, and
    the DC was able to match that IP address with one of the IP sub-
    nets forming a site.

3.   DC01 returns the fact that the workstation does not belong to the Munich site, but it belongs to the Houston site, which is not the closest DC available.

4.   With information about the site it belongs to, the workstation can make a much more specific request to DNS and ask for the DC in the domain that belongs to the Houston site. DNS returns DC02.

5.   The workstation can then log on to DC02, which is in the same site, and can store site information in its own registry.

Let us now imagine that the workstation is not really a workstation—it is a laptop, and this laptop travels to Munich. Let us assume that the Munich DHCP provides a new IP address. As shown in Figure 1.8, the following steps now occur:

1.   The laptop retrieves the site information that it previously stored in the registry and very naturally attempts to retrieve from DNS information about the DC in that site.

2.   The laptop goes back to DNS simply because the DC that it used previously may have been shut down or have been replaced with a different one, and if that were the case the SRV records in DNS would have been updated. The laptop asks DNS for a DC in the Houston site. DNS returns DC02.

Figure 1.8
Mobile user finding the closest site.

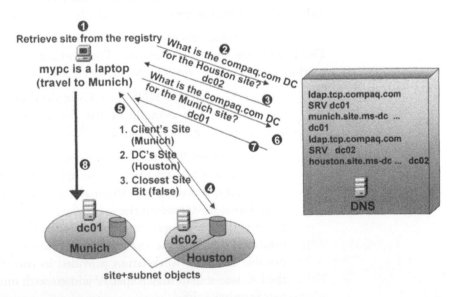

3.   Upon logon, the DC02 updates the laptop about the new site it belongs to, it mentions that it is no longer the closest site, and that the laptop now must log on to a DC in the Munich site.

4.   The workstation goes back to DNS and asks for the DC in the Munich site and DNS returns DC01. Now the laptop performs logons on DC01.

It is important to note in this example that the discovery of the closest site was performed automatically without administrator intervention.

Workstations can be set to contact the DCs that match their own IP subnet first. This can take considerably less time than contacting remote DCs. A site can, however, be composed of a number of IP subnets, and even if a DC and a client are in the same site, they could still belong to different subnets. In this case the above scenario would still apply.

1.12   Naming Conventions

The AD supports a number of naming conventions that are already widely used either on the Internet or in various DS implementations.

These include the following:

■   RFC 822 names are in the form of Johns@compaq.com. Anyone using the Internet or an IP-based network is familiar with these names, because they serve as e-mail addresses. In Windows 2000, these names can be used to log on, as they allow the concatenation of the user name and the logon domain. In a Windows 2000 implementation of a forest containing multiple trees and domains, it may be interesting to use a single logon name instead of having to remember the exact authentication domain. To provide this functionality, Windows 2000 uses the User Principal Name (UPN). UPNs are suffixes appended to the logon name of a user. These suffixes have a forest-wide scope. For example, we may have a forest with 12 different domains, with many users disseminated in those domains. We can create a UPN suffix called compaq.com. This suffix allows any user in the forest to authenticate using the RFC 822 convention, where the user name is followed by the chosen suffix, in this case, by @compaq.com. This has the benefit of reducing complexity, hiding long names, and prompting users to use a well-known domain name. It is also possible to add multiple UPN suffixes in the same forest.

- HTTP URL names allow access to AD data using Web browsers: `HTTP://SomeServer.compaq.com/Product/Sales/JohnS`.

- LDAP URLs. The AD supports access via the LDAP protocol from any LDAP-enabled client: `LDAP://SomeServer.compaq.com/CN=JohnS,OU=Sales,OU=Product,DC=compaq,DC=com`.

- Universal Naming Convention (UNC) names were the norm in Windows NT 4.0 and are still supported in Windows 2000: `\\compaq.com\product\sales\john\public\budget.xls`.

1.13 Protocols and APIs

The AD supports both LDAPv2 and LDAPv3 protocols (RFCs 1777 and 2251) and HTTP. LDAP is essential for interoperability reasons, since most of the DS implementations are supporting it.

The following APIs are supported:

- AD Service Interface (ADSI), a set of COM interfaces for searching and managing various DSs.

- LDAP API, a low-level C interface (RFC 1823). However, access to the AD via this interface is not recommended, since ADSI is available.

- The Windows Open Services Architecture (WOSA) Messaging API (MAPI). MAPI is supported for backward compatibility, largely to support access from MAPI clients such as Outlook 98 and Outlook 2000. Other messaging clients (e.g., Outlook Express) use LDAP.

In essence, LDAP is a lightweight version of the X.500 Directory Access Protocol (DAP). Over the past few years, LDAP has become the most commonly accepted DAP and is supported in implementations of X.500, the NetWare DS, and the Microsoft Exchange (5.0 and 5.5) directories. DSLDAPv3 is implemented in Windows 2000 and is used by applications to access the hierarchically organized objects in the AD.

Both DNS and LDAP are used by Windows 2000 to access data in the AD. Some explanation is required to outline why two protocols are required and when they are used. DNS is a very effective and well-proven protocol for locating host computers. Windows 2000 uses DNS to find LDAP servers within its network. In fact, the LDAP servers are DCs, and, once they are located, Windows 2000 then uses LDAP to access the data managed by the DCs. LDAP is most efficient at retrieving information organized in finely grained attributes, such as the properties maintained for objects in the AD. DNS is, therefore, used to locate the LDAP servers, and all further access to directory information is accomplished with LDAP. Accessing information via LDAP means performing one of four operations: read, write, modify, or delete.

1.14   DNS and AD integration

DNS is the Windows 2000 core naming service. AD uses DNS to name and locate AD domains and objects. Every Windows 2000 domain is identified by its DNS domain name. Remember that although an AD domain is identified by its DNS domain name, an AD domain and a DNS domain are completely different concepts: an AD domain stores objects; a DNS domain stores resource records. Consequently, every object member of the domain wears the domain name in its DN. The DNS parts of an object's DN are known as domain components and start with dc=. To illustrate this, look at the DN of the user object jdc member of the emea.nt.com-paq.com domain: cn=jdc, cn=consultants, cn=users, dc=emea, dc=nt, dc=compaq, dc=com (see Figure 1.9).

The cn= components of the object's DN reflect the container and OU structure of the emea.nt.compaq.com domain. In the above example, user jdc is part of the consultants OU, located in the users container. These common name (CN) components are not DNS based, but follow the

Figure 1.9
Locating objects in AD using DNS and LDAP.

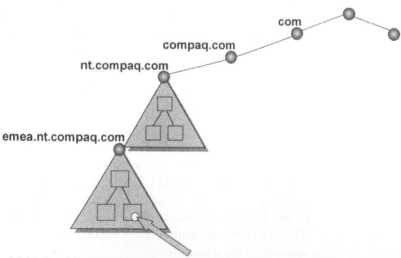

LDAP://cn=jdc,cn=consultants,cn=users,dc=emea,dc=nt,dc=compaq,dc=com

LDAP naming standards. Every Windows 2000 object's DN is thus a combination of DNS and LDAP names.

DNS can also be used to locate AD domains, AD objects, and core Windows 2000 services, such as a Kerberos Key Distribution Center (KDC), a global catalog, and so on.

DNS contains specific resource records pointing to AD domains or to the dc= portions of an AD object's DN. These records are simple, linking domain names to Windows 2000 DCs. Once you know the DC, you can query it for a particular domain object using LDAP. Every DC hosts the AD domain NC of a particular domain. You can easily test whether the DNS name of a particular domain is present in the DNS DB by pinging the domain name.

All of this shows the tight integration of the Windows 2000 AD namespace and the DNS namespace; in fact, the AD namespace is contained within the DNS namespace. Every AD forest can be mapped to a single contiguous namespace or to multiple disjointed namespaces; every AD domain tree can be mapped to a contiguous DNS domain hierarchy. Both namespaces can store their information separately (in the DNS zone files or in the AD DB) or in the same location (in the AD DB).

1.15 AD storage integration

The zone files of a Windows 2000 DNS service running on a DC can be configured to be integrated with AD. To integrate a DNS zone file with AD, open up its properties in the Microsoft Management Console (MMC) DNS snap-in and change its zone type to AD Integrated. This AD integration is an option; if you want, you can still run DNS as you did in NT 4.0.

Integrating Windows 2000 DNS zone files with the AD has two important consequences. DNS zone file data are stored in AD as AD objects and are replicated using AD replication mechanisms. The AD schema includes a set of generic objects that can be used to store DNS-specific information, such as zones, domain nodes, resource records, and general DNS configuration information, in the AD. Table 1.1 shows the principal attributes of the DnsZone and the DnsNode object classes. An AD integrated zone is stored in the AD domain NC, underneath the System\MicrosoftDNS container. This is a very important detail: It means that DNS zones are not replicated forest-wide but domain-wide.

Table 1.1   *Attributes of the DnsZone and the DnsNode AD Object Classes*

Object Class (Object Type) Attributes	Meaning
DnsZone (Container object)	Represents an AD integrated zone
ManagedBy	Administrator of DNS zone
DnsProperty	Stores configuration information
DnsNotifySecondaries	Support for notify messages
DnsAllowXFR	Support for incremental zone transfer
DnsAllowDynamic	Support for dynamic update
DnsNode (Leaf object)	Represents a host (a host can be a machine, a service, a sub-domain, etc.)
DnsRecord	Stores resource records linked to a particular host
DnsProperty	Stores configuration information linked to a particular host

1.16   AD replication integration

From a replication point of view, integrating DNS zones with AD offers the following advantages:

- *AD integrated DNS uses the same replication mechanism as AD.* Unlike NT 4.0, there is no need to set up other DNS replication mechanisms. The same is true for the replication topology; DNS can use the same replication topology as that used for AD replication.

- *Contrary to the classical DNS replication model, AD replication uses a multimaster replication model.* A major advantage of a multimaster model is that it eliminates a possible single point of failure: the primary zone server. AD integrated DNS does not use the concept of secondary zones; all zones are considered primary zones (at least on Windows 2000 DCs—a member server running a DNS server can still host a secondary copy of an AD integrated zone).

- *AD replication provides per-property replication granularity.* Classical DNS replication mechanisms had, in the best case (when using incremental zone transfers), per-object (resource record) granularity.

- *AD replication is secure.* It can take place across RPC or SMTP; both protocols can be secured and provide adequate authentication, confidentiality, and integrity services for the replicated AD data.

Obviously AD replication integration positively impacts the number of resources needed for the design of a DNS namespace and for administering and maintaining the DNS servers. You can leverage the efforts done for the design of your AD infrastructure, and your AD administrators can manage the DNS services as well.

Relying on AD replication for DNS data replication clearly has numerous advantages. One of the negative consequences of the AD replication model is the AD's constant state of loose consistency. In DNS terminology, this means that at any given moment different DNS servers hosting the same zone could return different answers to the same DNS query. After all, this is nothing new. This can also happen in a classic DNS replication model using primary and secondary zones.

1.17 DNS namespace design

The design of a DNS namespace is one of the AD architect's first crucial tasks. Because of the tight integration of DNS and the AD infrastructure, the namespace design will go hand in hand with the AD design. You will notice that both DNS and AD infrastructure design are iterative processes, which will influence one another continually.

In the following sections we provide some guidelines that may help you in your namespace design. First, it is important that you examine your business needs. Two main decision points in the namespace design will be whether you need or plan to integrate Windows 2000 DNS with a legacy DNS infrastructure and whether you need to consider the impact of an Internet presence for your corporate DNS namespace design. Throughout the design you may need to choose new DNS domain names; although this may look trivial, it is not an easy task.

1.17.1 Evaluating business needs

The following business factors may influence your DNS namespace design:

- *Current and future business needs.* The DNS design must cover both current and future DNS naming business needs. If your organization is planning acquisitions or mergers, provide as much flexibility as possible in your current DNS namespace design. DNS names are there to remain unchanged for a long time.

- *The need for an Internet presence.* Consider whether parts of your AD infrastructure will ever be exposed to the Internet. If they will, you will have to involve an official Internet name registration authority in your namespace design discussions.

- *Organization type and size.* The size and type of your organization will have an impact on the scope of the AD infrastructure. The AD infrastructure scope will obviously affect DNS namespace design. Depending on the size and type of your organization, you may want to include your core organization, subsidiaries, external partners, or even customers in your AD infrastructure design.

- *Legal and organizational constraints.* When choosing DNS names be sure that they are in accordance with the legal environment in which your organization is operating. For example, in the case of an Internet presence, make sure that the name is not already registered by another organization. Also, make sure that you have complete approval from the top-level management of your organization.

1.17.2 Choosing a DNS domain name

The choice of a DNS name is critical. If you plan to reuse your existing legacy DNS domain names, you may not need to do this as part of your Windows 2000 DNS namespace design. The following are some general guidelines that may help you in choosing a good DNS domain name:

- *DNS domain names must be unique in the DNS namespace.* If your domain will be exposed on the Internet, its name should be unique in the Internet namespace. If it is not, its name should be unique within your private DNS namespace. As will be explained later on in this chapter, most organizations prefer a separate external (Internet namespace) and internal DNS domain name (intranet-extranet namespace).

- *DNS domains also should be stable.* This is even more critical when you think about the integration of DNS with the AD infrastructure: a name change after the installation of a domain will impact your entire AD infrastructure.

- *DNS domain names should be meaningful.* Remember that DNS is a name resolution service, so it does not make sense to choose a domain name that is hard to remember.

- *The name should represent your entire organization or should at least be accepted by your entire organization.* This may not be the case in organizations resulting from a merger: They may require several DNS names, each representing part of the organization.

- *The choice of the DNS name of the root domain of a domain tree is critical.* The root domain's DNS name impacts the DNS name of all the child domains in the same tree. Also, once the root domain has been installed, it cannot be renamed without removing and reinstalling the AD.

1.17.3   Integration with legacy DNS systems

Many organizations already have a DNS infrastructure in place prior to the installation of an AD infrastructure. This may be an NT 4.0 DNS or a Berkeley Internet Name Domain (BIND) DNS (mostly UNIX based) infrastructure. More information on BIND can be found on the Internet Software Consortium (ISC) Web site: http://www.isc.org/products/BIND/. In the NT 4.0 DNS case, it is advisable to upgrade to Windows 2000 DNS, given the new functionalities.

Three different scenarios exist for how to integrate an existing BIND DNS infrastructure with an AD infrastructure:

1.   Reliance completely on BIND DNS;

2.   Reliance completely on Windows 2000 DNS;

3.   Coexistence between BIND DNS and Windows 2000 DNS. This scenario involves three alternatives:

   - Delegated subdomains from BIND to Windows 2000 DNS with namespace overlap;

   - Delegated subdomains from BIND to Windows 2000 DNS without namespace overlap;

   - Separate namespaces for BIND DNS and Windows 2000.

The first scenario (relying completely on BIND DNS) is an option when your BIND DNS is Windows 2000 DNS compliant. The compliancy requirements are as follows:

- The BIND DNS version must support RFC 2052 (SRV records). SRV records are supported in BINDv4.9.6 and higher.

- The BIND DNS version should support RFC 2136 (dynamic update) and RFC 1995 (IXFR). Dynamic update is supported in BINDv8.1.2 and higher. To see whether your BIND version supports dynamic update, use the `nsupdate` tool accompanying BIND. Although dynamic update is not an absolute requirement, not supporting it will lead to a lot of administrative overhead.

In a Windows 2000 environment, Microsoft recommends using BINDv8.2.1 or higher. This version supports SRV records, dynamic update, IXFR, and negative caching. If you do not want to upgrade to a higher BIND version and prefer to go with Windows 2000 DNS, read the following section on how to migrate (this brings us to scenario 2).

The second scenario can be used when your BIND DNS is not compliant, and your organization is prepared to migrate to Windows 2000 DNS. Migration from BIND DNS to Windows 2000 DNS involves the following steps:

1. Install a Windows 2000 server machine and add the DNS service.

2. Copy the forward and reverse lookup zone files from the BIND server to the `%systemdrive%\winnt\system32\dns` directory on the Windows 2000 server. To find out where the zone files are located on the BIND server, check out the named.boot (for BINDv4.x) or named.conf (for BINDv8.x) file in the `/etc` directory.

3. Start the new Zone Wizard from the DNS MMC snap-in and choose the Use This Existing File option. Point to the zone files that you copied over from the BIND server.

4. Install AD (using DCPROMO).

The third scenario contains three alternatives. They can be used when your BIND DNS is not compliant with Windows 2000 DNS, and your organization is not prepared to upgrade the legacy DNS to Windows 2000 DNS. Remember: Noncompliance means not supporting SRV records, IXFR, and dynamic updates.

In the first alternative, delegation with namespace overlap, the Windows 2000 domain uses the same DNS domain name, `cpq-corp.net`, as the one hosted on the legacy BIND DNS. This alternative is set up by delegating the Windows 2000–specific subdomains from the BIND DNS server to a

Windows 2000 DNS server, a member of the `cpqcorp.net` Windows 2000 root domain.

The second alternative, delegation without namespace overlap, uses a DNS domain name, `win2k.cpqcorp.net`, different from the one hosted on the legacy BIND DNS. This scenario is implemented by delegating the `win2k.cpq-corp.net` subdomain from the BIND DNS server to the Windows 2000 DNS server. In this alternative the name of the AD domain can be identical to the name of the delegated DNS subdomain. The Windows 2000 server running the Windows 2000 DNS service will be a member of the `win2k.cpqcorp.net` Windows 2000 domain (not the `cpqcorp.net` domain as in the previous scenario).

The third alternative, separate namespaces without delegation, uses a different DNS domain name for the Windows 2000 domain infrastructure: `compaq.com` on the BIND side and `cpqcorp.net` on the Windows 2000 side. Contrary to the previous alternative, this one is not implemented at the top level using delegation, but using separate namespaces.

1.18 Internet and intranet DNS namespace

Many companies have a separate Internet and intranet DNS infrastructure. Most even split their DNS namespace into private and public portions. The public portion is visible from the Internet; the private portion is not. A DNS name that is part of the public portion is known as an "external name"; a private portion name is known as an "internal name." The main reason for setting up DNS this way is to secure internal DNS host names and zones, which means hiding internal host names from the Internet and protecting internal zones against unauthorized modifications coming from the Internet. The protection is usually provided by a firewall or set of firewalls located between the intranet and extranet portion of the DNS infrastructure.

Also, in most cases the choice for hidden internal host names and zones is coupled with the choice of the private IP addressing scheme. Digital, for example, gave machines outside the firewall a name ending in `.digital.com`; the ones on the inside firewall had a name ending in `dec.com`. Digital used global IP addresses and allowed DNS queries to go through the firewall. After the merger, Compaq reorganized both its own and the Digital namespaces. The internal namespace of both merged companies was converted gradually to `cpqcorp.net`. As with Digital, Compaq's machines are known externally by the `compaq.com` domain name and internally by

Table 1.2   *Advantages and Disadvantages of Intranet and Internet Namespace Design Choices*

	Advantage	Disadvantage
Separate Namespaces	▪ Easier management ▪ Best security if set up correctly	▪ More complex to use for the end user ▪ Complex setup and configuration ▪ Need to register extra domain names
Single Namespace	▪ Ease of use for the end user	▪ No need to register extra domain names ▪ Complex administration and maintenance ▪ Need to duplicate data
Hybrid Model	▪ Contiguous namespace ▪ Ease of use for the end user	▪ Longer FQDNs

the `cpqcorp.net` domain name. Unlike Digital, Compaq uses a hidden internal DNS system: DNS queries coming from the Internet are not allowed to go through the firewall.

There are three different ways to set up the Internet and intranet DNS namespace: separate namespaces, a single namespace, or a hybrid model. The first model, separate namespaces, is the best way to go. When using separate namespaces, the internal and the external DNS domain have a different DNS name. If the internal namespace is meant to be visible only internally, we talk about a "private root." A private root scenario may require some special configuration to enable your internal clients to resolve both internal and external host names. The easiest way is to configure your internal DNS servers as forwarders to Internet DNS servers. The alternative is to provide smart clients that can decide whether a given host is located internally or externally—in other words, whether they should send a DNS query to the internal DNS servers or the Internet DNS servers.

Table 1.2 discusses the advantages and disadvantages of the three configurations.

1.19 DHCP and WINS integration

One of the important new features of the Windows 2000 DHCP server is its support for dynamic DNS update. This enables the DHCP server to register A and PTR records on behalf of Windows 2000 clients or, more importantly, on behalf of down-level clients (NT 4.0, Windows 98, etc.) that do not support the dynamic DNS update protocol. A DHCP server sends out a dynamic update request every time a lease is renewed. Deregistration is done only by a Windows 2000 client. Its DHCP client will automatically deregister a resource record when the DHCP lease expires.

The way DHCP dynamic update works between the DHCP client and server is based on some extra information that is added to the messages used during the DHCP protocol. (The DHCP protocol consists of four phases: discover, offer, request, and acknowledge.) This lets the DHCP client negotiate whether the DHCP server should do a DNS update on the client's behalf and how it should do it. The client and server set a special flag in the DHCP request and acknowledge messages. This flag can have one of the following values: 0, meaning that the client requests to set the A record itself and that the server set the PTR record; 1, meaning that the client requests the server to set both the A and PTR records; and 3, meaning that the server sets both the A and PTR records regardless of the client's request. By default a Windows 2000 client sends out the 1 flag. Depending on its configuration, the server can change this flag to 3. Depending on the way the DHCP server and client are configured, the DHCP server can register just the PTR record, both A and PTR records, or nothing at all. By default a Windows 2000 client registers its A record, and the DHCP server registers the PTR record because the client is considered to own its proper host name, while the DHCP server is considered to own IP addresses.

WINS is the dynamic NetBIOS name resolution service. Because of the importance of NetBIOS naming, WINS was a critical service in NT 4.0. Windows 2000 relies primarily on DNS for name resolution; nevertheless, WINS may still be required for backward compatibility.

Windows 2000 DNS still supports WINS lookup. This feature (introduced in NT 4.0) enables a DNS server to call on WINS if DNS name resolution fails. The WINS lookup method is based on two special resource records (WINS and WINS-R), which are added to the forward and reverse lookup zone files. To set it up, configure the WINS and WINS-R properties in your Windows 2000 forward and reverse lookup zone files. When an authoritative DNS server cannot resolve a forward lookup and it is configured for WINS lookup, it will strip the DNS domain off the host name and forward the host name to the WINS server. The IP address returned from the WINS to the DNS server is then passed by the DNS server to the DNS resolver. To the resolver it will appear as if the DNS server resolved the query.

Things look a little bit different in the case of a reverse lookup combined with WINS lookup. The problem in this scenario is that the WINS DB is not ordered using IP addresses (as is a DNS reverse lookup zone), but using

NetBIOS names. In fact, it is very misleading to talk about WINS lookup in this scenario. DNS will not call on WINS at all; it will use a node adapter status request. This is a special message the DNS server sends to the IP address to be resolved; if the machine is online, it can return its NetBIOS name to the DNS server. The DNS name will append the configured DNS domain name and forward this all together to the DNS resolver.

Windows 2000 allows an administrator to set up multiple WINS servers per zone and to configure different WINS servers for primary and secondary zones. Your organization may have different WINS servers depending on geographical sites. To do this check Do Not Replicate This Record in the WINS or WINS-R properties of the forward or reverse lookup zones. This will mark the resource record as local and exclude it from zone replication.

1.20 AD replication

AD replication is an important step to master when dealing with large corporate deployments. Many new applications will be relying on the consistency of the AD. Many will also store their own objects and attributes in the AD. An AD-enabled application will not worry about the replication aspects of the data it stores in the AD. Once the data are defined in the schema and instances of objects created in the AD, the application will attempt to access these objects, potentially in a distributed manner, but will not be involved in the replication of these data between DCs. An example of such an application is Exchange 2000. The Global Address List (GAL) in Exchange 5.5 is integrated in the AD in the Exchange 2000 release. This means that the directory portion of Exchange is stored in the AD; therefore, it is important to design a replication topology and avoid inconsistencies, which would affect Exchange greatly.

Replication in Windows 2000 has changed drastically from previous versions of Windows NT. For Windows NT, replication was a simple matter of copying information from the PDC system to the other computers that act as BDCs. Windows 2000 uses a multimaster, store-and-forward replication mechanism to allow changes to be made at any controller within an organization and have those changes successfully copied to all other DCs. Replication is the mechanism that ensures that data are copied in a robust and reliable manner so that DCs are updated in the most efficient and controlled way, no matter how distributed the organization.

One of the design goals of Windows 2000 is to accommodate the requirements of large enterprises. Windows NT replication was too simple to be able to match the scalability issues that are addressed in Windows 2000. The extensibility of the AD and the number of objects it can support far surpass the capabilities of the single-master replication model used in previous versions of Windows NT. A new replication strategy with the ability to sustain a large number of objects in an environment where domains are grouped together to form a global namespace had to be defined.

During the design phase of the site topology, architects must ask themselves the following questions:

- How many partitions (or domains) are composing the AD?

- What kind of data and how much must be replicated?

- How fast must replication be executed within the AD between two end points?

- What is the size of the user base and how distributed is it?

- How frequently are data stored in the AD modified?

- What is the network connectivity between the physical locations where the users reside?

This is the information that provides the basis for the site topology design. When dealing with namespace and domain designs, a number of domain models may be produced. Some of these models are due to political constraints. Some, however, are due to the business model in which the company operates. In other cases domain models are the result of security and legal constraints. The site topology will help identify how the different domain models are affecting the replication traffic. In some cases a particular domain model, which looked interesting at the early phases of the design, may not be implemented owing to the low network bandwidth available or the unreliability or latency of the network.

1.20.1   Replication basics

Windows 2000 DCs hold a replica of all the objects belonging to their domain and have full read/write access to these objects. Administrators can perform management operations using any DC in a domain. These operations affect the state or the value of an object and must, therefore, be replicated to the other DCs. Replication is the process of propagating object updates between DCs. The goal of replication is to allow all controllers to receive updates and to maintain their copies of the AD DB in a consistent state. Replication is not triggered immediately when an object has been modified, since this could trigger a flood of replication operations if the directory is being manipulated by programs that insert or update many records in a short period of time, such as directory synchronization procedures.

Instead, replication is triggered after a period of time, gathering all changes and providing them to other controllers in collections. Replication can be scheduled to control when these changes are disseminated to other DCs. Therefore, since replication is not instantaneous, in normal operation the AD on any controller can be regarded as always being in a state of loose consistency, since replication changes may be on the way from other controllers. Eventually the changes arrive and DCs synchronize with each other. However, when performing a management operation, an administrator does not know if another user or another administrator is performing the same operation on another DC. This could lead to a replication collision, which must then be resolved. We will see how these collisions are resolved in a later section.

The goal of the replication topology is to mirror the data stored in the AD so that these data are close to the users. The larger and more distributed the user community, the harder it is to design and implement a replication topology that fulfills the requirements of corporate enterprises. Because of this it is important to understand how replication works in detail.

1.20.2   DCs

In a Windows 2000 infrastructure, every DC maintains a copy of the AD DB with full read/write access to all of the objects belonging to the domain. This implies that if an operation is performed on one of the DCs, it must then be replicated to all other DCs in the domain. If domains are linked together to form a forest, some of the data from each domain must be replicated to the other domains to form a collective view of the forest. Windows 2000 introduces a multimaster replication model to support copying of data within the domain and, indeed, between domains. At the same time, AD replication is optimized, because only the data that are actually changed are replicated. In other words, if a user updates his or her password, then only the updated password is replicated to other controllers, instead of the complete object.

AD uses attribute-level replication. DCs are responsible for initiating and performing replication operations. Each DC serves as a replication partner for other DCs. Replication is always performed between DCs. Member servers do not play a role in the replication process (they do not hold AD information). Internally, DCs reference other DCs or replication partners using GUIDs, unique numbers that can be used to identify objects. A GUID is a 16-byte (128-bit) number introduced by the Open Software Foundation (OSF) to identify the unique application interfaces of the Distributed Computing Environment (DCE). The OSF called them Universally Unique Identifiers (UUIDs). Microsoft COM used the term GUIDs; however, the underlying algorithm for generating them did not change. Microsoft used them to identify COM interfaces, and GUIDs prevent two programs from defining the same API, even if the functions and callable routines have the same name.

GUIDs are by definition unique. This implies that they are generated using an algorithm that ensures their uniqueness even if they are generated at the same time on the same system. There are two GUIDs used internally by Windows 2000 to reference a DC:

1.   *Server GUID.* Replication partners use this GUID to reference a specific DC. The GUID for each DC is saved in the DNS DB as SRV resource records and is used by replication partners to locate the IP address of available DCs.

2.   *DB GUID.* Initially, this GUID is the same as the Server GUID and is used to identify the DB during replication calls. In the event of an authoritative restore, this GUID is changed to allow other DCs to realize that the DB was restored and, therefore, the state of the DC was changed.

GUIDs are more reliable than names, because their values remain constant even if systems are renamed. This ensures a safe rename environment. In other words, an object can be moved from one part of the AD to another without requiring the object to be deleted and then recreated in its new location.

It is important to note, however, that in Windows 2000, a DC cannot be renamed. To change the name of a DC, administrators must use the DC Wizard (DCPROMO) to demote the DC back to a member server first, and then change the name. Finally, DCPROMO can be run again to promote the renamed member server back to a DC. This can be a tedious operation if a number of DCs must be renamed or if the AD partition that they managed is large. Demoting a DC means getting rid of all AD information and generating a SAM DB for built-in security principals. Promoting the member server means replicating an entire domain to the local AD DB. This could take days if the domain is really big. So it is important to define the naming conventions during the planning and design phase of the Windows 2000 project.

1.20.3   Replication operations

A number of operations trigger replication between DCs. Depending on permissions, an administrator or a user performs these operations on objects stored in the AD. The operations that trigger replication are the following:

- *Object creation:* the creation of a new object in the DB, for example, a new user;

- *Attribute modification:* the modification of an object attribute, for example, a user changes his or her password;

- *Object move:* the moving of an object from one container to another;

- *Object deletion:* the deletion of objects from the DB.

OUs are special containers that help organize objects within the AD and often use the same names as departments within a company, such as "Sales" or "Marketing." A move from the Sales OU to the Marketing OU is an example of an object move that might happen as a result of reorganization within a company. Object move operations are very similar to attribute modification in that an object move implies the modification of an attribute, the DN of the object.

Object deletion does not actually delete the object immediately, but transforms it into a tombstone, a state of the object or flag meaning that the object has been deleted and is no longer accessible. Tombstones have a configurable lifetime of 60 days and then the object is really removed from the DB.

1.20.4   NCs and replication

NCs are a new concept introduced in Windows 2000. The scope of replication within a Windows NT domain is only domain-wide; therefore, this concept did not exist previously. An NC is a tree of objects stored in the AD. There are three NCs:

- *Configuration NC:* contains all the objects that represent the structure of the AD in terms of domains, DCs, sites, enterprise CAs, and other configuration-type objects.

- *Schema NC:* contains all the classes and attributes that define the objects and their attributes that are stored in the AD.

- *Domain NC:* contains all the other objects of the AD: the users, the groups, the OUs, the computers, and so on.

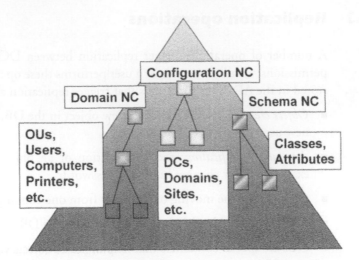

Figure 1.10
NCs and replication.

Domains act as partitions for the AD, but they are not the boundary of replication. NCs define the boundary of replication and define the replication scope. The boundary of replication indicates how far management operations performed on DCs are replicated to other DCs in the same domain or to other DCs in the forest. In other words, NCs define how far AD changes are replicated in an organization (see Figure 1.10).

There are two scopes of replication for NCs: forest-wide and domain-wide. In the former, the configuration and schema are unique in the entire forest and form a unit in the forest. This means that their NCs must be replicated to all the DCs in every domain comprising the forest. The configuration NC and schema NC are, therefore, said to have a forest-wide scope. Domain objects are replicated only within the domain to which they currently belong. Thus, the domain NC has a domain-wide scope. In other words, information stored in a domain is confined to an NC and is replicated in the domain itself. There is one exception to this rule: When the domain NC is replicated to a GC, its scope becomes forest-wide because GCs are available in multiple domains; therefore, domain NCs need the forest-wide scope to reach them. We will see later how the replication topologies will allow a domain NC to reach GCs in other domains.

NCs contain all the objects of the AD and are obviously held in the AD. Objects in the AD always have parents; they are contained in other objects, such as OUs, computers, and domains. The parents of these top-level objects are the NCs. Some NCs are the children of other NCs, as is the case of the schema NC, which is a child of the configuration NC.

The parent of the top-level NCs is the RootDSE. The RootDSE is a virtual container. It contains all the objects in the domain. It is the only object in the entire AD that does not have a parent object. The RootDSE object does not get replicated and does not hold any space. It is simply a virtual parent for the top-level NCs stored in the AD. The RootDSE could be viewed as the summit of the AD and is often used by applications to discover the NCs available at a particular DC.

1.21   DB sizing and design

One of the major benefits of migrating to Windows 2000 is the ability to consolidate servers. Consolidation is about reducing the number of domains and reducing the number of servers and DCs. The trend in Windows 2000 designs is toward fewer but larger servers. The rationale behind consolidating servers is to reduce the hardware costs as well as management and troubleshooting costs. In other words, the goal is to reduce the total cost of ownership.

Understanding the AD DB is an essential part of the Windows 2000 design and particularly of its consolidation efforts. The whole process of consolidation involves sizing DCs and GCs for large organizations with the goal of centralizing servers as much as possible. During this process, particular attention is paid to the choice of hardware and storage for these servers. The trend in scalable designs is to separate the server sizing and the storage design. This greatly simplifies the approach. In the server design, the CPU and memory considerations are addressed. In the storage design, the I/O subsystem and I/O performance are addressed.

1.21.1   Extensible storage engine

To create and maintain a large implementation of the AD, it is important to understand how the AD DB works and what happens when an object is created. Understanding how the DB works is key to tuning it for optimum performance.

The AD store is based on the Extensible Storage Engine (ESE). This is based on the same DB engine that is shipped with Microsoft Exchange. The ESE is not the Microsoft Jet DB, but a variant called "Jet Blue." Microsoft chose the ESE as the DB engine for the AD for a number of reasons:

- *Scalability.* Microsoft Exchange already uses this DB, and it is not uncommon to see 100-GB DBs deployed at customer sites.

- *Performance.* If well tuned, the DB is quite fast and can handle enterprise requests very well.

- *Recovery.* Most importantly, if something goes wrong—a disk crashes, the system crashes, or the software crashes—the ESE allows the recovery of the DB into a usable state.

The AD storage architecture is composed of multiple layers, as shown in Figure 1.11. The top layer is formed by a number of APIs to allow integration or applications with the Directory System Agent (DSA). This is the directory layer, which handles all access to the ESE engine through a DB layer.

The DSA handles the hierarchical namespace of the OU and other containers in the AD. The ESE layer handles a flat representation of the namespace via a set of tables and stores these tables in the ESE files. The role of the DB layer is to manipulate the hierarchical representation of the objects into a flat format, which can then be stored as tables in the ESE. The ESE is composed of the following files:

- NTDS.DIT is the directory store. This is the actual DB where the AD objects reside.

- EDB log files contain objects from transactions. These objects may not yet have been saved in NTDS.DIT. The ESE uses these files, called "transaction logs," to secure information on disk.

- EDB.CHK, or the checkpoint file, contains the current transaction state and is used when restoring log files. Information stored in this

Figure 1.11
AD DB architecture.

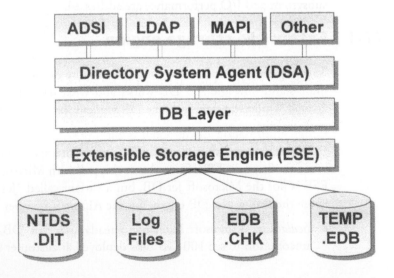

file indicates the latest transaction that has been saved in NTDS.DIT and can be used in a restore to reconstruct the DB to its original state by indicating the latest transaction from the log files that were saved.

- TEMP.EDB contains the transactions in progress while a new log file is being created. Transaction logs in the AD have a fixed size of 10 MB. Once this size is reached, a new transaction file is created. While the new file is being created, if there are incoming operations, they are saved in this file.

- RES1.EDB, RES2.EDB. These files have a total size of 20 MB. They are used only in case the disk is filled up. This allows an administrator to be informed that the disk holding the transaction logs is almost full while the services remain available. An administrator can then perform a backup of the transaction logs on the drive, causing their deletion by the system.

1.21.2 I/O patterns for the ESE

The files used by the ESE are fundamentally different. To understand these differences, we need to look at their I/O patterns. The I/O pattern is a combination of multiple factors, including the I/O size and how the DB is accessed. To adapt a storage solution for the AD and tune it to increase performance, it is important to understand the I/O pattern of these files because, depending on the I/O pattern, a particular tuning option will be used for the storage solution. Using the wrong tuning setting can result in a loss in performance. When building AD storage, this is the key knowledge that allows appropriate choosing of the settings for the various AD storage files to optimize access and, therefore, performance.

The I/O pattern for NTDS.DIT is the following:

- NTDS.DIT is a DB that is normally used for read-mostly operations. AD normal operations account for 70 percent to 90 percent of reads.

- Each record stored in the DB is exactly 8 KB.

- Access to the DB is done asynchronously. This means that a write operation will return immediately; however, the caller does not know immediately if the operation was successful or not.

- Access is performed in a multithreaded way. This means that multiple threads can access the DB to read and to write data. When put in perspective, the multithreaded and asynchronous access to the AD is clearly a very scalable design. Threads must perform tasks very quickly to scale to allow several hundred concurrent accesses. They are created to perform a specific task very quickly, and, once done, they can perform another task and respond to the queries of another client.

- Data are saved randomly in the DB. This means that if an object composed of multiple large (bigger than 8 KB) attributes must be retrieved, then the values of these attributes are spread in the DB and are not sequential.

The I/O pattern for the log files is as follows:

- The log files are intended for write operations only. Each record stored in the DB is exactly 8 KB, as with NTDS.DIT.

- Writes are synchronous. This means that the caller will wait until the operation is completed and will then know the result of the operation.

- Access is performed by a single thread, which means only one write operation is in progress at any time. If the LSASS needs to perform multiple write operations, it must queue them and wait for the current one to complete.

- Access to the data is sequential, which means that the data are stored contiguously in the log file.

Redundant Arrays of Independent Disks (or Drives) (RAID) is key for proper performance and protection of the AD DB. In a large AD implementation, an 18-GB disk drive will do no good for the performance of the DB even if it is half the size. This is because I/Os are the main driving factor for good AD performance. CPUs are always faster, and memory is becoming cheaper; however, storage is slower to improve. Special care must be taken when designing the storage subsystem.

RAID brings load balancing across multiple spindles. For multi-threaded, concurrent I/Os, it helps in eliminating "hot" spindles and can improve performance by factors of two, three, or even more, depending on usage. RAID also helps build large logical volumes that do not fill up as easily. Do not fill up storage to more than 70 percent; leave room for expansion. RAID, and in this case "parity RAID" (RAID5), protects you against hardware failures and prevents loss of information even if you lose an entire disk. RAID also allows for more disks and more spindles to provide more capacity to handle peak I/Os, and it brings better performance overall.

1.21.3 AD transaction logs

Logging is the action of saving data in a log file before these data are saved in NTDS.DIT. Data are written to the log file and to a cache in memory simultaneously. This is done as an atomic operation or transaction to ensure commitment from both sides that the data are safe before saving these data in NTDS.DIT. Logging is the fundamental technology underneath the ESE. The goal of logging is to be able to recover the DB in case of the following:

- Power failure;

- Disk crash;

- Software crash;

- Any other corruption.

Logging is intended to recover the data in a consistent state. To do so, the ESE uses the transactions to ensure commitment that the data have been correctly saved before discarding the copy in the log buffer in memory.

ESE transaction logs can be set into two modes of operations: circular logging and noncircular logging. Circular logging limits the number of log files that are created. By default, when circular logging is enabled, 20 log files are created. When the 21st log file must be created, the first one is deleted. This number can be modified in the registry. One of the advantages of circular logging is that storage size is under control. For 20 log files, a maximum of 200 MB are allocated on disk. Circular logging is the default and the recommended mode. When noncircular logging is enabled, files are created on an as-needed basis; as long as there is storage available, new files are created. Noncircular log files are removed when they are successfully backed up.

Windows 2000 is configured to use circular logging by default. While for Exchange a backup operation cleans the transaction logs, AD cleans the log files every 12 hours. This is known as the garbage collection interval. This means that backup procedures must take into consideration that rolling transactions forward to restore a failed DB may not be a viable solution. For this reason, it is important to keep the AD available by adding multiple DCs per domain. As long as a DC remains available, the AD is up and running. A restored DC from tapes will synchronize by replicating the missing data from one of the DCs in the domain. Therefore, a best practice in a production environment is to have at least two DCs per domain. The DCs can be configured in the following way:

- One DC for the infrastructure master, which can also be configured as the RID master.
- One replica DC configured as the PDC Emulator.

1.22   AD security

A solid understanding of the Windows 2000 security features is a key requirement for the creation of a secure and reliable enterprise AD infrastructure. Windows 2000 security is tightly integrated with the Windows 2000 directory system: the AD. This integration is implemented as follows:

- The AD is used to store security-related account information and security policy information.
- Access to the AD is secured via the operating system, which enforces the Windows 2000 access control model on all directory objects and authenticates every directory access.

Windows 2000 security is based upon numerous open standards. Open standards facilitate interoperability with other operating system environments. Some well-known open security standards supported in Windows 2000 include the following:

- Kerberos,[1] an authentication protocol for distributed systems;
- The security architecture for the Internet Protocol (Ipsec)[2] and Layer 2 Tunneling Protocol (L2TP),[3] two well-known tunneling standards.

Windows 2000 includes support for several strong security protocols and technologies. "Strong" means that it is very hard, if not impossible, to compromise the security of the protocol or technology. Windows 2000 incorporates Kerberos 5 as the default authentication protocol (the NT 4.0 default was NTLM). Kerberos 5 is widely regarded as a "strong" authentication protocol. Windows 2000 also comes with support for multifactor authentication using a smart card and PIN code and for public key infrastructures (PKI) and public key–enabled applications.

Windows NT has always provided a single sign-on. The purpose of single sign-on is to minimize the number of times the user must enter his or

---

1.   Kerberos V5 is defined in RFC 1510.
2.   IPsec is defined in RFCs 1825 through 1827.
3.   L2TP is defined in the Internet draft `draft-ietf-pppext-l2tp-14.txt`.

her credentials (his or her user ID and password). The user authenticates once at the beginning of a logon session; from that moment on, he or she should be able to access any resource in the domain or the domain tree (without an additional credential prompt). Windows 2000 extends the single sign-on process as follows:

- Windows 2000 now supports Kerberos as an authentication protocol;

- Windows 2000 supports the SSL and TLS protocols;[4]

- The X.509v3 certificates used in these protocols can be used as credentials for Windows authentication.

1.22.1   Kerberos authentication

Kerberos is embedded in Windows 2000 as the new default authentication protocol. Every Windows 2000 workstation and server include a client Kerberos authentication provider. Windows 2000 does not include Kerberos support for other Microsoft platforms: If you want your NT 4.0 or Windows 95 or 98 clients to authenticate using Kerberos, you will need to upgrade your workstation to Windows 2000 Professional.

The protocol is always dealing with three basic entities: two that want to authenticate to one another (i.e., a user and a resource server) and an entity that mediates between the two—"trusted third party," or, in Kerberos terminology, the KDC. The basic Kerberos protocol only deals with authentication. Microsoft's implementation of the protocol also includes extensions for access control. So far no Kerberos implementation has covered auditing. Later on in this chapter, we'll explain how one of the secret keys exchanged during the Kerberos authentication sequence can be used for packet authentication, integrity, and confidentiality services.

1.22.2   Access control

Although Windows 2000 includes quite a few new access control features, the access control "model" is basically the same as the one used in NT 4.0. It is based upon the following key concepts: access token, access mask, security descriptor, and impersonation. Windows 2000 also includes some important changes to ACLs, the associated Access Control Entries (ACEs), the way that access control is administered, and the ACL evaluation rules.

---

4.   For more information on SSL V3 go to http://home.netscape.com/eng/ssl3/ssl-toc.html; TLS V1 is defined in RFC 2246, available at http://www.ietf.org.

To enable a proper display of the ACE changes mentioned above, Microsoft provided a new ACL editor. This new editor was shipped for the first time with NT 4.0 SP4; it was installed together with the Security Configuration Editor (SCE). The most important characteristics of this ACL editor include its object independency (the same editor is used to set access control on different types of securable objects) and its support for Deny ACEs and the new ACL evaluation rules. The new ACL evaluation rules and how they affect what's displayed in the ACL editor will be discussed later on.

A fundamental difference with its NT 4.0 predecessor is Windows 2000's capability to display negative ACEs (also known as Deny ACEs). Although NT 4.0 supported negative ACEs, the ACL editor could not deal with them. If in NT 4.0 you set Deny ACEs programmatically, an error message was displayed when using the NT 4.0 ACL editor. The new ACL editor also has a brand new Graphical User Interface (GUI), consisting of a basic and an advanced view. The advanced view is used to set more granular access permissions, control inheritance, change ownership, and set auditing settings.

ACL inheritance is a mechanism that lets container objects pass access control information to their child objects. A container's child objects can be noncontainer objects, as well as other container objects. From an administrator's point of view, ACL inheritance simplifies access control management. The administrator can set the ACL on a parent object and, if inheritance is enabled, need not bother about setting ACLs on child objects. From a software-logic point of view, ACL inheritance makes access control evaluation much more complex. The software needs to consider multiple ACLs: not just an object's proper ACLs (also known as "explicit ACLs") but also all the inherited ACLs. Inherited ACLs can come from an object's immediate parent but also from parent objects higher up in a hierarchy.

A major difference with NT 4.0 is the Windows 2000 support for "dynamic" inheritance. In NT 4.0 inheritance was "static." This meant that an object inherited permissions from its parent object when it was created. Once created, changes to the parent object's permissions did not affect the child object unless the administrator selected Replace Permissions on Subdirectories and Replace Permissions on Existing Files in NT 4.0's Folder Permissions dialog box. The Windows 2000 support for dynamic inheritance means that Windows 2000 will automatically update the child's ACLs when the parent object's ACLs change. As in NT 4.0, a child object also inherits permissions at creation time.

Another important difference is that Windows 2000 does not overwrite the child's proper "explicit" ACEs with the inherited parent ACEs. Windows 2000 simply adds inherited ACEs to the child's ACLs and tags them with a special "inherited" flag. You can observe the presence of this flag in the advanced view of the ACL editor: To stress the fact that inherited ACLs cannot be edited in the ACL editor of a child object, Microsoft grays out the keys in the "type" column for inherited permissions; also, Microsoft added an explanatory text in the dialog box telling the user "this permission is inherited" and "you can edit the permission only at the parent object…" In NT 4.0, inherited permissions could be edited on the child object, because both the child object's proper ACLs and the inherited ACLs were merged, making the inherited ACLs unrecognizable.

Object type–based ACEs are a new feature of version 4 ACLs. Microsoft implemented them in Windows 2000 for AD objects. Object type–based ACEs include two new ACE fields: an "object type" field and an "inherited object type" field. Using these fields, an administrator can create fine-grain access control settings for AD objects in the following ways:

- He or she can define which object types an ACE applies to. The "object type" field of an ACE refers to an object GUID. The GUID can be linked to an object type, an object property, a set of object properties, or an extended right.

- He or she can define which object types will inherit the access control information defined in an ACE. The ACE field used for this feature is the "inherited object type" field. As with the "object type" field, it contains a GUID.

Object type–based ACEs can be used to set access control based on an object property or a set of object properties. Examples of user object properties are a user's First Name, Home Directory, City, and Manager's Name. Sample user object property sets are Phone and Mail Options, Account Restrictions, Personal Information, Public Information, and Home Address. An example of a property set is Public Information: it covers a user's E-Mail Addresses, Manager, and Common Name attributes. The Windows 2000 platform SDK explains how to create custom property sets for your organization.

Extended rights are special AD object–related actions or operations that are not covered by any of the standard Windows 2000 access rights (read, write, execute, delete). They are special because they cannot be linked to object properties. Good examples are the mailbox-specific Send As and Receive As extended rights. Although extended rights are not linked to

object properties, they are displayed together with the standard object permissions in the ACL editor. To get an overview of the extended rights, open
up the extended rights container of the Windows 2000 AD configuration
NC (you can look at the AD content using the ADSIEDIT tool). As with
property sets, an organization can create additional extended rights. The
Windows 2000 platform SDK explains the way to set this up.

All the access control changes listed in the previous sections forced
Microsoft to review the discretionary ACL evaluation rules and order. This
evaluation order contains three fundamental rules:

1.   Explicitly defined access control settings always have precedence
       over inherited access control settings. As mentioned earlier, this is
       a direct consequence of the discretionary access control model
       used in Windows NT and Windows 2000.

2.   Tier 1 parent access control settings have precedence over tier 2
       parent access control settings.

3.   Deny permissions have precedence over Allow permissions. If this
       were not the case, a user with a Deny access right could still be
       allowed to access a resource based, for example, on an Allow ACE
       for one of his or her groups.[5]

In what follows Windows 2000 objects can refer to any "securable"
object, which includes file system, share, printer, registry, AD, or service
objects. A securable object can also be a less "tangible" object, such as a
process or a Windows station. Some securable objects can contain other
securable objects; they are called "container" objects. A container object can
be a file system container (a folder), a registry container (a key), a printer
container (a printer contains documents), or an AD container (an OU).
Table 1.3 shows a subset of the securable objects available in Windows 2000
and which new access control feature is or can be applied to each object's
ACL.

In Windows 2000 the new ACL 4 has been implemented only for AD
objects. The main change in version 4 ACLs is the support for object-type
ACEs, which enable property-based ACEs, extended rights, and property
sets. The principal reason why Microsoft incorporated these changes was to
enable the definition of access control on AD objects in a more granular
way. These changes also enable fine-grain administrative delegation on AD
objects, another key feature of Windows 2000.

---

5.   In this case the evaluation order would be as follows: (1) Allow for the group, (2) Deny for the user. Because processing
       stops when all access rights in the access mask are granted, the evaluation process would not even get to the deny ACE.

Table 1.3   *New Windows 2000 ACE Features*

	Securable Object				
Access Control Feature	AD Object Permissions	NTFS Object Permissions[*]	Registry Object Permissions	Share Object Permissions[†]	Printer Object Permissions
New ACL editor	Yes	Yes	Yes	Yes	Yes
Fine-grain inheritance control	Yes	Yes	Yes	No	No
Object-type ACEs[‡]	Yes	No	No	No	No
Property-based ACEs[‡]	Yes	No	No	No	No
Extended rights and property sets[‡]	Yes	No	No	No	No
New ACL evaluation rules	Yes	Yes	Yes	Yes	Yes
ACL version	4	2	2	2	2

* NTFS object permissions require the NTFS file system.
† Share object permissions can be set on objects on the NTFS or on the FAT file system.
‡ New features included in new ACL 4.

1.22.3   Security management

In Windows 2000, the Event Viewer has also been extended: It includes a set of new folders[6] to gather auditing information related to certain OS core services (e.g., the Directory Service, the DNS Server, and the File Replication Service). Also, the description portion of the events has been extended, facilitating troubleshooting. Some events even include an HTTP pointer to the Microsoft online support site. Last but not least, the event logs can now also be accessed using the WMI management interface.

Using the SCA, an administrator can check a computer's current security settings against the values defined in a security template. The security templates can be defined using the Security Templates MMC snap-in. They contain all kinds of Windows 2000 security-related parameters: ACLs on file system and registry objects, event log settings, restricted groups (to set group membership), system service settings, and system account policy

---

6.   The services or applications that are logging their events to a particular folder can be found in the HKLM\SYSTEM\ CurrentControlSet\Services\EventLog\<Log-name>\sources registry entry.

settings. SCA uses a security DB (secedit.sdb) in which one of the security templates is loaded. The SCA engine can be run from the MMC snap-in or from the command prompt (using the secedit executable). The same engine is used for the security portion of the Windows 2000 Group Policy Object settings.

1.23   Public key infrastructure

The PKI software shipping with Windows 2000 offers a great level of flexibility and scalability to organizations planning to deploy public key–based security solutions within their enterprises. Microsoft has clearly chosen the open-standards track to implement its PKI solution, which is very important from an interoperability point of view. A critical factor that can drive the decision to set up a Windows 2000–based PKI is cost: Windows 2000 PKI is substantially cheaper than products from other vendors.

A PKI can use a directory to store certificates and certificate revocation lists (CRLs). Most PKI products (including Windows 2000 PKI) require the directory to be LDAP and X.500 compliant. The presence of a directory is not always a requirement. In Windows 2000, for example, you can build a PKI based on standalone certification authorities. In this scenario, a much simpler certificate and CRL sharing mechanism (e.g., a shared folder) can be sufficient.

If you plan to use a directory in a Windows 2000 environment, it is wise to use the AD, which is tightly integrated with the Windows 2000 OS. AD is also a good choice from a TCO point of view: You can leverage the investment for your corporate Windows 2000 AD. Integration of Windows 2000 PKI with another directory system (e.g., the Isocor or Netscape directories) will demand more resources.

When using a directory in a PKI, a critical requirement is availability. PKI users should have access to other users' certificates and revocation lists on a permanent basis. In most environments, availability of the directory is even more critical than the availability of the certification authorities. In addition, if you're planning to implement a Windows 2000–based PKI, remember that just as with any other PKI product, a large amount of the planning, design, and administration work related to a PKI is nontechnical. Also, remember that a PKI is an infrastructure, which not only affects different applications but also all entities dealing with your corporate IT infrastructure, from simple users to your CIO.

1.24   Migration and integration issues

A successful migration strategy integrates users and computers seamlessly, without disrupting business operations. Documenting each step and testing contingency plans will reduce migration risks. Before attempting a migration, it is crucial to understand the current environment and have a well-designed Windows 2000 infrastructure. The migration phase in a Windows 2000 project will define the necessary steps to move from the current environment to the new Windows 2000 infrastructure.

Migrating to Windows 2000 involves a number of preparation steps and a thorough understanding of the various migration techniques and their implications. Before the actual migration is even attempted, a full design of the future Windows 2000 infrastructure must be achieved. In other words, the design phase in the Windows 2000 project will define what the future infrastructure will look like. The migration phase will define the steps involved in getting there.

The migration phase must provide a strategy for migrating the current infrastructure to Windows 2000 without interrupting daily business. This is a very challenging aspect of the migration. Global corporations may have a large existing infrastructure composed of many Windows NT 4.0 domains. Compaq, for example, had 13 account domains and more than 1,700 resource domains. Corporations or conglomerates often do not really know how many domains exist in their infrastructure. One of the design goals is to reduce the number of domains and store the resources they contain in OUs. These containers may replace resource domains, since Windows 2000 provides the ability to delegate administrative rights at the level of OUs. Collapsing domains into OUs is not something that can be achieved overnight. The migration phase of a 100,000-seat company may take several months. It is not possible to stop all operations while the migration phase is in progress. Therefore, the migration of these domains requires accepting a coexistence phase, where some of the accounts or resources have already been migrated to Windows 2000, while some have not.

1.24.1   Preparing for a migration

Performing a migration involves choosing a strategy and defining contingency plans for each migration step. Preparation is necessary and basically involves going through the various phases of a Windows 2000 project. These phases can be broken down as follows:

- *Assessment planning, design pilot implementation, and migration assessment phase.* The assessment phase of the project evaluates the infrastructure in place and provides critical information essential for learning about current administrative practices. This information will also be used for reducing the risks associated with the migration. The assessment phase is a discovery phase where the following information is gathered:

  - *Business drivers for migrating to Windows 2000.* The goal is to understand the role and scope of the new infrastructure. Many companies will migrate to reduce costs, some will be interested in building a foundation for Exchange 2000, and others will want a stronger and more flexible environment for an e-business strategy. Understanding the business drivers allows the project team to design the new Windows 2000 infrastructure accordingly.

  - *Network operating system infrastructures (Novell, IBM mainframes, OpenVMS, existing directory structure).* This information will be used to design the AD schema and to define the source for directory information. Some companies will want to continue using their current directory for the management of user data. Synchronization between heterogeneous directories may then be required to publish and update the records in the AD. From a security perspective, a step toward single sign-on may be desired to integrate the various operating systems' security principals.

  - *Windows NT 4.0 infrastructure (number of domains, their purpose, and administrative model).* The NT 4.0 infrastructure and the administrative model will give clues to the current administrative practices and delegation requirements. This information will also form the base for the migration strategy.

  - *Network infrastructure (DNS, DHCP, WINS, bandwidth between physical locations, user population, network usage, and growth rates).* This is critical information for the network elements and site topology designs.

  - *Systems (DCs, member servers, client systems, their configuration, storage settings, and backup solutions in place).* This is information used to determine which systems can be reused. The disaster tolerance aspects and requirements will be gathered here.

  - *List of installed applications.* If some legacy applications require NetBIOS names, then the WINS infrastructure may not be shut down, and it could be desirable to review it. Knowing which applications are certified or supported on Windows 2000 helps in defining a migration path for them. Some applications may require a development cycle and, therefore, spin off a new project. Some systems may not be able to run Windows 2000 for the following reasons:

— Systems may be too old. For instance, Intel 486–based CPUs are not supported by Windows 2000.
— Systems are not sized correctly to support a consolidated design. For example, they may not have enough memory or enough I/O throughput.
— Components such as network adapters or controllers may not be certified to run in a Windows 2000 environment.
— Applications may not be certified or supported in a Windows 2000 environment.

These reasons may impact the migration strategy and may force companies to upgrade their systems or take a particular approach. In this case, some companies prefer to migrate the server infrastructure first, if the systems are ready. Migrating a server infrastructure also requires making a choice between migrating account domains or resource domains first.

- *Planning and design phase.* The planning and design phase is composed of an analysis of the requirements and a detailed design of the Windows 2000 infrastructure. The analysis evaluates a number of possible solutions for addressing the requirements and provides recommendations for the adoption of a specific technology. The detailed design defines how the selected technology can be applied to address the needs as defined by the requirements. This phase shapes the look of the Windows 2000 infrastructure and designs, in detail, the various components, such as DNS, forests, group policy objects, OU and administration models, capacity planning and sizing, networking, site topology, and more. The planning and design phase defines the strategies used for migrating objects from the current infrastructure.

- *Pilot phase.* The pilot phase produces a semiproduction environment to prove the concepts defined in the planning and design phase. Generally, these concepts are tested in special proof-of-concept labs during the design phase; however, the pilot phase provides the ability to test the new infrastructure with real users, often in various physical locations. The pilot phase will test the critical aspects of the new infrastructure, such as new Windows 2000 clients and associated applications, as well as server functionality and server-side applications, similar to Exchange 2000. Once the pilot phase is completed, the implementation and migration phase can begin.

1.24.2 Migration strategies

Which migration strategy will work best for a specific company? Some companies will be concerned that the employees will not see the immediate benefits of the migration, in which case they may prefer to start with the client migration. Some companies, on the other hand, will prefer to upgrade the servers first and perform the client migration later to avoid affecting users before a stable infrastructure is provided. Finally, some companies will run the two migration projects (client and server) simultaneously, with independent schedules.

Migrating clients also involves migrating the installed applications. While some of these applications are easy to migrate, some may require a development cycle. Microsoft has provided a certification path for Windows 2000, and many ISVs are already porting their applications to Windows 2000. Microsoft is hosting a Web site providing the list of applications tested to run on Windows 2000; this site can be found at http://www.microsoft.com/windows2000/upgrade/compat/search/software.asp. It should also be noted that many companies have home-grown applications that will require development efforts to be migrated.

Migrating the Windows NT 4.0 domains requires selecting between starting with the account domains or the resource domains. In any case, it is strongly recommended to start the migration with the smaller or less-important domains first, the rationale being that if a problem occurs, a smaller community will be affected. As experience grows, the larger or critical domains can be migrated.

Migrating the infrastructure has a number of benefits:

- *Establishment of the foundation.* Windows 2000 provides a number of benefits to reduce operational costs while increasing performance and reliability over Windows NT infrastructures. The total number of domains is likely to decrease and many servers will be consolidated. The trend in Windows 2000 designs is fewer but larger servers.

- *More flexibility.* Windows 2000 allows delegation of administration at a very granular level. The flexibility to define policies and disseminate them to a large number of users and computers is important, as is the flexibility to change these rules easily by editing group policy objects.

- *Easy integration.* Adoption of standards allows companies to integrate with their partners in a heterogeneous environment.

- *Stronger security by using authentication protocols such as Kerberos.* This benefit is not, however, fully implemented while clients are still running Windows NT 4.0.

- *Easier trust relationship management.* Windows 2000 trusts are transitive.

- *Visibility of benefits.* Users see the advantage of running Windows 2000.

- *Greater reliability and performance.* Windows 2000 requires far fewer reboots than Windows NT 4.0 and is much more stable.

- *New features, such as hibernation and plug-and-play.* Hibernating is similar to standby, in that it allows for saving power by shutting down system functions, such as spinning disks, without closing applications. Hibernation goes further than standby, however, and the system is completely shut down—that is, the power is turned off. Turning the power back on restores the system state, and applications are found in the same state that they were in prior to the hibernate operation.

- *Encrypted File System (EFS).* EFS protects the data stored locally on the client system.

- *Easier user interface.* The Windows 2000 interface is far more user friendly.

The infrastructure migration can be accomplished using two techniques: an in-place upgrade or restructuring. The in-place upgrade involves upgrading the existing infrastructure to Windows 2000; the restructuring technique involves moving or copying the data from one infrastructure to another. Each technique has pros and cons with implications for the approach taken and the tools used.

In-place upgrade

The in-place upgrade technique involves upgrading every DC, member server, and client in a Windows NT 4.0 domain structure. In other words, the domain structure remains unchanged, because each domain is upgraded to Windows 2000. This is probably the quickest path to Windows 2000 and is a recommended approach for small network infrastructures.

Generic steps involved in an in-place upgrade migration

The in-place upgrade can be broken down into four main steps:

1.   Preparing for the migration;

2.   Upgrading the PDC;

3.   Upgrading the BDCs;

4.   Switching to native mode.

Preparing for the migration

Preparing for the migration involves checking that the DCs can run in a Windows 2000 environment. This verification must be performed on both the hardware and the software running on the servers. To verify that the systems can be upgraded, the following questions must be answered:

- Is the server on the hardware compatibility list for Windows 2000? As mentioned, Intel 486–based systems are not supported by Windows 2000.

- Are the peripheral components supported in a Windows 2000 environment? If not, then the systems must be upgraded and the peripherals replaced before the migration can occur.

- Are the drivers for these components certified? If not, there are possibilities that the drivers have not been thoroughly tested, which could lead to a system halt, hang, or the "blue screen of death."

- Are the systems sized correctly? Windows 2000 requires more memory than Windows NT 4.0. The minimum recommended amount of memory for DCs is 256 MB, and 128 MB is the minimum recommended amount for clients.

- Are the applications supported and certified? If not, can they be moved to a member server? Windows NT 4.0 member servers can be members of a Windows 2000 domain.

- Is a DNS infrastructure in place? This is required by Windows 2000.

If DNS has not been implemented correctly, the Windows 2000 domain will not function properly.

Some protective actions must be performed before starting the upgrade. An easy protective action is to synchronize the entire domain and shut down one of the BDCs. This DC will remain offline until the upgrade of the PDC. If an error occurs during the upgrade phase of the PDC, then the offline BDC can be rebooted and promoted to the PDC role. It is important to note that once DCs have been upgraded to Windows 2000, a downgrade is not possible.

Upgrading the PDC

The in-place upgrade must be initiated on the PDC. The PDC is the only DC with read/write access to the account DB. The reason for starting with the PDC is that when the first DC in a domain is upgraded to Windows 2000, it inherits the domain-wide operation master roles. One of these roles is the PDC Emulator. If you start the upgrade with a BDC, you effectively have two PDCs in a domain, which is not possible.

Once the upgrade of the PDC is performed, a number of advantages become immediately available. These are all related to the fact that the server is now running Windows 2000. This means that administrators can start using Windows 2000 management tools, such as the MMC. Administrators can also keep using the Windows NT 4.0 management tools. The PDC Emulator acts completely like a Windows NT 4.0 PDC and all the NT 4.0 tools can be used seamlessly. From the perspective of the NT 4.0 BDCs in the domain, the PDC emulator is a Windows 4.0 PDC.

It is strongly recommended that you perform the upgrade on a second BDC shortly after the upgrade of the PDC. This allows two systems to run Windows 2000, and, if something happens to the first DC, the second Windows 2000 DC can become the PDC Emulator, thus preserving the upgrade phase and allowing the domain to carry on business operations. Also, in the case where workstations are upgraded to Windows 2000 Professional first, these workstations are able to log on to Windows 2000 DCs only when the domain is changed from NT 4.0 mode to AD mixed mode, because they need to use Kerberos as authentication protocol, which is not supported on NT 4.0 BDCs in an AD mixed-mode domain.

The new Windows 2000 DCs in the domain replicate using AD replication. This means that they are replicating in a multimaster fashion. The PDC Emulator uses NT 4.0 synchronization to replicate information to the BDCs. When the NT 4.0 PDC is upgraded to Windows 2000, the domain is transformed into a Windows 2000 domain from the perspective of the PDC and all Windows 2000 member servers and workstations; however, it remains an NT 4.0 domain from the perspective of the NT 4.0 BDCs and member servers. This mixed environment is called a mixed-mode domain.

Upgrading the BDCs and switching to native mode

Once the PDC has been upgraded to Windows 2000, it is now the BDC's turn to be upgraded. You must upgrade all the BDCs to allow the domain to be switched to native mode. This is a one-way operation: It cannot be reversed. The operation is initiated on any Windows 2000 DC and is replicated to all the DCs in the domain. Native mode implies that Windows NT 4.0 BDCs are no longer accepted in the domain. NT 4.0 member servers and clients are, however, accepted in the domain. Therefore, the domain mode affects only the DCs and not the member servers or clients of the domain.

Table 1.4   *Differences between Mixed and Native Mode*

Feature	Mixed Mode	Native Mode
Location of security principals	Active Directory for Windows 2000 DCs, SAM database for NT 4.0 BDCs	Active Directory
Scalability beyond 65-KB accounts	No, due to SAM database limitations	Yes
Universal groups (security)	No	Yes
Distribution groups	Yes	Yes
Global groups	Yes	Yes
Domain local groups	No	Yes
Local groups	Yes	Yes
Group nesting	No	Yes
Transitive trusts	Yes, with restrictions when using NTLM	Yes
NTLM authentication	Yes	Yes
Kerberos authentication	Yes (for Windows 2000 clients and DCs)	Yes (for Windows 2000 clients)
Management Console	Yes, for Windows 2000 DCs in the domain	Yes
NT 4.0 synchronization	Yes, between the PDC Emulator and the down-level BDCs	No
Active Directory replication	Yes, between Windows 2000 DCs	Yes
Hierarchical organizational unit structure	Yes, for Windows 2000 DCs	Yes
Group policy objects	Yes, for Windows 2000–based servers and clients	Yes, for Windows 2000–based servers and clients

Table 1.4 *Differences between Mixed and Native Mode (continued)*

Feature	Mixed Mode	Native Mode
Microsoft Software Installer	Yes, except for Windows 3.11	Yes, except for Windows 3.11
Security Configuration Manager	Yes	Yes
LAN Manager Replication (LMRepl)	Yes, on Windows NT 4.0–based servers; no, on Windows 2000–based servers	Yes, on Windows NT 4.0–based member servers; no, on Windows 2000–based servers
File Replication Service (FRS)	Yes, on Windows 2000–based DCs	Yes, on Windows 2000–based DCs
sIDHistory attribute in security principals	No	Yes
User principal names	No	Yes
NetBIOS names support	Yes	Yes

A mixed-mode domain does not have all the features available in Windows 2000. There are a number of restrictions, because BDCs in the domain may not understand or function appropriately using some of the objects that can be generated in a native-mode domain. For example, group nesting is only available in native mode, because in a mixed-mode domain the PDC Emulator would replicate nested groups to BDCs that would not be able to understand them. Table 1.4 lists the differences between the mixed and native modes.

Trust relationships in a mixed-mode environment

Trust relationships are used to allow security principals of one domain to access the resources of another domain. Trusts do not grant permissions; they simply make security principals stored in trusted domains visible to other domains. Permissions are granted by modifying the ACL of a particular resource. In Windows NT 4.0, trusts were one-way, nontransitive, and explicitly created by administrators. If a trust relationship is not physically available between two domains, then the security principals of one domain are not visible to the other domain. The transitivity characteristic of Windows 2000 trust relationships is independent of the authentication protocol, but it depends on the version of the DC used. Trusts can only be transitive if the trust path between the physically trusted domains is composed of a Windows 2000 DC.

The trust path is verified by following the physical trusts in place from the source domain and the target domain. In some cases, the transitivity is not available. This is the case when a down-level DC is in the trust path. In this case, the administrator must create a shortcut trust between two domains not physically trusted. Let us review the different scenarios in more detail and see what the solutions are.

Let us assume that we have a forest composed of three domains. The root domain is called Root. The Root domain has two child domains: Accounts and Resources. The Accounts domain is in mixed-mode domain. This means that in the Accounts domain, there are potentially down-level BDCs accepting authentication requests. Let us assume that the Accounts domain contains a number of workstations running either Windows NT 4.0 Workstation or Windows 2000 Professional. In that domain there are two DCs: One is a Windows 2000 DC with the PDC Emulator operation master role, and the second is a Windows NT 4.0 BDC (see Figure 1.12).

The second child domain in the forest, Resources, is in native mode and contains member servers running Windows 2000. The physical trust relationships in place are those automatically generated by Windows 2000 when the forest and the domains were put in place. There are two two-way transitive trusts in place: one from the Root domain to the Accounts

Figure 1.12
Mixed-mode domains and trust transitivity.

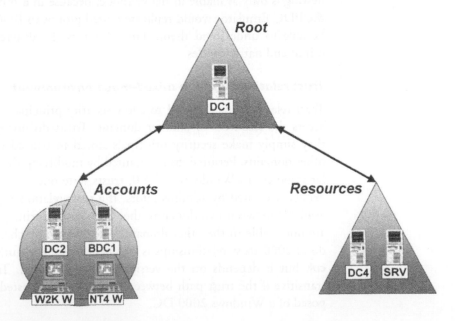

domain and one from the Root domain to the Resources domain. Trust transitivity allows the Accounts domain to trust the Resources domain and vice versa.

Given this environment, there are three scenarios for when users authenticate, depending on the client and the DCs used:

1.   A Windows 2000 client authenticates to a Windows 2000 DC. The authentication protocol is Kerberos.

2.   A Windows NT 4.0 client authenticates to a Windows 2000 DC. The authentication protocol used is NTLM.

3.   A Windows NT 4.0 client authenticates to a Windows NT BDC. In this scenario the authentication protocol used is NTLM.

Let us now assume that a user authenticates in the Accounts domain using a Windows 2000 client. As we have seen, the authentication protocol used is Kerberos. During the authentication process, the KDC running on the Windows 2000 DC provides the client with a Ticket Granting Ticket (TGT), which contains information about the user credentials. This information is encrypted using a special key called the domain master key. Only the Windows 2000 DCs of the authenticating domain know this key. Using the TGT, the client can request from the DC of its own domain a session key to access resources in the domain. For example, a user requires a session key to access his or her own client system or requires access to a resource server in the same domain. The session key is provided to the client, which, in turn, will provide it to the resource system. The resource system will not need to contact the DC as it must in Windows NT 4.0, because the session key provides the credential information and is protected in such a way that only the DC could have created it and only the resource system can decrypt it. The session key is protected by a secret between the DC and the resource system. Since only the DC and the resource system share the secret, allowing encryption and decryption of the session key, the resource system can trust its content—that is, the credentials of the user.

This mechanism provides a secure and fast authentication in a distributed environment. Once the resource system has decrypted the session key, validated the user's credentials, and verified the allowed permissions, it can provide access to the resource to the user. If the client in the Accounts domain attempts to access a resource in a remote resource domain, it will request a session key to a DC in its own domain, the Accounts domain. The KDC on the DC in the Accounts domain cannot provide a session key to the client, because it is not authoritative for the Resources domain and must therefore create a referral request. In order to process the referral, the DC must verify the physical trust relationships in place and will use the closest trust to the target domain for this operation. In our scenario, such trust is established between the Root domain and the Accounts domain. The client then contacts the DC in the Root domain to request a session key to the resource server in the Resources domain. The KDC on the Root domain is not authoritative for the Resources domain and will in turn verify the established physical trust relationships. This time, the KDC can create a referral to the Resources domain, because a physical trust exists between the Root domain and the Resources domain. Finally, the contacted DC in the Resources domain can provide a session key to allow the client to provide credentials to the resource server and access the resource.

The transitivity provided by transitive trusts is only apparent. Under the hood, a physical connection must be established between domains physically connected by trust relationships, as shown in Figure 1.13. In a forest with multiple domain levels and multiple trees, it is recommended that you establish shortcut trusts, alleviating the referral process and increasing the authentication speed.

The Kerberos protocol allows a client to access a resource in any domain in the same forest or in physically trusted forests or non-Windows 2000 Kerberos realms. Kerberos realms are security boundaries: a Windows 2000

Figure 1.13
Trust transitivity referrals.

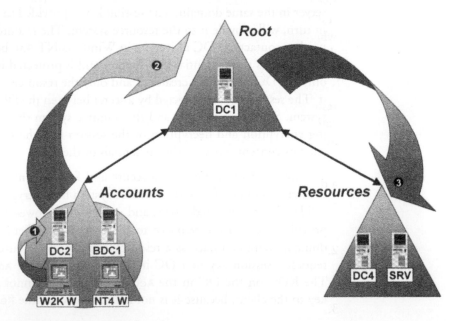

Kerberos realm is a domain, regardless of the domain mode of the domains involved. It will not, however, allow authentication between a Windows 2000 domain and a trusting Windows NT 4.0 domain. For this Windows 2000 supports the NTLM protocol. The NTLM protocol is used when either the DC, the client, or both are running Windows NT 4.0. NTLM is a token-based authentication protocol. When using the NTLM protocol, a DC provides the client with a token containing a list of SIDs. These SIDs are the user's own SID and the list of SIDs of the groups in which the user is a member. When a client requires access to a resource server, this system must verify the credentials of the client by contacting a DC. The DC provides the resource domain with a token containing the user's credentials. After matching the SIDs in the token with the ones stored in the resource ACL and verifying the allowed permissions, access is granted to the client.

When a client requires access to a resource in a remote domain, the resource server must establish a connection to the client's domain. In order to do this, a trust relationship must exist between the two domains. In our scenario the Resources and Accounts domains trust each other using a transitive trust established with the Root domain. A trust path will be established from the resource server to the Accounts domain. Because the Accounts domain is running in mixed mode, however, the trust path may be established with either a Windows NT 4.0 DC or a Windows 2000 DC. If the trust path is established with the Windows 2000 DC, then the transitive trust will allow the DC to provide authentication information to the resource server. This means that even when using NTLM authentication where Windows 2000 DCs are involved, the transitivity of the trusts is validated and the client can access the resource in the remote domain. If, however, the trust path is attempted with a Windows NT 4.0 DC, this DC cannot verify the transitivity of the trust relationship, and access to the resource will be denied. In order to allow access to the resource, administrators must establish an explicit trust between the Resources domain and the Accounts domain.

To summarize, when a client in a domain requires access to a resource in a different domain trusted via a transitive trust, there are three golden rules:

1.   If any of the three systems is running Windows NT 4.0, then the authentication protocol used is NTLM.

2.   If one of the two servers runs Windows NT 4.0, then the trust is nontransitive. A shortcut trust is required to allow access to the resource.

3.   In all other cases, the trust is transitive.

Limitations of the SAM DB in mixed-mode domains

It is often the goal to consolidate domains in order to reduce the physical resources used, such as DCs. Security principals are stored in the AD and are replicated between all DCs in a domain. Windows 2000 can scale up to a theoretical 4 billion objects (2^{32}), accommodating the requirements for most, if not all, companies. A mixed-mode domain can, however, contain Windows NT 4.0 BDCs. Although Windows 2000 DCs will use AD replication to replicate directory information between DCs, Windows NT 4.0 BDCs will contact the PDC to perform Windows NT 4.0 synchronization. A Windows 2000 DC performs the PDC Emulator operation master role. It establishes the connection with the down-level BDCs and synchronizes the data stored in its own DB—the AD. The down-level BDCs store security principals in the SAM DB, which is still limited to 65 MB even in a mixed-mode Windows 2000 domain. If the amount of data stored in the AD exceeds 65 MB, then the PDC Emulator will perform the synchronization with the down-level BDCs in the domain, which will result in exceeding the limitations of the SAM DB and potentially making the BDCs unavailable.

Therefore, it is important to take into consideration the existence of Windows NT 4.0 BDCs while in the process of consolidating domains. Switching to native mode will remove this limitation, because NT 4.0 BDCs will no longer be accepted in the domain. It is, therefore, recommended to consolidate domains within the limitation of the SAM DB. If the number of security principals resulting in a consolidation effort exceeds the maximum supported size of the SAM DB, then it is strongly recommended to wait until the target domain for the consolidation is running in native mode. Another advantage of switching to native mode is to allow interdomain movements of security principals.

Pros and cons of an in-place upgrade strategy

The in-place upgrade is the fastest path to Windows 2000. There are, however, other benefits associated with it. These benefits are related to the fact that there is no change in the infrastructure as it is known to the users:

- Many small companies are likely to want to reuse the same domain name to reduce impact on employees. These impacts are related to the requirement to inform users of the new authentication domain.

- The migration is transparent to users.

- There is no need to use migration tools, since the domain is unchanged and all its security principal SIDs are preserved during an in-place upgrade.

There are, however, some risks to adopting this strategy. These risks are related to the fact that the production domain is being upgraded to Windows 2000. The systems running in the domain may not be able to run correctly in a Windows 2000 environment. There are many parameters to be determined to achieve a successful migration, including the following:

- Is the hardware compatible with the Windows 2000 Hardware Compatibility List?

- Are the drivers for the peripherals certified to work in a Windows 2000 environment?

- Are the applications supported on Windows 2000? Are they certified?

- What if the upgrade of the PDC fails?

- What if there is a need for an NT 4.0 BDC once the switch to native mode has been made?

- What are the contingency plans in each phase of the migration, and have they been tested?

Addressing each of these questions will certainly help reduce the risk of a poor migration, but no one can be absolutely sure of the success of the migration until the last user or resource has been migrated. Preparing a contingency plan is crucial. For example, the domain could easily be synchronized and a BDC shut down to prepare the primary DC for the upgrade. If something happens during the upgrade, the PDC can be removed from the domain, rebooted, and promoted to PDC. It is also worth upgrading a BDC shortly after the PDC has been upgraded. The Windows 2000 PDC Emulator operation master role can easily be transferred from one DC to another provided that they both run Windows 2000 and are part of the same domain.

When multiple domains must be upgraded, it is strongly recommended to start with the smallest of the domains. If something goes wrong, a smaller population of users will be affected, and as the administrators are performing the migration, they will gain experience for larger and more complex domains. In all cases we strongly recommend using proven tools tested in a lab and documenting each migration step with an associated tested contingency plan.

Restructuring

Restructuring is a strategy that allows migrating to Windows 2000 by performing one of the following actions:

- An in-place upgrade of the existing Windows NT 4.0 domain structure, followed by a restructuring of the domains and their objects;
- A direct migration by generating a brand new forest and copying (cloning) the security principals from the old domains.

This migration technique relies on the ability of the AD to do the following:

- Scale potentially to millions of security principals, hence allowing fewer but larger domains;
- Retain the SIDs belonging to security principals moved from other domains, hence allowing coexistence between migrated domains and down-level trusted or trusting domains.

Probably the biggest advantage of the restructuring technique is the ability to leave the current NT 4.0 environment intact, thereby reducing the risk of migrating to Windows 2000.

The current Windows NT 4.0 structure of domains may have been the result of either of the following:

- The limitations of the SAM account DB, forcing administrators to create multiple domains for the largest companies;
- The inability of NT 4.0 to delegate administrative management or provide a more granular delegation.

During the design phase of a Windows 2000 infrastructure, it is common practice to start with a forest composed of a single domain, then look at valid reasons to split that domain into either child domains or multiple trees. Those reasons, as mentioned, are mostly political, due to a trust between business units; security reasons can be due to the inability to export particular pieces of information outside of a country, and business reasons can include, for example, a conglomerate requiring multiple namespaces.

Eliminating domains provides the instant advantage of having to manage far fewer DCs, which reduces the cost of hardware, administration, and troubleshooting for these servers. It also allows an easier and more flexible structure in which to deploy policies and applications.

During a restructuring migration, while some people have yet to be migrated, some have already been migrated. Some resource domains have been eliminated while others are still up and running and require the SID of the security principals of the former account domains to grant or deny access to resources. This means that if we have an account that has been migrated from a former Windows NT 4.0 account domain to a new Windows 2000 domain, the domains containing the resources of that account may still be running NT 4.0 and not know about the new domain. Not knowing about the new domain means not having the SID from the new domain in the ACL protecting the resources. A user with a new Windows 2000 account may still require access to resources in a Windows NT 4.0 domain. If this user cannot access the resources, then the migration strategy is failing to maintain normal business operations. The goal is to ensure that the migration is as transparent as possible to users. To accomplish this, Windows 2000 has the ability to retain old security principal identifiers from the former NT 4.0 account domains. Old SIDs are stored in the AD as part of a security principal attribute. The attribute is called sIDhistory. The sIDHistory attribute is multivalued and can contain up to 255 SIDs. This attribute is only available if Windows 2000 is running in native mode. This means that if the in-place upgrade technique is used with a Windows NT 4.0 domain, the domain will be in mixed mode; restructuring other domains into this mixed-mode domain while maintaining the sIDhistory will not be possible. The migrated accounts to this mixed domain will not have sIDhistory information.

The sIDHistory attribute allows security principals to be cloned. No, not with DNA samples, but with SID samples. Windows 2000 migration tools inject SIDs into the sIDHistory of a Windows 2000 security principal. This allows Windows 2000 users to use their new Windows 2000 accounts, since the authentication process will store the list of SIDs the users are entitled to, including those stored in the sIDhistory, as part of the PAC of a Kerberos ticket or an NTLM token. In other words, this allows a Windows 2000 user to access resources protected with the SID of his or her old NT 4.0 account. This is transparent to the user, who seamlessly continues to access his or her resources once the account has been migrated.

Cloning versus moving

The clone operation copies the attributes of an object from one domain to a Windows 2000 native-mode domain and populates the sIDhistory of the new object. From a Windows 2000 perspective, the object cloned is a new one, since it receives a new GUID. The GUID will be used to identify the object internally.

The moving operation, on the other hand, is a destructive operation, which creates a new object in the target domain with the GUID of the old object and destroys the old object. Moving objects has a rather important consequence for the objects in the source domain. If, for example, you need to move a group, then the members of this group must be moved as well. If the group resides in a native-mode domain and contains nested groups, then the nested groups and their members need to be moved as well. This is because the move is a destructive operation, and destroying the group without moving all its members would result in a loss of data. The worst-case scenario occurs when users and groups are so linked together that moving one of them requires moving the entire domain. A way around this constraint is to create parallel groups on the target domain—that is, the users will be moved, but not the groups, resulting in a duplication of groups that need to be managed. Another possibility is to transform the groups into a universal group. This is only possible if the source domain is in native mode and has the effect of making the group available in the entire forest. Universal groups are stored in GCs. One last possibility around this constraint is to use the cloning technique for the groups and move the users only. During a move operation the target domain can be either in mixed or native mode.

As previously mentioned, however, the sIDHistory attribute will only be preserved if the target domain is in native mode. The source domain mode does not matter in either scenario, but during a move operation, the source and target domains must belong to the same forest. There are some differences and restrictions depending on whether a moving or cloning strategy is adopted. These differences are summarized in Table 1.5.

Restructuring Account Domains

The restructuring technique differs for account and resource domains. For account domains, the following generic steps are involved:

1.   Creating a Windows 2000 forest or defining the target Windows 2000 native domain;

2.   Establishing a trust relationship between the former account domain and the Windows 2000 domain;

3.   Global groups cloning;

4.   Account cloning.

Creating a Windows 2000 forest

In a restructuring migration, the target domain may exist or may need to be created. If the domain must be created, it is then recommended to perform

Table 1.5   *Cloning versus Moving*

Feature	Cloning	Moving
Source domain	Windows NT, Windows 2000 from different forest	Windows 2000 domain from same forest. No Windows NT.
Source domain mode	Mixed or native	Mixed or native
Target domain	Windows 2000 from different forest	Windows 2000 from same forest
Target domain mode	Native	Native
Password preserved	Yes, depends on the tool	Yes
Security Principal SID from source domain	Must not exist in target domain and must not be found in the sIDHistory attribute of any object.	Must not exist in an sIDHistory attribute (there can't be a second primary SID)
Object GUID	A new GUID will be generated.	The same GUID will be preserved.
Tools	ADMT, ClonePrincipal, third party based on DsAddSIDHistory API	ADMT, third-party tools supporting DsAddSIDHistory API, MoveTree

the necessary planning and design steps to define the purpose and scope of the new domain. Windows 2000 domains cannot be renamed, and the design phase must define the name of the domain and how it coexists in a company's global namespace. Adopting a design without such considerations may lead to a second restructuring phase. Designing a Windows 2000 infrastructure is a step that may take several months for the largest companies.

The restructuring technique requires a native-mode domain to allow the sIDhistory to be populated; therefore, selecting a target domain that is in mixed mode is not an option. Transforming that domain into a native-mode domain is also not something that can be performed lightly. As we saw earlier, it is a one-way operation with no point of return. It is in the best interest of users to plan their migration and target domains and avoid multiple restructuring operations in order to "get it right."

Establishing the trust relationships

Before migrating the users and groups, it is necessary to establish the same trust relationships that exist between the resource domains and the former account domains with the new Windows 2000 domains. The Windows 2000 domain will need to be trusted by the resource domains to allow users to access their resources. This is an operation that may take a long time to perform manually and it can be automated using specific tools.

Cloning the global groups

Once the trust relationships have been established between the resource domain and the target Windows 2000 domain, the global groups can be cloned. The global groups are cloned before the users to allow memberships to be retained during the cloning phase of the users.

Cloning the accounts

Cloning users can be done in an incremental fashion. Some organizations may decide to clone groups of users instead of the entire set. Once all the users and groups have been cloned, it is generally recommended to disable the accounts in the former account domain. This will reduce administrative costs and will help in ascertaining that users are really using the new account domain prior to the shutdown of the Windows NT 4.0 account domain. In some cases, there is a possibility that both the former and the new account can be enabled. However, it is important to note that the profiles for the users will not be the same, and customizations of the old profile may not be accessible by the user when the former account domain is disbanded.

Restructuring resource domains

For resource domains, the migration steps are more complicated due to the need to clone security principals, which may be stored in shared local groups. These are local groups created on the PDC and are available on BDCs. These shared local groups store information about the domain and require the DC for that domain to authenticate the SID. In this case, it is not possible to eliminate the resource domain before performing additional steps. The main steps of a resource domain migration are as follows:

1.   Establish trusts between the resource domain and the target Windows 2000 domain.

2.   If the account domain has not been migrated yet, establish additional trust relationships between the new Windows 2000 domain and the Windows NT 4.0 account domain.

3.   Clone local and shared local groups

4.   If applications are running on BDCs, demote these systems to member servers. This is an operation that can be performed during the upgrade of Windows 2000 on the system.

5.   Move member servers to the Windows 2000 domain.

Establish trust relationships

As with master account domains, resource domains require trust relationships to be established with the target domain. In addition, if the target domain needs to be accessed by accounts stored in other domains, such as Windows NT 4.0 account domains that have not been migrated yet, trusts must be established between the target Windows 2000 domain and those domains. This technique will allow organizations to adopt different schedules for their migration. Some resource domains may be migrated before the account domains. Establishing these trusts will allow accounts in downlevel domains to continue to access migrated resources. Again, tools such as AD MIGRATION TOOL (ADMT) will allow generating the required trust relationships.

Clone local and shared local groups

There are two types of local groups: those that have a machine scope and have been created on member servers or workstations and those that have a domain scope and have been created on the PDC. While the former are stored in the SAM DB of member servers and workstations, the latter replicate from the PDC to all the BDCs in the domain. Shared local groups require at least the PDC of the domain in which they belong to authenticate and validate their SIDs. In other words, if shared local groups are cloned to a Windows 2000 domain, the sIDhistory will be populated with the shared local group SID of the source resource domain. This resource domain cannot be eliminated until the SID is tracked and replaced in the new domain. If this operation is not performed and the resource domain is eliminated, then the SID cannot be authenticated, resulting in a denial when accessing the resource in the new domain. The access denial is produced because the SID cannot be validated and Windows 2000 will assume that the SID is unknown. To track and replace these types of SIDs, administrators can use the SIDWalker tool available from the Windows 2000 Resource Kit. SIDWalker will allow administrators to search for resources for a specific SID and replace it with another SID.

Demote DCs

Demoting DCs is not a standard operation in Windows NT. Administrators are required to reinstall the OS in order to demote a BDC. In Windows 2000, however, promoting a member server to a DC is an operation performed using the AD Installation Wizard (DCPROMO). Demoting a Windows 2000 DC can also be performed with the AD Installation Wizard.

Demoting DCs in our restructuring migration context means performing an in-place upgrade of the NT 4.0 BDC. The Windows 2000 installation procedure will detect that the system is a DC, and once the system has been upgraded, the Wizard will automatically launch the AD Installation Wizard. During the execution of the AD Installation Wizard, it is possible to cancel the operation. As a result of this, the NT 4.0 domain SAM information is lost, while the new AD data have not been replicated locally. A SAM DB with built-in security principals has been generated and the system is a member of the same domain.

Move member servers

Moving member servers can be performed using Netdom, ADMT, or third-party tools. This operation involves creating computer accounts for member servers in a Windows 2000 domain. Some third-party tools provide the ability to move the data of specific servers in an effort to consolidate shares.

Pros and cons of a restructuring strategy

The restructuring strategy provides the benefit of starting with a brand new forest. This forest is the ideal one, designed without the limitations of NT 4.0 and with the business and security objectives in mind. Obviously, since this forest is created in parallel with the current infrastructure, there is no risk for the Windows NT 4.0 production domains, because they remain untouched. Creating a new infrastructure, however, is not free; there are hidden costs related to managing two infrastructures. There are also additional costs due to the additional hardware. Cloning tools must be tested, and although they perform similar functions in principle, they are not the same and do not cost the same amount. Coexistence will also be problematic, and migrated users living in the new infrastructure may be required to access resources in the old infrastructure and vice versa. This is the recommended approach for large corporations.

1.25   AD administration tools

Windows 2000 uses the MMC as the common infrastructure for management tools. The management tools designed for the MMC are snap-ins or COM-based applications, which snap into the MMC. Snap-ins are easy to use, because they are based on a GUI. All the Windows NT 4.0 management tools have been migrated to snap-ins. The MMC allows a customization of the loaded snap-ins and allows saving the console with the snap-ins loaded. This way, administrators can create custom management consoles

Figure 1.14
*MMC with four
snap-ins loaded.*

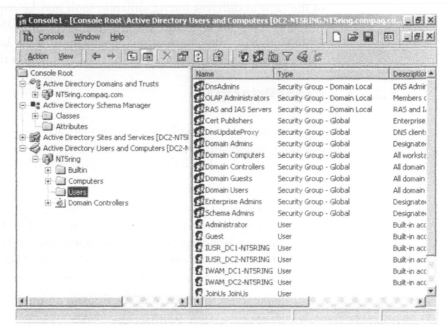

dedicated to particular tasks. Figure 1.14 shows a console with the following four snap-ins loaded:

- AD Domains and Trusts, which manages the trust relationships between domains;

- AD Schema Manager, which is the snap-in used to modify the content of the schema;

- AD Sites and Services, which is used to manage the replication topology and connectivity between DCs and sites;

- AD Users and Groups, which replaces User Manager for Domains and manages users, groups, and the hierarchical organization of a domain.

Many more snap-ins exist and applications will provide add-ins to manage objects that are added to the AD. Tools provided in Visual Studio 6.0 allow programmers to write additional add-ins, if required.

1.26   AD migration tools

Migration tools can be categorized according to the type and scope of the operation that needs to be performed. Depending on whether you will be moving an object within a domain of the same forest or between domains of the same or different forests, different tools may be required. In all cases, it is always possible to write custom scripts based on ADSI. ADSI is a set of COM interfaces allowing scripting languages to easily bind to a container and perform management tasks on the objects stored in the container.

1.26.1   ClonePrincipal

ClonePrincipal is a collection of Visual BASIC scripts based on the DsUtil Component Object Model (COM) object. DsUtil can be found in the clonepr.dll dynamic link library and provides three main interfaces:

1.   Connect. Allows a script to authenticate and connect to the source and target domains. The bind operation in the source domain must be performed on the primary DC if the domain is running Windows NT 4.0. This operation can be performed on DCs on source domains running Windows 2000. It is important to note that the source and target domain must not belong to the same forest. Auditing must be enabled on the target domain.

2.   AddSidHistory. Provides the ability to copy SID information from a security principal in the source domain to a new object in the target domain. AddSidHistory populates the sIDhistory attribute of the target object with the SID of the source object.

3.   CopyDownlevelUserProperties. Copies all attributes from the object stored in the source domain to the equivalent attributes in the object in the target domain. ClonePrincipal is an interesting set of samples for those wishing to learn and modify the scripts to provide additional functionality. It is not, however, an adequate tool for migrating large numbers of users and groups. ClonePrincipal cannot be used between domains of the same forest, and this restricts its use for cloning objects in interforest migrations. A tool recommended for large migrations is AD Migration Tool.

1.26.2   MoveTree and Netdom

MoveTree is a tool that allows migrating OUs, users, and groups between domains of the same forest. MoveTree cannot be used for interforest migrations and cannot be used with Windows NT 4.0 domains. It will preserve the old security principal SIDs in the sIDhistory of the new security principal objects, will reuse the GUID of the original object, and will preserve the password of the original users. MoveTree cannot, however, be used for migrating computers. For this task, administrators can use Netdom.

In addition to migrating computers, Netdom can be used to list and establish trust relationships between Windows 2000 domains and down-level domains or Kerberos realms.

1.26.3   AD migration tool

ADMT is available for free and was codeveloped by Microsoft and Mission Critical Software. It uses a GUI in the form of an MMC snap-in. ADMT provides all the features of ClonePrincipal, but also provides convenient wizards to allow the program to guide the administrator in the choice of options during the migration. ADMT also establishes the necessary trust relationships and can be used for both cloning and moving strategies. Furthermore, the task of enumerating trust relationships and establishing them can be performed by ADMT and Netdom. ADMT is pretty unique among the Microsoft migration tools, because it can migrate user profiles, service accounts, and update ACLs on migrated resources.

1.26.4   Third-party tools

Third-party vendors have developed management tools based on the AddSidHistory API. DM/Manager and DM/Consolidator by FastLane Technologies allow migrating the resources, such as shares. FastLane Technologies provides reporting tools, migration tools, and management tools bundled in the DM/Suite. The DM/Reporter is capable of impressive reporting and is very useful in the discovery phase of a project. For example, it can be used to track client and server configurations and verify the conformance of groups and users given a naming convention. DM/Manager provides the ability to migrate passwords and can merge accounts from different sources. This tool is also capable of converting the ACLs on the shares and can schedule computer membership in the new domain as well as the reboot. Finally, it is capable of converting a BDC into either a Windows 2000 DC or member server.

Bv-Migrate by BindView and Domain Migration Administrator by NetIQ are cloning tools capable of preserving the original password for security principals. This tool also provides extensive logging and reporting capabilities as well as security translation on shares and Exchange mailboxes. Bv-Migrate from BindView also preserves passwords. This tool is capable of migrating profiles and allows you to model the AD on top of Windows NT.

NetIQ also provides a tool for managing Windows 2000 and Windows NT using a unified console called the Directory and Resource Administrator. This tool uses a set of predefined rules to enforce AD security and integrity and provides easy delegation of administration. In terms of management and monitoring, NetIQ offers AppManager, a comprehensive systems and application suite providing monitoring for Windows 2000 and BackOffice applications, such as SQL, Exchange, IIS, MTS, and more.

1.26.5   Moving objects within a domain

When an object must be moved between containers in the same domain, such as moving users between OUs, then the MMC can be used. For example, if a user, group, or computer must be moved from one OU to another, then the Users and Computers snap-in can be used.

1.26.6   Moving objects between domains of the same forest

When moving objects between domains of the same forest, the following tools can be used:

- `Movetree`, a tool provided in the Windows 2000 support tool kit, can move a tree of objects from one domain to another. For example, `Movetree` can move the objects in an OU, including child OUs and their content, to another OU. `MoveTree` will preserve SIDs in the `sIDhistory` if the target domain is running in native mode and will also preserve passwords.

- AD Migration Tool (also available from the support tool kit) can be used to move computers from one domain to another.

1.27   Summary

Windows 2000 is a lot more than a major upgrade—it is a whole new operating system that was designed clearly with the enterprise in mind. The AD is the most important technology introduced in Windows 2000. It provides the foundation for the enterprise infrastructure. Before attempting to design a Windows 2000–based infrastructure, one should carefully understand the replication topology required for effectively disseminating data throughout the enterprise so that these data remain available at a reasonable cost. Understanding how the schema must evolve, what objects should be published in the AD, and who needs to have access to what are prerequisites for a successful Windows 2000 design. Always keep in mind that designing a Windows 2000 infrastructure involves designing the DNS namespace, the domain, the OU structures, and, possibly, the Exchange Server and other AD-enabled application infrastructures.

Novell NDS eDirectory
by Mark W. Foust

I connect to my ISP while traveling in France (I'm using any PC on any OS) and point my browser to http://myserver.mycompany.com. I am then presented with a dialog box asking for my name and password, which, when provided, will enable me to access my files. What OS is the server running on? Linux, Solaris, Windows 2000, NetWare, IBM mainframe, or TRU64: The point is, it does not matter (as long as the OS supports eDirectory). Did I mention that I do not need a 20-some megabyte Novell client or that I do not need a virtual private network (VPN) connection? Sounds too good to be true, right? That is the compelling reason Novell is presenting you with for upgrading to its eDirectory product (or "solution," as they prefer to call it).

Novell's new flagship product (it's not NetWare anymore) is the cross-platform answer to solutions that require authentication or some sort of digital ID for access. This was Eric Schmidt's dream for a while—he wanted to challenge the concept of using a firewall. The logic was that you could deny everything and allow access only to authenticated users through whatever means using standard protocols. You can point your browser to http://www.cnn.com and see the shocking Novel Directory Services (NDS) eDirectory advertisement at the bottom of the page to see that Novell does have some current mind share for using the directory for more than just local LAN file and print access—Eric's dream realized.

My two years as a consultant employed by Novell taught me that most of you are far from upgrading to Novell's newest eDirectory version. I, therefore, have fashioned this chapter to help you with the DS.NLM versions starting with NetWare 4.11 support until present day. I have included best practices and plenty of links to more information. You probably know that Novell has evolved into a semiservice company (they would prefer that I call it a "solutions" company) after acquiring Cambridge Technologies Consulting Company.

Hopefully, by now, you understand what a directory service (DS) is and its importance, so I will skip most of that in this chapter and stick to the topics I needed to know about as a consultant in the heat of the battle: design recommendation, security, tools and utilities, and tuning and optimization recommendations. If you are an administrator, you can gain insights that I have gained through experience by going to some of Novell's largest NDS clients. Novell's eDirectory Web site, www.novell.com/products/nds, links to a new eLearning online seminar. I also want to recommend that you read my other book, published by Digital Press, *NetWare Administration* (it covers NDS too). I go into more detail there about NDS and the overall NetWare platform as well as other Novell products.

2.1   NDS, or eDirectory

Novell often describes NDS as a distributed, hierarchical-naming, object-oriented, global, replicated, and partitioned database. Novell has made NDS (or eDirectory as they now call it) the centerpiece of its future—at one time that centerpiece was, of course, the NetWare OS. You know, by now, that a DS is a special database that allows logical, immediate access to objects (printers, servers, applications, policies, and whatever else you define as an object) based on access privileges and regardless of physical location. Roughly, the NDS database works as follows:

```
A resource is requested by some client→response from
server→the object is located in NDS→location of
resource→validity and authority of requesting client
verified→client is connected to resource
```

For more information on NDS or other Novell products mentioned consult http://www.novell.com/documentation and http://www.novell.com/products/nds. Novell has banked its future on NDS/eDirectory. I have not seen any news on a server OS past NetWare 6.

Understand that a DS is apparently not a compelling reason to buy a NOS. If it were, you would see Sun, IBM, and Linux adopt one more readily. Microsoft's Active Directory (AD) certainly is a good 1.0 directory, but even Microsoft has not ported SQL, SMS, and many of their other applications completely to AD because the market has not demanded it. Novell is betting the farm on a DS being the central "identity" or authentication point, and they, seemingly, are the only ones doing so. You will remember a company called Banyan VINES that did the same thing years ago. Time will tell if Novell is a visionary or horribly wrong.

2.1.1 NDS Administration Guide

Novell now publishes the eDirectory Administration Guide online. I highly recommend it. It is currently 504 pages long and free—great news. Find it at www.novell.com/documentation/lg/ndsam/pdfdoc/taoenu.pdf.

2.1.2 NDS versions and types

NDS, unlike AD, which is integrated into the OS, runs as a separate application on top of the OS/NOS. Therefore, NDS may be upgraded without always having to upgrade the NOS.

The legacy NDS database we most often refer to is NDSv7 for NetWare 4.11. NDS in NetWare 4.11 was as solid as a rock. Clients tell me they could golf and never worry about their NOS or NDS DS.

Versions

NDS comes in the following versions:

- *NDS:* Just plain NDS is referred to as versions 6.x and 7.x.

- *SKADS or NDSv8:* SKADS was the code word for NDS 8 and stands for super kick-ass DSs—seriously.

- *TAO—NDSv8:* The latest version of NDS, TAO supports filtered replicas, DirXML, and other advanced feature sets. Also, look for information on iMonitor—the new NDS troubleshooting utility—found in NetWare 6.

- *eDirectory—Version 8.5 and beyond:* These support Federation and DirXML and can run on various operating systems, such as NT 4.0, NT2000, Linux, Solaris, OS390, and so on. NDS eDirectory has no support for file and print integration; it is solely used for the entry and authentication point into your Internet and intranet.

- *Novell Account Management version 2.x (formerly called Corporate Edition):* Novell Account Management NDSv8 is Novell's new supercharged, billion-user object DS. BrainShare demos have shown billion-user trees on servers and one Solaris server. NDSv8 exists in two forms, Novell Account Management and eDirectory. Novell Account Management distinguishes itself as a file and print-plus-user account management DS. It is the evolution of NDS 7.x versions. Novell Account Management has been enabled to run on several platforms (and is scheduled to be able to run on more) and is managed by ConsoleOne/NetConsole.

2.1.3   Which NDS version should you use?

The latest. I do not mean to be smart, but being in the field working with some of the largest NetWare/NDS clients has shown me the need for fresh code. Obviously, fresh code does not fix every bug, and new code introduces new bugs, but the evolution of Novell products has taught me that newer is generally better. Having said that, let me clarify: I mean the latest of the current version you have. If you are running NDSv7, you may not need version 8.5, but it is likely that you will need the latest version 7 release or version 8 of the DS.NLM.[1]

Even if you do not need a billion-user tree with millions of objects in each partition, you should consider using NDSv8. This is a no-brainer for clients who use the directory for more than just network access, file, and print. If you are using DNS/DHCP, or any ZEN product or other directory-enabled product, you are putting double or triple the amount of objects into the tree. Novell's internal IS department reports (found in the Novell Beige Papers—http://www.tinypineapple.com/luddite/beigepapers) that it went from 18,000 NDS objects to 120,000 after implementing DNS/DHCP. The size of the old database was almost cut in half (before adding DNS/DHCP) from 200 MB to 110 MB by using NDSv8—pretty cool to add more than five times the objects and still cut the amount of space used by the database. This is possible due to the power of the FLAIM database used first by Novell's GroupWise, now NDS (Microsoft uses their JET database for AD, which was first used by, and made for, Exchange).

NDSv8 uses the Direct File System (DFS), which lets the database control the data directly. NDSv8 is also more scalable, more stable, more reliable, faster, smaller, and supports more advanced features (LDAPv3, Filtered Replicas, DirXML, etc.) than its version 7 cousin. If that does not excite your upper management, use Novell's marketing stuff online at http://www.novell.com/products/nds and tell them it is a free upgrade—nothing can get a budget-monger's attention faster than the words "free upgrade."

Upgrading to NDSv8

The following are my recommendations for upgrading to NDSv8. You may upgrade through a file or CD ROM, using :NWCONFIG→Product Options,

---

1.   The DS.NLM and sometimes supporting NLMs (e.g., DSREPAIR, etc.) are versioned and easily seen on your OS by simply going to the server console and typing "mds"; you will get a response that shows the server version. If you want to look at multiple servers, use a utility such as CONFIG Reader shareware, found on www.netwarefiles.com.

or you may upgrade DS versions through an OS upgrade to NetWare 5.1 or 6—each of which gives you the option of upgrading to NDSv8. I would recommend upgrading your OS to the latest and greatest, especially if you have purchased upgrade protection from Novell. NetWare 6, though, may be the exception. NetWare 6 mostly provides multiprocessor upgraded NOS modules and other minor pieces, which may not be necessary for many smaller installations.

Before you upgrade, you should perform the following tasks:

- Verify time synchronization in DSREPAIR, and fix it if it is broken. Also, verify that you are using the same TIMESYNC.NLM on your servers—that is, on the same versions of NetWare.

- Repair the database until you have no errors (though sometimes NDS will always report a couple of errors). Troubleshoot all synchronization problems. Verify that you are using the latest DSREPAIR.NLM version available; if you are not, download it and put it on your server. Some older versions do not fix database errors properly. DSREPAIR→Time Synchronization will list the DS.NLM versions.

- Back up your old database. Use your backup software to back up NDS. Afterward, create a dump file. Realize that a large database may take a couple of minutes to create the file

  ```
  :DSREPAIR→Advanced Options→Create a database dump OR
  :DSREPAIR -rc
  ```

- Verify that you have IPX running on the server for NDS running the IPX stack—Novell requires it for an upgrade from versions prior to NDSv8.

- Start upgrading at the ROOT. There are many arguments about where to start. Some say never at the ROOT; some say always at the Master of the ROOT. I like to start, at least, somewhere in the ROOT partition—I like the Read/Write. You are, obviously, going to do all testing in a lab first.

- Finish upgrading the ROOT partition, then work your way through the tree at your discretion. Work at upgrading within replica rings completely before going to the next, if possible.

- Know that a mixed-version NDS tree (NDSv8 and NDSv6 or NDSv7) will experience some errors and problems. Most are fixed in some new DS version that Novell will release for free.

- Force a replica sync and update your backlinks after you finish the upgrade.

```
:SET DSTRACE=*U
:SET DSTRACE=*S
:SET DSTRACE=*SSA
:SET DSTRACE=*H
:SET DSTRACE=*B
```

- After you upgrade to NDS eDirectory, you may see -601 errors on NetWare 4.11 servers trying to authenticate to the NDS eDirectory server. Verify that you have the latest DSREPAIR.NLM support (usually on the eDirectory download site) on each of the NetWare 4.11 servers in the same replica ring and select Verify Remote Ids.

- Stay on top of your NDS health by doing NDS health checks.[2] Net-Pro provides a great solution for your NDS health check needs—DS Expert at http://www.netpro.com.

2.2   NDS terminology

Dilbert teaches us how to talk like managers; router boy talks in routing algorithms of shortest path; NetWare NDS techies need to learn NDS lingo. If you work with NDS every day, you need to read and understand this section.

2.2.1   Tree

Objects can exist singly and access resources globally within an authenticated domain called a "tree." There can be only one ROOT. The ROOT represents a single namespace. This is from the X.500 standard.

Best Practice: When naming a tree, use the format <NAME_TREE> (e.g., ACME_TREE) as it is easier to distinguish in sniffer traces and other server display settings for troubleshooting.

---

2.   I cannot overstate the importance of NDS health (and monitoring utility for medium to large enterprises). Working with developers has convinced me of the need to monitor your NDS health constantly and to be proactive with problems. I learned the term "code rot," which simply means that code sits around until it breaks. Your job is to monitor, patch, work around, and proactively fix it, before it breaks. Relax, it is a theoretical joke.

2.2.2   Partitions

The NDS database can be broken into smaller pieces called "partitions." Partitions are managed by NDSManager in the SYS:PUBLIC\WIN32 directory or, recently, through ConsoleOne/NetConsole. Any user with supervisor-level rights to the partition object (partitions are made at the container level, which is the ROOT, O, or—most of the time—an OU) can completely manage the partition; without full supervisor rights to the partition object the user will not be allowed to manage the partition.

A partition should not usually span a WAN—though this is nearly impossible. "Never span the WAN," Novell used to say.

The information replicated is based upon time stamps. Using time stamps means that your entire enterprise of NetWare servers must share the same time.

An NDS tree can contain many (hundreds) partitions. You may view the partitions on any server by using one of the aforementioned management tools or :DSREPAIR→Advanced Options→Replica and Partition Operations.

Best Practice: I like the DS Designer third-party utility to document and model the NDS tree(s)—http://www.dsdesigner.hypermart.net.

Partition root entry information

Successful NDS operations need information contained in the partition root entry. This attribute and value information must include the following:

- *Replica pointers:* a pointer, stored on the local server, to the remote servers that contain a replica of this partition (the replica ring servers) and contain the server's ID, address, and the type of replica (master, read/write, subordinate) stored on the server and other attributes and values;

- *Partition control attribute:* the attribute that tracks the progress of operations, such as splitting and joining partitions and repairing time stamps;

- *Partition status attribute:* local server attribute that stores information about the success of the last synchronization cycle;

- *Synchronized up to attribute:* the attribute that stores time stamp information indicating the last update the local replica received from each remote replica (NetWare 4.x servers only);

- *Transitive vector attribute:* the attribute that allows servers to store information about each replica in the ring and includes a modification time stamp. It is used to make NDS replication more efficient (introduced in NetWare 5.x).

Do not concern yourself with partition ROOT entry information. It is not information you will need; it is background information that you do not really see and used to teach the concepts of NDS.

2.2.3   Replicas

To provide fault tolerance to a partition, replicas, or copies, of the partition may be made. It is possible, though not advisable, to make many copies of a partition. A server may contain an unlimited amount (theoretically) of replicas. I think the most I have seen is 130—which is about 125 too many. It is hard to give specific numbers, since your design is dependent upon many variables. Realize that an inefficient replica design can cause server thrashing (to try to keep constant synchronization) and tons of unnecessary network traffic. The best tool to use to model your tree/upgrade or new design is through DS Designer at http://dsdesigner.hypermart.net.

NDS replica design and placement principles—VERY IMPORTANT

The replica design principles are slightly different for NDSv8 than for previous versions. Check the Novell Web site for basic information at http://www.novell.com/coolsolutions/nds/basics.html.

Your replica design should give you the following:

- Fault tolerance and high availability (more than one replica of a partition);

- Fast user login and name resolution (local name resolution when possible);

- Low WAN impact (do not "span the WAN"—you will have to sometimes, but the principle says not to when you can help it; realistically, larger bandwidth WAN links of 256 KB and up are not usually a problem, unless you are swamped with other network traffic);

- Bindery service access (any server that supports BINDERY emulation must have a replica of the bindery context it is supporting).

Best Practice: Separate the ROOT partition from your top organizational partition for better protection from corruption, fault tolerance, disaster recovery, and ease of backup.

Realize that there are tradeoffs to every design need. Your job is to determine the points of diminishing return. Of course the best fault-tolerance idea is to have a replica on every server, but you cannot afford the network traffic or the possibility of the replica having too many partners to finish its mandatory sync every 30 minutes, and therefore within 30 minutes. If a replica ring does not finish syncing in 30 minutes, it keeps running the sync process until it can finish. I have been to clients where the sync process rarely ever finishes owing to problems with the client's NDS design (i.e., too many replicas).

2.3   NDS design guidelines

Novell's NDS recommendations for NDS versions 6.x and 7.x are as follows:

- Three replicas minimum for fault tolerance.

- Fast authentication of clients (clients need an NDS server [SAP type 278] to authenticate to).

- No more than 15 replicas per server in an NDSv7 implementation. Novell has recently updated its recommendation to 20 per server. This is an important number, since outbound synchronization is a multithreaded process, while inbound replication is a single-threaded process. Thus, a server with many replicas might show a high CPU server utilization because of the queued synchronization processes waiting for a chance to update their partitions. The server that I mentioned earlier that had 130 replicas on it stayed at above 80 percent utilization all of the time. Note that using a multiprocessor server would do no good, since the inbound sync process will still use only a single thread. The only answer is to split the partitions between several servers. I recommend staggering the master replicas among several central servers wherever the administration is being done (I like the central design versus the decentralized design most of the time). I still recommend keeping a copy of a replica off-site for disaster recovery. To do this, you will need a fairly fast link between the sites

(256 K, hopefully, but less can work if the partition is small and SAP traffic is confined).

NDSv8 says that a dedicated replica server (a server used for NDS only—no file and print, user home directories, etc. . . . you get the idea) may have 150 to 200 replicas. I have never seen or heard of this kind of design, but I guess it must be possible if Novell published the numbers; they will be responsible for supporting it, too. An NDSv8 nondedicated replica server is limited to 50 replicas.

- No more than 10 replicas per partition. NDSv8 says unlimited, but I would not believe it.

- Replica placement designed around your WAN infrastructure.

- No more than 5,000 objects per partition (1,500 maximum is recommended). Novell has updated its site to say 10,000 objects.

- Minimum server RAM of 64 MB. I recommend a minimum of 128 MB RAM. RAM is cheap; better yet, use 512 MB and fast I/O access. Look for tuning ideas at the end of this chapter. If you have 50+ NetWare servers, you should consider 256 MB RAM as a minimum. Remember, NetWare is a cache and I/O-intensive NOS—it is not CPU intensive.

Note: The eight-byte NDS entry field limits 64,000 entries per partition as a technical limit.

2.3.1   NDS design ideas

I presented Novell's recommendations for NDS tree designs. Seeing many trees—many of Novell's largest NDS trees in the world—allows me to make the following recommendations based on a few of my favorite design ideas:

- Separate the ROOT into its own partition.

- Separate the O into its own partition.

- Separate any SLP container into its own partition.

- Place a replica of its SLP partition on each DA in order for it to work properly.

- Keep all search policies—from ZEN and licensing—from extending past the immediate partition, if at all possible.

- Use OUs and other container objects to administer group rights when possible and avoid the NDS group object, since it may have to walk the tree to resolve rights and names (a major cause of slow logins).

- For larger installation, use a dedicated server for NDS only.

- Cache your entire local NDS database (explained earlier in this chapter and in Chapter 9 of *NetWare Administration*, Digital Press).

- Keep your replicas down to between 3 and 5 per partition, if possible.

- Remove bindery dependencics ASAP.

- Use alias objects to organize printers, servers, and other administrative objects in their own containers.

- Use alias objects to support the old context when you move user objects into a different context; clean up the alias objects with the freeware alias object cleanup utility on Novell's cool solution site.

- Look for other design ideas in Novell AppNotes.

- Upgrade to NDSv8 and NetWare 5.

2.3.2   **NDSv8.x (eDirectory) design**

NDSv8 breaks many of the existing rules. Your directory design should be predicated on variables not considered in earlier versions. Novell publishes some great guidelines in AppNotes at http://developer.novell.com/research. Also, Novell's Cool Solutions NDS site has several design guidelines and troubleshooting articles.

First, you will have to define what you are using the directory for. If it is just for network authentication, file, and print, you would design your tree the same way you would in NDS versions 6.x and 7.x but without the numerical partition restrictions—NDSv8 is more scalable. If, however, your directory needs go beyond normalcy—LDAP, DirXML, NDS for NT, and so on—you will need to evaluate your design based on many new variables. The general rule is that you want local access without clogging WAN links with synchronization traffic. Use a third-party tool such as NetPro's DS Analyzer to verify the efficiency and effectiveness of your tree design and to document NDS traffic patterns.

Types of replicas and how they relate to synchronization

Replicas are designated as master, read/write, read-only, and subordinate. Again, replicas are best viewed by NDSManager ConsoleOne or the third-party software DSDesigner. NDS must sync every 30 minutes, and trying to sync too many partitions in 30 minutes will probably cause NDS sync problems and errors that will manifest themselves in different ways. Synchronization between partitions causes all servers in the replica ring to contact each other—subordinate replicas are included in the sync process. Therefore, a replica ring of a partition put on 20 servers equals 380 routes: 20 servers each contacting 19 partners. Consider 380 routes, some probably across WAN links, each needing to contact and update each other. Again, outbound synchronization is multithreaded; inbound synchronization is single threaded.

Availability of the directory

Novell provides the ability to partition off small pieces of the database at any OU level for redundancy and load sharing. Users may notice faster logins when a replica of their partition exists on their LAN. Replication provides performance enhancements based on directory queries, too.

Replica ring

All servers given copies of any particular partition participate in a replica ring. NDS synchronization requires that all partitions communicate constantly to share NDS database changes.

Master replica

The master replica is the authoritative source for all replicas in any partition. NDS is, therefore, a single master design. AD, for instance, has a multimaster design—all domain controllers are authoritative for updates. The master replica is the first-created replica type of any partition. The master initiates and controls partition operations; answers object reads and writes, and accepts client updates, bindery information, and tree authentication and connectivity. Any replica can be promoted to a master replica through DSREPAIR, NDS Manager, or ConsoleOne. When you promote a replica, the old master is demoted to a read/write replica.

Read/write replicas

Read/write replicas do everything that the master replicas do but are not the authoritative source of information and do not initiate synchronization. Fault tolerance and increased performance—at the expense of synchronization traffic—are the read/write replica's purpose in life. Novell recommends that there be at least two read/write replicas for every master. Do not exceed ten replicas in NDSv7, if possible. Try not to "span the WAN"—which means do not put a copy of a replica across a slow link, if possible (which is not possible, I know).

Read-only replicas

Read-only replicas are for object reads, fault tolerance, and tree connectivity. Do not use or concern yourself with the use of read-only replicas; they are part of the X.500 standard. Design your tree with a master replica and at least two read/write replicas, taking into account the reduction of subordinate replicas. AD uses a read-only replica for its global catalog partition on its domain controller servers.

Subordinate replicas

Subordinate replicas are made automatically, never manually, when a parent replica of a partition is placed on a server without the child. Subordinate replicas are like icons: they are shortcut pointers to where the real information is. They are used for tree connectivity and do participate in NDS synchronization. Subordinate replicas contain only a partition ROOT object.

Subordinates are to be avoided, but not treated like the plague. Do not delete them. Larger implantations cannot help but have them—just keep subordinates to a minimum. Reduce the number of subordinates by reducing the number of parent replica partitions.

Replica states

Replica states are used to troubleshoot replica and synchronization problems—by experienced, advanced administrators. Replica states may be viewed when looking at DSREPAIR information.

On
New
Dying
Locked
Change type 0, 1
Transition on
Split 0,1
Join 0, 1, 2

Logins affect replicas

When a user authenticates (logs in successfully), user properties—network address, login time, last login time, and revision—are updated. An authenticating client needs a master or read/write replica to update these property values. As these values are updated in a replica, they are synchronized to the rest of the replica ring. When a user logs out, the `network address` and `revision` property values are updated. To see the effect of logins on NDS, use NetPro's DS Analyzer at http://www.netpro.com. This is the only tool I know that can effectively relate the impact of group membership and ZEN policies on login, which are probably the two largest "slow logon" culprits.

Note: For more information about tuning and optimizing your NetWare client software, please see my Digital Press book, *NetWare Administration*.

2.3.3 Synchronization and replication

A directory is read to, maybe, a hundred times more than it is written to. Therefore, a directory is optimized by the vendor for reads. Realize that your server, to be optimized, must therefore support fast I/O functions (I go into more detail at the end of this chapter). Data in directories is loosely consistent, which means that it is possible to have different information in the directory in two places. At the determined synchronization time, NDS automatically updates all information in a partition with the master replica. Some attributes, such as user passwords, are flagged to synchronize immediately—DS_SYNC_IMMEDIATE—while other information is not as important, such as phone numbers, and will be synchronized at the preset Novell NDS 30-minute interval. The 30-minute interval makes it difficult (though not impossible) to synchronize with more than ten replicas in one partition replica ring; thus, it is recommended to have no more than ten replicas—three to five are actually recommended—for any one NDSv7 partition.

Changes to any object must be time stamped (via Timesync) and updated to all parts of the partition, or replica ring. Time must be consistent throughout the tree. Synchronization requires network bandwidth and server CPU cycles. For example, each login triggers a synchronization of the entire partition within minutes and causes a slowdown for each server holding the partition. As with AD, outbound synchronization is multithreaded, but inbound replication uses a single thread.

An immediate sync occurs ten seconds after a save, such as a password change. The DSTRACE command forces the following actions:

- Slow sync 22 minutes after a change (similar to a logout);
- Schema synchronization every four hours;

- Heartbeat every 30 minutes;

- Limber five minutes after boot, then every three hours;

- Backlink two hours after boot, then every 13 hours;

- Connection management;

- Server status check every six minutes.

Synchronization is an NDS background process that is event driven. It can be triggered manually, as you will see later. In the NDS code, syncing is sometimes referred to as skulking, which is the process to make sure that all replicas have the same information when no changes have occurred. The heartbeat process is an example of skulking.

```
:SET DSTRACE=ON
:SET DSTRACE=*H
```

Each server must authenticate to the other servers in its replica ring to send and receive changes. Disabling login (through the server console command :DISABLE LOGIN) will not only keep users from logging in but will also keep servers from authenticating to each other.

Synchronization traffic

Realize that syncing takes up network bandwidth (although NDS is very efficient). The following NDS processes generate network traffic:

- *Immediate sync*—with only changes (deltas) sent;

- *Slow sync*—viewed by the following:

```
:SET DSTRACE=ON
:SET DSTRACE=+SYNC
:SET DSTRACE=+IN
```

- *Heartbeat process*[3]—forced by:

```
SET DSTRACE=*H
```

- *Schema sync process*—forced by:

```
:SET DSTRACE=*SS
```

Viewed by:

```
:SET DSTRACE=+SCHEMA
```

---

3.   Read-only and subordinate replicas participate in the heartbeat process.

- *Limber process*—forced by:

    : SET DSTRACE=*L

  Viewed by:

    : SET DSTRACE=+LIMBER

- *Backlink process*—forced by:

    : SET DSTRACE=*B

  Viewed by:

    : SET DSTRACE=+BLINK

- *Connection management process*—viewed by:

    : SET DSTRACE=+VCLIENT

- *Server status check process*

Fast synchronization

Fast synchronization occurs 10 seconds after a selected client update occurs on the server. Property values that cause a fast sync are defined by the NDS internal code. A password change is an example of a fast sync process.

Slow synchronization

Slow sync works at 30-minute intervals. Every replica must synchronize every 30 minutes. The slow sync is sometimes called the heartbeat. You may initiate a sync heartbeat with : SET DSTRACE=*H.

Password change effect on synchronization

I am often asked how a password change affects NDS and the sync process. After a user changes a password, the public key for the user's object is updated. The password is immediately synced (ten seconds after it is saved to the database) to all servers in the replica ring. Servers with external references to the object also need to be updated, but this is not done automatically. When a user request hits a server with an external reference, the server returns a -669 error to a server holding the object. The replica server holding this object should then know that the server holding the external reference needs an updated public key and should synchronize, which will then allow the user to authenticate to that (external reference) server with the new password. If this process gets held up (which it sometimes does for a number of reasons), the backlink process will automatically resolve the problem when it runs (within 13 hours).

2.3.4 **Synchronization design considerations**

How do you know if your tree design is working optimally? Novell does not have a utility to tell you how to design your tree; it only provides guidelines. NetPro is a third-party vendor that sells two great NDS products. DS Analyzer is an NDS sniffer. DS Expert is a health and alerting application.

Designing your NDS tree is the most important part of your NetWare deployment, migration, or upgrade. Novell did not put out too much information about designing NDS trees in the past—they charged big time money for a consultant (me) to come out and do it. You are stuck if you have a big tree, because there are very few people outside of Novell that can give you good information. I have been involved with several other consulting firm "experts" who have done more damage than good for their clients. You are going to have to go with Novell Consulting for the best information if you have a medium to large tree. Novell has recently put some great design information on its Cool Solutions site at http://www.novell.com/coolsolutions.

Again, outbound synchronization is multithreaded, but inbound replication uses a single thread. When planning replica placement, realize that each replica server must contact all of the others with the same replica (called a replica ring). This includes even subordinate replicas of a partition. So the formula would look something like the following: O (n^2) (that's the order of n squared). Thus, 20 replicas on a server with 20 other replicas per partition would equal about 400 sync patterns—which is too many.

Make sure that router boy does not block IPX SAP types 278 (used by servers to locate other replica servers), type 4 (used by servers to identify other NetWare servers), or type 26B (used by the NetWare servers for time synchronization). Never, ever let router boy filter IPX RIP broadcasts.

Some additional guidelines I would suggest include the following:

- For disaster recovery reasons, always keep a replica "off-site" in a place with a fast connection, and never put all master replicas on one specific server. Use at least two servers.

- For centralized control, choose two central servers with enough RAM to cache at least half (better to have the whole tree cached) of the server's DIB set (sum of all partition information on the server). To find out how big your server's DIB set is, type :DSREPAIR -RC at the server console. You may have to wait several minutes as the NDS information is written to a file on the server. Use a file viewer (CPQFM.NLM freeware, if you are on the server) to find the size in

`SYS:SYSTEM/DSREPAIR.DIB` for NDSv7 or in `SYS:DSR_DIB` for NDSv8 DIB files. You can then dictate to NDS (via SET DSTRACE commands) the amount of NDS you want placed in RAM (more on this later).

TAO—the newer, but not the newest, NDSv8

The latest version of NDS, TAO supports filtered replicas, DirXML, and other advanced feature sets.

Filtered replica types

The filtered replica types include the following:

- *Sparse read/write:* contains only desired classes;
- *Fractional read/write:* contains only desired attributes.

Sparse replicas can be created only if the master partition is on a TAO NDS version server. The `ERR_ILLEGAL_REPLICA_TYPE` error message will otherwise be generated.

DirXML and LDAP use sparse/fractional replicas, which are useful to do the following:

- Permit administrators to limit the amount and type of data per server;
- Custom tailor applications to access local data more efficiently;
- Decrease search time;
- Decrease synchronization of undesired attributes;
- Decrease size of NDS database on the server;
- Customize indexes (which enhance performance).

Read/write replicas allow modifications to attributes and classes if all mandatory attributes are within the filter. Read-only replicas do not allow local modifications.

TAO filtered replica synchronization

A replication filter contains a list of wanted classes and attributes. Each server may have only one filter; therefore, every sparse/fractional replica on a server must use the same filter. Inbound synchronization occurs on all types of replicas, regardless of NDS version. Outbound synchronization must be controlled, since replicas contain only a subset of NDS information. Outbound changes are not dependant upon NDS versions but do have limitations. For example, changes can only be synched to partition roots. TAO can outbound filters to reduce network traffic. Two new DSTRACE commands are introduced:

- To disable outbound filtering—`:SET DSTRACE=*OD`

- To enable outbound filtering—`:SET DSTRACE=*OE`

2.3.5 Bindery emulation

Bindery emulation is a no-no in the realm of NDS. It automatically requires a replica on each server supporting bindery services and causes the server to support bindery connects that are single-threaded, unlike NDS connections. All bindery requests to the server are made over a single bindery thread, which can monopolize the CPU. NDS is multithreaded and uses the CPU more efficiently.

Bindery access is very limiting as well. A bindery user is limited to access resources only inside the bindery contexts the user has an object in. Access to resources outside the user's context requires a replica on the server accessed or the object has to be redefined. Bindery objects are able to recognize only NDS users, groups, print queues, print servers, and bindery objects. The `:CONFIG` command displays the bindery context for any server. NDSv8 (eDirectory) provides two bindery QoS parameters. Search for a TID if you are having problems with bindery emulation using NDSv8.

I have experienced several significant client problems with bindery emulation. Several clients use Microsoft's NetWare services with bindery emulation, which causes many users to use the same NetWare bindery client login connection (this is a bad thing). You read that right: one connection. You cannot really scale past ten users using the same connection. Another client was using Microsoft's SMS desktop management product, which used the NetWare server as a workstation software staging point, but used one bindery connection for all users—at the same time. It drove the NetWare server's utilization to 90 percent plus.

Best Practice: Upgrade or replace all bindery-dependent software programs and hardware devices. Major culprits are old NetWare workstation clients and older print devices.

2.3.6   Schema

Schemas are rules. A DS has rules about what is allowed in the directory. For instance, every user object requires a password, a login name, and a `login time` property. Schemas define the rules as to what objects can exist in an NDS database tree, the relationships between object types (e.g., users can go into groups, groups do not have passwords, etc.), and the information (stored as attributes) that can and must be maintained by the NDS object.

NDS uses an extensible schema format, which defines the rules for data types—what kinds of objects can exist in NDS. There are three data types:

■ *Object classes.* Each object belongs to an object class that specifies which properties or attributes can be associated with an object.

■ *Attribute type definitions.* These identify and define the syntax for the values for each object's attribute store of information.

■ *Attribute syntax definitions.* These define the type of data that an NDS object stores.

Other good schema information includes Novell's Developer Notes "NDS Schema Overview" of October 1998 at http://developer.novell.com/ research and the Logic Source CDs (there are two CDs for NDS).

Extending the NDS schema

The NDS schema, as with any LDAPv3-compatible DS schema, is extensible. This allows for greater use of the directory as a policy and management tool. Novell lets you use ConsoleOne/NetConsole, Schemax, or Schema Manager to extend the NDS schema—you must have write rights to the ROOT to extend the schema.

As you add directory-enabled products, you extend the schema. For example, when you load DNS/DHCP from the product OS CD-ROM, you copy a .SCH file from the CD that extends the database schema. Schema extension should be loaded at the ROOT of the NDS tree—that is, one of the servers holding the master or a read/write replica of the ROOT partition. Schema extensions are replicated across the tree and down—they do not travel up the tree. These extensions will automatically be copied down the entire tree, and every DS server needs to accept the schema extension change. Sometimes these changes do not get replicated down the tree and later cause problems. Later in this chapter, I will discuss how to force schema synchronization down the tree. My consulting friends also recommend the Novell freeware schema-compare utility DSDIGN.NLM with the DS switch or the third-party DSDESIGNER tool, mentioned later, with the SCHCMP.EXE program. Never consider a tree merge without checking and rechecking that the schemas are exactly the same.

Specialized schema files are available from the NDS eDirectory download site. The following applies to a schema file (*.SCH) to NDS (the .SCH file is not copied to the NDS files):

```
:NWCONFIG.NLM→Directory Options→Extend Schema.
→You will be prompted for the Administrator's name,
password, and the location and name of the schema file.
```

This is also how you copy schema between disparate trees to begin a tree merge.

Novell also provides Schemax, a free download that lets you extend the directory schema by dragging and dropping, with no programming. ConsoleOne also now integrates this ability (the product manager for ConsoleOne was the owner of Schemax before Novell acquired it).

What sort of things would you want to extend the schema for? Easy: for a user's Social Security number, employee number, employee badge number, cell phone number, photograph, contract number for a workstation, asset tag number for a workstation, and so on. The possibilities are endless. The trick to getting this information into NDS is to get the user to enter this information or bulk load it into NDS versus having someone typing it in. The Schemax free utility gives you the ability to make users enter their own information.

Schema Manager tool in NDS Manager

Although schema is now controlled via ConsoleOne for eDirectory, many of you are still using the NDS Manager with an older version of NDS, so I will quickly discuss the older NDS Schema Manager, which is a Windows-based GUI utility from the Object menu in the NDS Manager tool (Figure 2.1). It allows you to manipulate the NDS schema in the following ways:

- By creating a new class;

- By deleting a class;

- By adding an optional attribute to a class;

- By managing classes;

- By running a tree compare schema utility—very important to use before tree merges;

Figure 2.1
*NDS Schema
Manager's look at a
user object.*

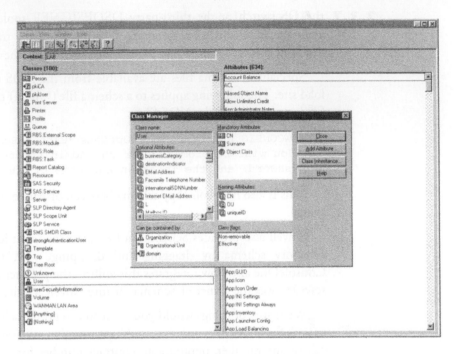

- By running a schema report utility—my test lab shows 100 classes with 634 attributes.

Schema problems

Many schema problems occur simply because of mismatched versions of NDS (the DS.NLM) or schema extensions getting "stuck" somewhere in the tree. If you have standardized all servers in the tree on the latest DS.NLM, you need to check the schema with the following:

```
:SET TTF=ON
:SET DSTRACE=ON
:SET DSTRACE=*R
:SET DSTRACE=+SCHEMA
:SET DSTRACE=*SS
→toggle to the DS server console screen
→wait to see that all processed=yes or no
→:TTF=OFF (saves the log file)
→look in the SYS:SYSTEM/DSTRACE.DBG to decode problems
```

Again, you may also use the Schema Manager to compare schemas between trees, but there is a need to compare schemas between servers sometimes. Novell also publishes a schema compare tool, DSDIAG.NLM–DA (for server-to-server compares) freeware.

2.3.7 Auxiliary classes

Auxiliary classes are added to the `object class` attribute of individual objects in the NDS database. For example, a pager number and Social Security number can be added to the user class NDS object. The `pager` and `social security` attributes are auxiliary classes, and the values of these properties (the actual numbers) are auxiliary attributes. Auxiliary classes can be optional or mandatory attributes. To extend the NDS schema, you must have write rights to the ROOT. To add an auxiliary class, you must have write rights to the `object class` attribute. Auxiliary classes are not supported on non-NDSv8/eDirectory servers.

Auxiliary classes can be a lifesaver if, for example, you only want to modify a subsection of your users. If you extend the user class with an additional attribute, all users will inherit that attribute, and it cannot be removed. With an auxiliary class, you need only apply it to the users you want and you can remove it at any time.

2.3.8 External references

External references are temporary placeholders on a server containing information about an NDS object the server does not hold locally in one of its replicas. Simply put, external references are created to track all NDS objects not physically residing on a server. The external reference life span is 192 hours, by default (do not change it). Two types of information about an external reference object are stored: relative distinguished name and local object ID. The external reference information is stored in the server's partition and held by a server that does not hold a replica of the NDS object.

External reference problems

External references are another NDS problem area. For some reason, they often have a hard time clearing themselves. Novell provides a great TID (at http://support.novell.com) that uses the STUFKEY.NLM process to generate a report on replica information and external references automatically.

Find external reference errors as follows:

```
:SET TTF=ON
:SET DSTRACE=ON
:SET DSTRACE=*R
:SET DSTRACE=+BLINK
:SET DSTRACE=*B
→wait until the server's DS screen says all processed=
yes or no
```

```
:SET TTF=OFF
→look in SYS:SYSTEM/DSTRACE.DBG and decode
```

Remove a server's external references as follows:

```
:LOAD DSREPAIR -xk3⁴
→Advanced Options Menu→Repair local database
choose <Yes> to rebuild operational schema and check
local references
then <F10> to repair
```

Use the following DSTRACE commands to start the backlink process (since the server must rebuild its external references, which we call backlinking):

```
:Set DSTRACE=+blink
:Set DSTRACE=*b
```

If you wanted to watch the backlink process, you would, of course, begin the DSTRACE commands with :SET DSTRACE = ON. Always work on one server at a time with external reference errors, and work within a replica ring before going on.

2.3.9 Backlinks

Backlinks are created by NDS to point to an external reference. A backlink is a logical pointer to information contained somewhere else—much like an icon on your desktop. Backlinks verify external references and remove them when they are not needed. Each object has an attribute for backlinks and backlink obituaries. Because backlink is an attribute of an NDS object, it is synchronized between replicas, and you can query its value with the NLIST command. For example, a group object contains a membership list. When users are contained within a partition outside the location of the group object's partition replica ring, NDS creates external references and backlinks for each of those user objects. The backlink process runs every 780 minutes.

You can use NLIST to see what objects have a backlink by typing the following at a workstation:

Syntax: NLIST <Class Type> Where "Back Link" EXISTS

Example: NLIST "Directory Map" Where "Back Link" EXISTS

---

4.   The –xk3 option is for advanced administrators who understand the ramifications of such an extreme repair.

To see what objects do not have backlinks type the following:

Syntax: `NLIST <Class Type> Where "Back Link" NEXISTS`

Example: `NLIST "Directory Map" Where "Back Link" NEXISTS`

2.3.10 Obituaries

Obituaries are pieces of information (object attributes) that have been changed and need to be removed from DSs—they are part of the synchronization process. When an object is deleted, moved, or renamed, a new obituary value is added to the object. It normally takes four synchronization cycles to eradicate a deleted or changed object or attribute.

Obituary problems

Obituary problems are among the most frequent you will see when troubleshooting NDS. They are quite common in mixed tree environments—in which you have more than one version of NDS.

Best Practice: As much as humanly possible, upgrade all of your NetWare servers to the latest DS.NLM version.

Obituaries do take some time to clear by the NDS janitor process (`SET DSTRACE=*J`). Obituaries get stuck because servers in the replica ring have not acknowledged the NDS change associated with that NDS object. In other words, the sync process got stuck on the deleted or changed information.

Obituaries go through four NDS flag stages:

1. `0000`: Not modified;
2. `0001`: Notified;
3. `0002`: Okay to purge;
4. `0004`: Purgeable.

There are three types of obituaries:

1. `Type=0002`: Moved—attached to an object that has been moved from this container;
2. `Type=0003`: Inhibit_Move—attached to an object that has been moved from another container to this one;

3.   Type=0006: Backlink—attached to an object that points to another server holding an external reference to the NDS object to be notified as the object is edited (modified, moved, deleted, renamed, etc.).

Best Practice: Obituary problems rarely occur on the server with the master replica of the partition because it is the master's responsibility to process obits. You may promote a read/write partition with obituary problems to a master replica, and then run a DSREPAIR on it, which should clean up all of the obit problems. You may then demote the master back to a read/write. Otherwise, look up support TIDs to help troubleshoot obituary problems.

The following will generate information on obituaries:

```
:SET DSTRACE=ON
:SET DSTRACE=*sto
```

The following will clear obituaries:

```
:DSREPAIR→Advanced Options Menu→Check External
References
```

The following will verify that obituaries are gone:

```
:SET DSTRACE=ON
:SET DSTRACE=+S
:SET DSTRACE=+J
:SET DSTRACE=*H
:SET DSTRACE=*F
```

Then run the DSREPAIR from the Advanced Options menu to check external references. The obits should purge within the next couple of minutes.

DSREPAIR.LOG file

Found in the SYS:SYSTEM directory, the DSREPAIR.LOG file contains information about database repair processes. You are able to read it with any text editor.

Best Practice: The DSREPAIR.LOG is populated with more detailed information when you load DSREPAIR with the –A switch.

An example of the DSREPAIR.LOG follows:

```
Found obituary at VID: 00054980, EID: 11000FE8, DN:
CN=PHARVEY.OU=LABRATS.O=ACME.ACME_TREE
TV: 1999/12/06 06:45:01 0004, Type = 0001 DEAD, Flags =
0000
```

The following are some helpful decodes:

- *VID = Value ID:* This is a record number in the Value.NDS file that has been used as an `obituary` attribute for the object identified by the EID.

- *EID = Entry ID:* This is a record number in the Entry.NDS file that specifies the object that has the `obituary` attribute assigned by the VID.

- *DN = Distinguished Name:* This is the full distinguished name of the object identified by the EID.

- *TV = Time Vector:* This is the time stamp that denotes when the `obituary` attribute was created.

- *Type:* This indicates both a number and a text description. There are three type categories: primary, secondary, and tracking:

  - A primary obituary indicates one of the following actions on an object:

    — 0000 `Restored`;
    — 0001 `Dead`;
    — 0002 `Moved`;
    — 0005 `NEW_RDN` (New Relative Distinguished Name);
    — 0008 `Tree_NEW_RDN` (Tree New Relative Distinguished Name—specifies a partition ROOT name, not an NDS tree name);
    — 0009 `Purge All`.

  - Two secondary obituaries indicate the servers that must be contacted and informed of the primary obituary action:

    — 0006 `Backlink`: This specifies a target server that needs to be contacted regarding an obituary.
    — 0010 `Move Tree`: There is one Move Tree obit, which is similar to the Backlink obit, for every server that needs to be contacted regarding a Tree_NEW_RDN operation.

- A tracking obituary is associated with certain primary obituaries. The following is a list of the valid obituary types:

  — 0003 Inhibit Move;
  — 0004 OLD_RDN (Old Relative Distinguished Name);
  — 0007 Tree_OLD_RDN (Tree Old Relative Distinguished Name —does not specify an NDS tree name but rather a partition ROOT name).

- *Flag:* The following valid flags indicate the level or stage that the obituary is processed to:

  - 0000 ISSUED: Indicates the obituary has been issued, created, or is ready for processing.
  - 0001 NOTIFIED: Indicates that the obituary is at the notify stage—the servers identified in the Backlink or Tree Move obituaries have been contacted and notified of the operation or action of an NDS object.
  - 0002 OK-TO-PURGE: Indicates that the obituary is being cleaned up on the local database of each server identified in the Backlink or Tree Move obituaries. The cleanup includes resolving all objects that reference the object with the obituary and informing them of the change (deletion, rename move, etc.).
  - 0004 PURGEABLE: Indicates that the obituary is ready to be purged. The purge process essentially recovers the value to the free chain and enables it to be reused. Check for a backlink trying to notify a server that is no longer in the tree. Remove the dead server's objects with NDS Manager. The obituary should then process.

Find obituary errors

To find obituary errors, you can do the following:

```
:SET TTF=ON
:SET DSTRACE=ON
:SET DSTRACE=*R
:SET DSTRACE=+J
:SET DSTRACE=*J
→toggle to the DS server console screen
→wait to see that all processed=yes or no
→:TTF=OFF
→look in the SYS:SYSTEM/DSTRACE.DBG to decode problems
```

You may also start a purge process on obituaries that have not finished purging:

```
:SET DSTRACE=ON
:SET DSTRACE=+J
:SET DSTRACE=*F
```

2.3.11 Janitor process

The janitor is an underpaid, underappreciated worker—there is little glamour for dirty work. The janitor keeps DS clean, running the flat cleaner process at 60-minute intervals. Some of the other janitor tasks are run every two minutes. The process is run after a synchronization process occurs. Intervals may be seen with the following commands:

```
:SET DSTRACE=ON
:SET DSTRACE=*P
→toggle to the Directory Services screen
```

Janitor processes include the following:

- Verifying connectivity to all servers in the NDS databases;

  ```
  :SET DSTRACE=*U
  ```

- Temporarily setting the UP and DOWN flag status of the NetWare server NCP entries. (Servers whose status goes back to down usually indicate that there is a communication problem between your server and the server showing down; use the DISPLAY SERVERS server console command to see if the server entry is still in your server's SAP cache table; try to PING the server, too [IPXPING.NLM or PING.NLM]);

  ```
  :SET DSTRACE=*U (yes, the same *U)
  ```

- Taking calls from the flat cleaner process, as well as scheduling the flat cleaner;

  ```
  :SET DSTRACE=*J
  ```

- Issuing synthetic time errors.

2.3.12 Flat cleaner

The work of the flat cleaner process is simple. It performs the following tasks:

- Generates server Certificate Authority keys;
- Returns deleted space from bindery and external reference partitions;

- Updates `status` and `version` attribute values of NCP server objects (e.g., SAP table cleanup when entries time out);

- Validates the UP status of servers of which it holds the master copies:

      :DSREPAIR→Advanced Options→Servers known to this
      database→Local Status

2.3.13   Limber process

The automated limber background process runs every three hours—unless it does not finish; then it retries every five minutes, performing the following:

- Verifying the server network address for all servers in the partitions the server holds;

- Maintaining the `version` attribute for the server in the NDS database;

- Changing the NDS tree name when the server receives a request or when server boots or NDS is restarted:

      :RESTART SERVER

or

      :SET DSTRACE=*

This information is stored in the server's local system partition. The limber process is started manually by `:SET DSTRACE=*L` and is viewed by `:SET DSTRACE=+LIMBER`.

2.3.14   NDS background processes

NDS background processes are checked with the following:

```
:SET TTF=ON
:SET DSTRACE=ON
:SET DSTRACE=*R
:SET DSTRACE=+IN
:SET DSTRACE=+S
:SET DSTRACE=+SCHEMA
:SET DSTRACE=+LIMBER
:SET DSTRACE=+MISC
:SET DSTRACE=+AGENT
:SET DSTRACE=*H
→toggle to the DS server console screen
```

```
→wait to see that all processed=yes or no
→:TTF=OFF (saves the log file)
→look in the SYS:SYSTEM/DSTRACE.DBG to decode problems
```

2.3.15 Unknown objects

If you have ever spent any time with NetWare Administrator or Console-One/NetConsole, you have probably seen objects with question marks next to them. These indicate that NDS cannot read required information from the object or that the management utility (ConsoleOne or NetWare Administrator) is missing a snap-in. For example, every user object requires a last name (or surname). If, somehow, the object gets corrupted and the property value for the last name disappears, the object becomes unknown.

Many times, I can update the schema, manage the snap-ins, or open the NWAdmin/ConsoleOne directly from the master replica of the object to resolve the unknown objects into readable objects. You may delete unknown leaf objects if you know how to restore them, but do not delete unknown container objects. I inadvertently deleted some unknown objects for a client and later found out that they were the objects added by the client's backup program. Needless to say, the backup program did not run and generated a significant error log, so be careful. Also, unknown objects can appear during NDS syncing processes. This is normal and should be worked out automatically by NDS. When they do not resolve, however, they can prevent the sync process from completing.

You may use the NetWare Administrator to search for unknown objects. You can also query for unknown objects with `C:\>NLIST unknown /D /S /C /R >filename.txt`. When you cannot, use DSDIAG.

Using DSDIAG to report on unknown objects

DSDIAG does not fix the unknown objects; it only reports on them.

```
:DSDIAG -DA→Distributed Repair→Mutate Unknown
Objects→<On>→Delete unknown class base <On>→Resend
Mutated Entries <On>
```

2.3.16 NDS startup

When the DS.NLM loads, for instance upon boot up or a SET DSTRACE=*., the DS.NLM automatically starts a heartbeat and limber process (which is equal to a SET DSTRACE=*H and SET DSTRACE=*L). You can prevent NDS from loading upon boot with `:SERVER -NDB`. Other useful NDS startup commands include the following: :SET DSTRACE=*A clears the NDS database cached in RAM, and :SET DSTRACE=1 resets all of the DSTRACE switches.

2.3.17 Transaction Tracking System

Novell uses the Transaction Tracking System (TTS) to preserve the integrity of data. A transaction in the process of being written to the hard drive when the system crashes is backed out upon reboot, preserving the integrity of the original data. TTS is a simple file attribute. Administrators may optionally flag any file with the TTS flag, although this flag is intended for NDS and useful for other databases, typically those that have no rollback features. NDSv7 must use TTS, which is why the SYS volume may not be an NSS volume, as NSS did not support TTS until NetWare 6. You must leave extra room on the SYS volume for TTS, or it may shut down, taking NDS with it. TTS tracks 10,000 transactions, by default. Each TTS write uses a small piece of memory.

2.4   SYS:_NETWARE hidden directory

Best viewed from either RCONSOLE or CPQFM.NLM (my preference), the SYS:_NETWARE hidden directory houses the NDS database.

2.4.1 NDS versions 6.x and 7.x

The following files are found in the NDSv6.x and v7.x directories:

- *PARTITIO.NDS:* This file contains information on all partitions used within the database on this server—schema, system, external reference, and bindery.

- *ENTRY.NDS:* The entry database contains records pertaining to bindery, schema, and user-created objects. The object's name and its location within the schema, bindery, or tree are among several fields held by an entry record. In short, it is the object database.

- *VALUE.NDS:* This file contains information on specific object attributes; it is the attribute database.

- *BLOCK.NDS:* The block database contains records referenced by the value database. It also holds overflow information from the value record (VALUE.NDS) file when the data field of an attribute exceeds the record length of the value record. Numerous blocks may be assigned to a given value record. This file holds the overflow for values and blocks.

- *STREAM FILES:* These files contain such information as login scripts, printer control files, and print job definitions. The link between a specific stream file and its owning attribute is determined by the name of the file. The first eight characters of the name (standard DOS 8.3 naming convention) references an offset within the value database. The record in the value database at that offset is the owning attribute. ZENworks for Desktops' application objects extends the stream files in NDSv7; this is not the case in NDS 8.

- *MLS.000:* This is the license file.

- *VALLINCEN.DAT:* This is the license validation file.

.DIB files

A .DIB is an unofficial backup of the NDS database. It is unofficial because there is no restore mechanism short of calling Novell technical support and getting them to do a restore with their specialized DSDUMP utility.

How big is a .DIB file? A client had one partition that contained the following:

- 32 groups;

- 1 organization role;

- 32 print servers;

- 31 printers;

- 16 profiles;

- 27 queues;

- 34,980 users;

- 37 containers;

- 4 file servers.

The .DIB file on a NetWare 4.11 server running NDSv7.47 was about 335 MB. This same configuration on NDSv8 uses only 74 MB. The biggest difference is in the stream files.

2.4.2   NDSv8 files in SYS:_NETWARE

The structure of the database in NDSv8 is very different. The database scales to more than a billion objects (tested) on one server. This is because the underlying foundational database for NDS (called FLAIM and developed at Brigham Young University) has changed.

- *_NDSDB.INI <DIR>:* Holds the tunable parameters for DS (seen by SET DSTRACE=*P) and cache information:

  ```
  _NDSDB.NST <DIR>
  CONNHAND.DAT
  ```

- *NDS.01:* Holds all records and indexes. When this file reaches 2 GB, another starts—NDS.02.

- *NDS.DB:* The control file that contains all of the rollback information for incomplete entries:

  ```
  NDS.LCK
  ```

- *NDS00001.LOG:* Roll forward file to apply completed transactions not yet written to disk:

  ```
  NLSHAND.DAT
  NLSLIST1.DAT
  NLSSECUR.DB
  ```

- *SERVCFG.000:* All server SET parameters:

  ```
  SERVHAND.DAT
  EMGRCFG.INF
  XMGRCFG.KS0
  XMGRSEED.INF
  ```

NDSv8 .DIB files found in SYS:DSR_DIB

This specialized directory stores your .DIB files from NDSv8. The directory stands for DSREPAIR_DIB. A .DIB is an unofficial backup of the NDS database—unofficial, since there is no restore mechanism short of calling Novell technical support and getting them to do a restore with their specialized DSDUMP utility.

2.5   How to manipulate the NDS directory

Novell provides the following tools to expand, maintain, and troubleshoot the NDS database:

- *ConsoleOne/NetConsole:* This is the single, future one-stop utility for all of your NDS needs.

- *NetWare Administrator:* You may add, delete, and rename objects and their corresponding properties with the NetWare Administrator. As

Novell's products are expanded, NetWare Administrator becomes less of a player. Novell's newest products are ported to ConsoleOne only. The NetWare Administrator 5.19f, according to Novell, is the last release of the utility. From now on, you must use ConsoleOne.

- *NDS Manager:* Partition and replicate the directory database with this utility. This utility will go the way of the dinosaurs too. ConsoleOne, because of its Java cross-platform ability, will now contain all future NDS management functionality.

- *DSREPAIR.NLM:* This is a server-centric database-repair utility. Notice the words "server-centric," since this utility will not fix the NDS tree, only the partitions contained on the server you are running it on.

- *DSTRACE SET commands:* These commands force specific parts of the database to sync or display on a screen. This is a great trouble-shooting utility but will not repair the database; it will only force specific NDS synchronization or background processes. Great TIDs for DSTRACE commands include 10011026 and 10011027. Note that TID numbers sometimes change when Novell's support staff updates them; in such cases, search on DSTRACE or SET DSTRACE commands.

- *DSBROWSE:* The DSBROWSE utility lets you dissect NDS objects, schemas, and attribute values. This is for the advanced NDS administrator. The utility also lists all NDS error codes—a great, great, great feature. Just press <F7> to display a list of error codes.

- *DSMERGE:* DSMERGE's APIs do not match the NDSv8 DS.NLM; it is for DSv6 and 7.x. DSMERGE lets you rename or merge NDS trees.

- *TREEINST.NLM:* This new module merges one-server trees into any-size trees. This is great for staging the OS at a central site, sending the server to its home, and merging it into the production tree. The TREEINST.NLM needs no subtree move to accomplish the merge, which is a huge plus. Find this .NLM buried on Novell's developer site.

The following third-party tools are worth mentioning:

- *NetPro:* I hesitate to give too much space to third-party products, but this company makes two very important DS monitoring and alerting utilities. DS Expert proactively monitors and alerts you about NDS problems. DS Expert can monitor 30+ NDS conditions and provides

SNMP alerts. I will discuss these utilities in greater detail later in the chapter.

- *DSDesigner:* This is a utility that no medium- to large-sized NDS shop can do without. It is cheap and extremely useful. I used it often as a consultant for Novell (http://dsdesigner.hypermart.net).

- *Bindview:* Bindview's products do not manipulate the NDS tree, per se; they audit and query it. I love the Bindview product and have seen some very large clients use it. Its only drawback—it is expensive.

2.5.1   ConsoleOne

The ConsoleOne utility has evolved so quickly that an explanation of all of the menu items seems useless. Major renovations have been done to its speed and functionality. Look for downloads of newer versions of Console-One (maybe renamed NetConsole) on Novell's Web site at http://www.novell.com/download.

ConsoleOne may be used for the same functionality as NetWare Administrator, Schemax, Schema Extension Manager, specific product management (ZEN for Desktops, ZEN for Servers, DirXML, etc.), and as replacement for the old NDS Manager utility.

2.5.2   NetWare Administrator

The NetWare Administrator manipulates the object and property values of NDS. It is not really for NDS troubleshooting.

2.5.3   NDS Manager

This utility is replaced by ConsoleOne for NDS database partitioning and management. As an interesting side note, Novell published an NDS tuning guide using NDS Manager (in an AppNote—look it up online), although I know of no one who would use NDS Manager for detailed troubleshooting. I always use DSTRACE and DSREPAIR, as does every consultant I know.

2.5.4   NWCONFIG

The NWCONFIG utility allows you to add or remove NDS. You may remove NDS from a server without having to supply an administrator's password with :NWCONFIG -DSREMOVE (this is very, very dangerous; therefore, always secure your server physically).

2.5.5   DSDIAG.NLM

DSDIAG Tool Manager is not an intuitive tool but does include four important report types:

1.   *Check NDS Versions*: provides information about servers that may relate to the NDS database. The information provided by this report includes the following:

Version;

Server name;

Address;

NDS version;

Replica depth;

Network cost.

2.   *Check Partition Status:* provides information about servers and their partitions. The data provided by this report include the following:

Partition status;

Number of readable rings;

Subordinate references in each ring.

3.   *List Replica Rings:* provides a logical view of NDS partitions. The report includes the following information:

Documentation of replica rings;

Cursory consistency check;

Unreachable partitions;

Location partition roots by NDS or servers.

4.   *List Server's Partition Table:* documents the association of the servers and their partitions and grants a physical view of the logical NDS database. The information provided by this report includes:

Server partition;

State;

Type.

2.5.6   DSMERGE.NLM

Use DSMERGE.NLM to change your NDS tree name or merge two NDS trees (the latter does not work for NDSv8). DSMERGE uses low-level APIs, such as DClient and CIA. It merges the source tree into the destination tree at the root. It first compares the schema in the two trees to ensure they are exact prior to doing the merge. If differences are present, the utility will warn you that it cannot continue. TREEINT (a freeware utility on Novell's developer Web site used to merge a single server tree into any other tree) also compares the schema and will attempt to reconcile those differences by modifying or extending the destination tree's schema. If reconciliation cannot be achieved, you are warned of this fact and given the choice to continue or end. DSMERGE can merge any two NDS trees and can recover from a merge stopped or stalled due to error(s) by backing out the changes made through the transaction tracking system regardless of tree size and the number of servers in either tree.

Tree merging

To merge trees, you should look up Novell TIDs first. Plan carefully for a tree merge. I have seen a month of planning, lab work, and NDS patching take place before the merge for one customer. The production merge process took only 15 minutes.

You need to make sure that your schemas match. Go through DSRE-PAIR and import the schema both ways twice. All relevant OS and NDS patches need to be installed. Lab testing should be done until the tree merge becomes second nature. Clean up any NDS errors in both trees before you start, and verify that timesync is consistent in both trees. I would recommend using the same time source for both trees. Verify licensing and make sure every replica server is either up or removed from the tree. NDS will need to contact every replica server to complete the tree merge.

There is, of course, a little more to the process, but these are the most important concerns. You can perform tree merges from the information in Novell's TIDs—that's where I got tons of my NDS information as a consultant for Novell (and you thought it was mostly secret information).

2.5.7   TREEINT

Use this freeware utility to stage a server in a central location with a bogus tree name and then merge it into your production tree (prune and graft) at the local site. Realize its one server tree limitation and read the readme file. Search for it at http://developer.novell.com.

2.5.8 DSREPAIR.NLM

DSREPAIR.NLM is a server-centric tool for repairing the global NDS database. This is important. There is no global tool to repair the database. NetPro, a third-party company, makes the DS Expert and DS Analyzer tools, which give you better management and reporting of global NDS information but still do not repair the database globally.

Best Practice: Download and use the latest NDS versions, which often include updated DSREPAIR.NLMs.

The ability to repair the database is an integral part of NDS health. The first most important piece of NDS health is to upgrade to the minimum patch listed version of NDS. Go to http://support.novell.com/misc/patlst.htm. *Warning:* Know what you are doing before running the XK killer switches!

DSREPAIR switches

DSREPAIR switches are formatted as follows: `:DSREPAIR -switch`. Note that not all of the switches listed below work on all versions of DS.NLM:

- −41x: deletes the 41x files after an upgrade;

- −CV #: enters a number to show attributes with more than # values (e.g., `DSREPAIR -cv 75` shows all attributes with more than 75 values);

- −A: enables advanced mode (I use this often);

- −D: requests alternate DIB files mode (`dsrepair -ext`);

- −INS: extends schema

- −xk2 *(secret switch—do not use unless told to by Novell support):* destroys all replica roots by doing the following:

  Making all objects external references;

  Zeroing the creation and modification time stamps;

  Clearing all flags except `EF_PRESENT`;

  Class = −1 (not backlinked).

- −xk3 *(secret switch—do not use unless told to by Novell support):* clears backlinks EF_BACKLINKED:

  Flags = 8001, which is present and verify creation timestamp;

  Class = id_invalid =FFFFFFFF=-1;

  All ext-ref attribute time stamps set to zero.

Note: It is advisable to run the backlinker after this DSREPAIR switch to rebacklink: SET DSTRACE=*B.

- −L: sets a flag so the file will be deleted and a new log file name created;

- −M: reports move inhibit obituaries;

- −MR: removed;

- −N#: sets number of days before deleting user object Net address—if it is older, it is deleted (default is 60 days) (e.g., to release connections that are older than one day, on NetWare 4.x, go to the Master replica→DSREPAIR -N1→Advanced Options→Repair local DS→ <F10>);

- −P: marks all unknowns per replica as referenced;

- −RC: remote load create .DIB dump file (use this in STUFF-KEY.NLM scripts);

- −RD: repairs local database (automated) (use this in STUFF-KEY.NLM scripts);

- −RI: verifies and repairs remote server IDs (dependent upon IPX or SLP);

- −RL: specifies an alternate DSREPAIR log file name; the first one is deleted (to keep the old one and append to it, use the −L switch);

- −RM <partition_root_ID>: makes this server the master for the specified partition ID (I prefer doing this manually through DSRE-PAIR→Advanced Options→Replica and partition opera-tions→<Enter on partition>→Designate this server as the new master replica.) (use this to troubleshoot external reference and backlink problems);

- −RN: repairs network addresses (dependant upon the server's IPX SAP table or your SLP infrastructure);

- `-RR <partition_root_ID>`: repairs replica with specified partition ID;

- `-RS <server_ID><partition_root_ID>`: removes specified server ID from the specified partition ID;

- `-RV`: repairs volume objects and trustees;

- `-736`: terminates the 0.DSB file (used to troubleshoot a specific 736 NDS error);

- `-V`: ignores API version checking;

- `-wm`: clears the `wm:registered` workstation attributes that can some-times cause high utilization from ZEN for Desktops registry entries when the workstation is not being imported into the NDS database as a workstation object.

Some of the switches that I use most often include :`DSREPAIR -RC -RD`, which repairs the local database and dumps a .DIB set of the database, and :`DSREPAIR -A`, which opens advanced options in DSREPAIR.

DSREPAIR's menu screen includes the following options:

- *Unattended full repair.* When you run an unattended full repair, you check the following:

  - *Records.* The validity of links between entry, value, block, and par-tition records is verified. There are pointers between these four files, and running the repair checks all of the pointers to be sure they are accurate.
  - *Structure.* The links of all entry records to the ROOT and all properties linked to the corresponding entry record are verified.
  - *Schema.* Existing schemas are compared with base class schemas, objects missing mandatory attributes are changed to unknown, and illegal containment is checked for.
  - *External references* (discussed earlier).
  - *Mail directories* (a holdover from the bindery days).
  - *Stream syntax files.*
  - *Network addresses.* (*Warning:* If you are using IP in NetWare 5, the network addresses are verified via SLP. If you have a poor SLP design, you will have problems.)
  - *Remote IDs.*
  - *Replica ring.*
  - *Volume object and trustees.* This option will temporarily lock the database. Users logged in already will be able to continue to work;

new users will not be able to log in until the repair process unlocks the database. I have seen the server hang doing unattended full repairs. Therefore, before you run the repair, back up your current database with the following command, just in case: `:LOAD DSRE-PAIR -RC`.

■ *Time synchronization.* This option checks the time synchronization health of your servers. Realize that you can run this option five times and get five different results. I always start an NDS health check here. Troubleshoot all time problems. You cannot have stable NDS health without almost perfect time synchronization.

Best Practice: Use a Network Time Protocol (NTP) utility to keep your NT servers in time with your NetWare servers. One utility is Time Lord for NT http://www.cix.co.uk/~ossytems/os_syst/time_lord.html.

■ *Report synchronization status.* This option reports the replica ring status and is a very important troubleshooting screen. Document all errors and go to Novell's TIDs to look for answers.

■ *View repair log file.* This option displays the SYS:SYSTEM\DSRE-PAIR.LOG file, which is updated each time you run a repair.

■ *Advanced options menu.* This option provides a portal to a whole new range of options. Use the DSREPAIR –A switch to enable even more advanced menu choices.

■ *Exit.* Sortie in French.

DSREPAIR→*Advanced Options menu*

This choice includes the following options (Figure 2.2):

■ *Log file and login configuration:* includes self-explanatory items concerning the DSREPAIR.LOG file;

■ *Repair local DS database:* checks the local records, structure, and schema and encompasses basically the first three parts of an unattended full repair (this option will temporarily lock the database);

■ Servers known to this database

■ *Replica and partition operations* (window to other advanced features covered later);

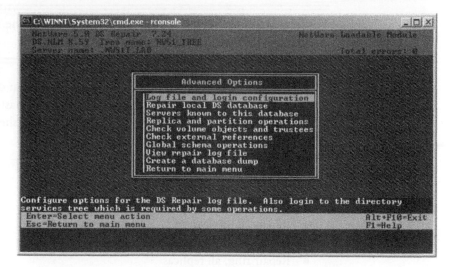

Figure 2.2
The
DSREPAIR.NLM
Advanced Options
menu.

- *Check volume objects and trustees:* makes sure all volumes are mounted as all links to rights and trustee assignments are verified;

  - Check external references
  - Global schema operations

- *View repair log file:* views the SYS:SYSTEM\DSREPAIR.LOG file;

- *Create a database dump:* shows a path to the dump file, which is a snapshot of NDS that only Novell support can restore (do not use this in place of regular backups, because you can only restore the dump file by placing a support call to Novell).

  - Return to main menu

DSREPAIR→Advanced Options→Replica and Partition Operations→Partition Name <Enter>

Options accessed via `Replica and Partition Operations→Partition Name` include the following:

- *View replica ring:* displays the replica ring and opens to other choices if you press <Enter> on a replica;

  - Report synchronization status on the selected server
  - Synchronize the replica on the selected server
  - Send all objects to every replica in the ring
  - Floods the network with NDS traffic temporarily

Best Practice: Use Send all objects to every replica in the ring to fix inconsistencies in your replica ring; run from the master only.

- Receive all objects from the master to this replica: only for use on servers with read/write replicas to receive from master replicas
- View entire server name: shows the full distinguished NDS name
- Return to servers with replica list

  — Return to previous screen

- Report synchronization status of all servers
- Synchronize the replica on all servers
- Repair all replicas
- Repair selected replica
- Repair ring, all replicas
- Repair ring, selected replica

- *Schedule immediate synchronization* (why do you schedule something that is starting immediately?);

- *Cancel partition operation* (it is easier to hit <Cancel> during an operation, although either choice may take a while to register—just be patient);

- *Designate this server as the new master replica:* a great troubleshooting tool;

- *View entire partition name:* full distinguished NDS name.

  - *Return to replica list*

Repairing NDS with DSREPAIR.NLM

DSREPAIR.NLM is a server-specific utility for troubleshooting NDS problems. Remember, with DSREPAIR.NLM you are not troubleshooting the tree, but replica(s) of partition(s). DSREPAIR does not resolve global problems with the NDS database.

How often do you need to run DSREPAIR.NLM? When you find an error. You do not need to run it every week or every day as maintenance. Verify that the replica rings are clean (e.g., that there are no replicas in a non-ON state. The fastest place to check this is DSREPAIR→Report Sync Status).

2.6   LDAP support

LDAP is supported in NDSv8 or eDirectory, as well as in later versions of NDS 7.x. Novell is embracing many open standards. ConsoleOne is the management utility for LDAP integration. Realize, though, that NDS, unlike AD, is not a "pure" LDAP DS. NDS uses the NLDAP.NLM to provide LDAP support. Is this a big deal? No, but it does require a bit more work when communicating with a pure LDAP directory, such as mapping the NDS attribute names to the LDAP attribute names. This can also be done with Novell's DirXML product, which is made for you to use NDS as the central directory to publish selected content to other DSs.

The term LDAP has four meanings:

1.   LDAP is a protocol riding on top, or within, an IP packet.

2.   LDAP is an API for developers to hook into directory-enabled applications.

3.   LDAP is a format defining data in a directory.

4.   LDAP is a format to exchange information, referred to as LDIF.

LDAPv3 is supported by NDS. The complete LDAPv3 specification can be found in RFCs 2251 through 2256.

LDAP is an open-standard protocol riding within IP to access any DS that supports the LDAP standard; it rivals Novell's proprietary Novell Directory Access Protocol (NDAP). Novell includes LDAP support, which has taken center stage as the new de facto standard to allow clients access to DS—any DS—information.

For LDAP to return data to an unauthenticated client (such as Netscape Communicator or Microsoft Internet Explorer), the NDS (public) trustee must have appropriate NDS rights, including the browse object right. In addition, the compare and read property rights must be on all property rights on the specific set of attributes that need to be searched on or read. If the entire tree is to be accessible from LDAP, these rights should be granted at ROOT.

Administrators should grant property-rights access only to those properties and portions of the NDS tree they want to be publicly accessible, which should not be much. Administrators should also consider the security advantages offered by the Proxy User feature of LDAP services. LDAP may use an SSL connection for security.

For applications that authenticate with a distinguished name via LDAP, the appropriate rights should be granted to the authenticating DN.

2.6.1 Auxiliary classes

Auxiliary classes are not supported on non-NDSv8/eDirectory servers. You may create Auxiliary classes in mixed environments. Schema extensions will synchronize from the point of installation, down the tree. The non-NDSv8/ eDirectory servers will accept the schema extensions as unknown but without error.

LDAP provides for the following:

1.   *A data form:* defines the kind and means for updating information put into an LDAP-compatible directory;

2.   *A naming form:* defines how to organize the information in the LDAP directory;

3.   *A security form:* defines how to access information based on rights.

LDAP also defines the LDAP Data Interchange Format (LDIF) format, which provides a text-based means for describing directory information. Using LDIF, you can import and export bulk information between directories (similar to the OIMPORT and OEXPORT NDS tools).

2.6.2 LDIF support

The LDAPv3 specification defines LDIF as a text-based bulk-loading format. LDIF file creation, in NDSv8, is comprised of BT.EXE, which creates three files:

1.   Filename.add;

2.   Filename.del;

3.   Filename.mod.

Looking at the extensions, you can probably figure out that you may add, delete, or modify database entries. As with any technology, LDIF does have limitations. It is great, however, for importing and exporting directory information from, say, AD to NDS, or vice versa. Novell also supplies a BULKLOAD.NLM, which may be used to add many users at once to NDS, a great feature for lab scenarios.

LDAP protocol operations

LDAP offers nine basic protocol operations:

1.   *Search:* a query function;

2.   *Compare:* a query function;

3.   *Add:* an update function;

4.   *Delete:* an update function;

5.   *Modify:* an update function;

6.   *Rename:* an update function;

7.   *Bind:* a security function equivalent to a login;

8.   *Unbind:* a security function equivalent to logging out;

9.   *Abandon:* a security function equivalent to closing a connection— similar to the watchdog process logging you out of NDS.

BULKLOAD.NLM

BULKLOAD imports LDIF format information into DSs—much like OIMPORT.

To use the BULKLOAD.NLM, do the following:

1.   Copy LDIF files to the SYS:SYSTEM.

2.   Load BULKLOAD.NLM.

3.   Log in with proper rights; admin is always preferable.

4.   Select Apply LDIF File to run.

5.   Output creates a .LOG file.

Best Practice: Using a password will eat up about 250 ms for each object created, versus 5 ms for those without. The process will also run faster if you cache DS.

TAO introduces a new import/export feature called ICE. This is run from ConsoleOne and will allow import/export via LDIF. It will also allow you to import from any LDAP server.

2.7 NDS objects

NDS objects are the building blocks of the database, which is an object-oriented database. Objects are manipulated by NetWare Administrator and ConsoleOne/NetConsole. A user object represents a physical person authenticated to the network. The user object contains the following properties, among many others:

- Login restrictions;

- Intruder detection limits;

- Password;

- Password restrictions;

- Security equivalencies;

- Account balance;

- Last name;

- Last login;

- Login script;

- Minimum password length.

When you create a user object, you can create a home directory for that user, who then has default rights to that home directory. You can also provide default property values by applying a user template object to new user objects as they are created.

2.8 Repairing NDS

1. The first step to checking anything with NDS is checking time synchronization: :LOAD DSREPAIR→TIME SYNCHRONIZATION. NDS allows for a + or − 2-second time differential. Anything within this differential is considered synced. This two-second standard can be changed through the set command: :SET TIME-SYNC SYNCHRONIZATION RADIUS = 2000. The default setting is 2,000 milliseconds.

2. The time synchronization screen in DSREPAIR.NLM will show you the DS.NLM version number—hopefully they are all the same. Make sure that your versions are all up-to-date. This is a very important point. Remember that many DS version updates

are part of a support pack update. In the README.TXT file that comes with the support packs, Novell recommends applying the entire support pack and not individual modules or files within the support pack.

3. Troubleshoot any time problems. Check whether you have configured sources on or off on your servers. Check to see if your servers are pointing to the right time source. Ping servers that report errors, then work from finding trouble spots. Ping the router interfaces. Try to ascertain whether you have a network communication problem.

    ```
    : LOAD IPXPING
    : LOAD PING
    ```

4. Use the DSTRACE commands to check for NDS synchronization errors and troubleshoot them. Look up Novell's support TIDs for information on specific errors.

2.8.1 NDS error codes

Instead of listing all of the error codes and possible causes here, I will recommend going to Novell's support site and looking up the appropriate support TID for a given error code to get the information you need. The following is a general guideline:

- *−1 through −255:* DS OS error codes;

- *−301 through −399:* Client error codes;

- *−400 through −599:* NLM client library error code;

- *−601 through −799:* Agent error codes—you will probably see these most.

Other NDS resources include the LogicSource CDs (I and II for NDS), although they are not free.

2.9 NDS health check

Novell publishes some TIDs and AppNotes on NDS health checks. I have not included them, however, as there have been too many changes to NDS lately to do a thorough job. Instead, go to Novell's site and look up the TIDs on NDS health.

NetPro's DS Analyzer and DS Expert can perform constant NDS health checks automatically. I prefer using one of these automated applications to performing a manual health check.

DSDesigner is used by some to do NDS health checks, although it is not really made for it—it is an NDS design and documentation tool.

2.10   NDS dependence on SLP

If you are wondering what SLP is, then either you have not moved to Net-Ware 5/6, or you have and are running only IPX. I say that because name resolution has changed for NetWare 5 running IP. IP is the preferred proto-col, meaning that with both IPX and IP running, the OS is going to use IP for everything it can. NDS can name resolve by looking into itself (its own database).

I am often asked, "When do I need to plan for SLP?" The answer is as soon as the second NetWare 5.x/6 server is added into your network, because SLP is used to locate other servers in an IP network. An IP network may be either IP-only or a dual IP/IPX stack. NetWare 5.x is tuned to prefer an IP connection over an IPX connection, even if both protocol stacks are loaded; therefore, it needs a service resolution and namespace provider in the IP world. NetWare 5.x provides the functionality of SLP to locate net-work resources via multicast. SLP is a distant cousin to DNS. I explain SLP and give design recommendations in detail in my other Digital Press book, *NetWare Administration*.

NDS doesn't need SLP to discover other servers or NDS information. NDS can resolve names within itself because it is a database of names and because NDS object properties, such as IP addresses and IPX addresses, provide the information that NDS needs to be a name resolver. NDS is its own namespace provider, as is DNS. NDS needs no assistance to resolve server names when a server holds a replica copy of all the other serv-ers in the tree, although it is nearly impossible to do and would be a very inefficient design in medium to large sites. A NetWare server can resolve any name it holds in the NDS database that it houses locally. NDS tree information is partitioned, distributed, and replicated across the enterprise. For NDS to resolve an object, it must rely on the referral list, which is a list of the network addresses of the servers that hold a master or R/W copy of the partition that the object resides in. NDS can accomplish this if, and only if, every server in the NDS tree has a replica on it with a copy of the partition of the server's own NDS context, because NDS already has the network addresses of all the servers in the tree.

For example, a request to resolve a name is made to an NDS server. The server scans its local database to find the object. If the object is there, then the server returns the referral list to the client with its own network address in the list. If the local database doesn't hold the object, the server's responsibility is to create a referral list for the client—the server acts like a client itself. The server has its own view of the tree and a connection table viewable via MONITOR.NLM→Connection Information. The server uses the network address information in the connection table, contacts the servers in the list one by one, and asks them if they hold the object. As soon as the server finds another server with a copy of the object, it receives the referral list and sends the list to the client. If the server queries all the servers in the connection table and doesn't find a server with a copy of the object, the server "falls back" to its bindery information and either multicasts for a service or unicasts, depending on the bound protocols:

- IPX: NDS uses SAP to build its bindery table;

- IP: NDS either uses SLP to multicast for an NDS replica server service or contacts a DA by unicasting to the address(es) listed in the server's SLP.CFG to query for a replica server service—ndap.novell.

When an SLP infrastructure, using a DA, is set up, every server's service agent should know about the IP addresses of all the DAs. DAs are found via the 224.0.1.35 multicast by DHCP queries on options 78 and 79 (which the NetWare server can operate as a DHCP client to query for DAs within the DHCP database) or by statically configuring the DA in the server's SYS:ETC\SLP.CFG file. DAs know about all of the services in their scope (because all of the SAs register with the DA) and normally hold the top NDS partition layers of the tree.

Best Practice: Pick servers that have the top layers of the NDS tree on them to be DAs.

A referral list is built by looking at the Replica attribute, since it holds the replica type (master, read/write) and the network address of each server—UDP, TCP, and IPX if both protocols are bound.

SLP is dependent upon IGMP multicast, much the same as IPX is dependent upon SAP/RIPs. You may statically configure the server's SYS:\

`ETC\SLP.CFG` to unicast directly to a DA, thereby avoiding router boy's possible decree that no multicast is allowed on the enterprise. A pure IP implementation is dependent upon an SLP infrastructure. SLP is used for the following:

- Server-to-server discovery (remember you do not have SAPs);

- Client discovery of servers (upon boot up, multicasts are sent to look for services, i.e., servers);

- Support for browsing network neighborhood;

- Support for "IPX" short names (may be resolved a number of ways):

  - By allowing IGMP multicast across the network;
  - Through the SLP.CFG if you have implemented a DA;
  - Through NDS if you partitioned the SLP OU and have it on a server that you can get to;
  - Through the server's HOSTS file;
  - Through a DNS lookup, if the name exists in the same DNS sub-zone.

2.11   NDS dependence on time synchronization

A distributed database has constant changes occurring at about the same time, hence the dynamic nature of NDS. How do you make sure that the most recent change is the one that takes effect in such a dynamic system? You have to time stamp every database (NDS) transaction. To ensure time consistency across all servers and partitions, all times must be the same. For times to be the same, logic dictates that all server times must come from the same source. That is where timesync comes in. Every time a password is changed or an object is renamed, NDS requests a time stamp. Time stamps ensure that the order of events written into the database is correct. When you troubleshoot NDS, first verify time synchronization by :`DSRE-PAIR`→`Time Synchronization`. If you get errors here, troubleshoot them before looking at NDS. Many NDS errors are symptomatic of timesync problems. The primary time servers make up to a 50 percent correction in their time-per-polling interval.

In NetWare 5, the TIMESYNC.NLM works differently than it does in a 4.x environment. The native IP nature of NetWare 5 allows references to Internet sources, via NTP (UDP port 123), that we could not use in Net-Ware 4.x (at least, not without a third-party NLM or extra hardware).

Time synchronization should be administered centrally.

2.11.1   NetWare 4.x

RDATE.NLM, a shareware utility, has been used with great success by many of my clients. The RDATE.NLM allows for NetWare IPX servers to sync to IP time sources. Check the favorite NetWare shareware sites for this utility.

2.11.2   NetWare 5.x and 6

NetWare 5.x provides the legacy TIMESYNC.NLM and the new NTP.NLM. TIMESYNC.NLM version 5.12 and above can support older IPX dependencies, as well as NTP reference sources. RFC 2030 outlines the NTP specification. I recommend TIMESYNC.NLM and configured sources.

Best Practice: If you have an Internet connection, use TIMESYNC.NLM to sync your reference server to an atomic clock resource.

2.11.3   NTP and TIMESYNC

New in NetWare 5 is the NTP.NLM. Use it when you want to set up NTP relationships. I have not had a need to use the NTP.NLM, since I can do NTP from the TIMESYNC.NLM. TIMESYNC.NLM can poll an NTP time source without the need for NTP.NLM and NTP relationships. I find the complexity of NTP.NLM and the NTP.CFG unnecessary for many of my clients.

2.11.4   TIMESYNC server types

- *Reference:* The definitive time source time provider on the network. Use reference time servers in implementations of more than 12 servers. Set the reference server's time to an NTP time source for best results. Only one reference server is needed on the network. Use with primary time servers, too. Uses a multiple of 16 (overrides every other type) to vote on time. I normally use one reference: two to five primaries and the rest secondary.

- *Single Reference:* Standalone definitive time provider for use in smaller networks that use only this server and secondary time servers.

- *Primary:* Time providers that need to connect to one other time provider—primary or reference—to adjust their network time and set the time synchronization flag. Uses a multiple of one to vote on time.

- *Secondary:* A consumer or subscriber. Must set time according to received values.

2.11.5   SET commands relating to TIMESYNC

The following server SET commands are related to TIMESYNC.

```
:SET TIMESYNC Configuration File = SYS:SYSTEM\
TIMESYNC.CFG
```

`:SET Time Zone = EST5EDT`

```
:SET Start Of Daylight Savings Time = (APRIL SUNDAY FIRST
2:00:00 AM)
```

```
:SET End Of Daylight Savings Time = (OCTOBER SUNDAY LAST
2:00:00 AM)
```

`:SET Daylight Savings Time Offset = +1:00:00`

`:SET Daylight Savings Time Status = OFF`

`:SET New Time With Daylight Savings Time Status = OFF`

`:SET TIMESYNC Correction Floor: 1` (Minimum default clock value, in milliseconds, before time correction is applied.)

`:SET TIMESYNC Configured Sources = OFF` (Default uses either SAP type 26B for IPX or SLP timesync.novell for IP. Turn configured sources on for better reliability.)

`:SET TIMESYNC DEBUG: 0` (A value of 7 will enable a server console screen to show timesync messages. This is a great troubleshooting tool.)

`:SET TIMESYNC Directory Tree Mode = ON`

`:SET TIMESYNC Hardware Clock = ON` (If your NetWare server is set up as a reference server and pointing to an external time source, be sure to turn this hardware clock parameter to OFF.)

`:SET TIMESYNC Immediate Synchronization: OFF`

`:SET TIMESYNC Maximum Offset: 600`

`:SET TIMESYNC Offset Ceiling: 315532800`

: SET TIMESYNC Polling Count = 3

: SET TIMESYNC Polling Interval = 600 (Default of ten minutes [600 seconds] to poll other servers.)

: SET TIMESYNC RESET = OFF (Change to ON every time a time sync value is changed.)

: SET TIMESYNC Restart Flag = OFF (Change to ON every time a timesync value is changed.)

: SET TIMESYNC Service Advertising = ON (Using configured sources enables you to turn this value off and decreases network traffic.)

: SET TIMESYNC Short Interval: 10

: SET TIMESYNC Synchronization Radius = 2000 (Default of two seconds for server to adjust time.)

: SET TIMESYNC Time Adjustment = None scheduled (Used to set the tree time—never use "set time" to adjust server/tree time.)

: SET TIMESYNC Time Sources = ;

: SET TIMESYNC Type = SINGLE

: SET Default Time Server Type = SINGLE

2.11.6   TIMESYNC troubleshooting

Look at a single server by typing :TIME and reading the resulting info. Query the network's time health through DSREPAIR.NLM :DSRE-PAIR→Time synchronization. Turn on the timesync debug screen by :SET TIMESYNC DEBUG=7. Toggle to the Timesync Debug screen and look for error messages.

2.12   The NDS security model

NDS security includes object and object property rights. NDS is an object-oriented database that assigns each object various attributes (e.g., a user object has a full name, phone number, fax number, password, etc., all of which are properties or attributes of the user object). Novell allows security permissions to be placed on objects and each property of an object. For instance, when a user object is created, the object automatically inherits the read right to the OU's login script property.

User objects are created to assign each person a digital identity on the network. Network and resource access is based on rights assigned to the user object. Some rights are given explicitly, while others are inherited. For instance, the earlier example of a user gaining the read right to the OU's login script property is one assigned in NDS by default. It is, therefore, considered an inherited property.

Enforcement of rights is automatic and immediate. Unlike NT 4.0, where each user logs in and gets a token to keep during the entire login process, NDS permissions are dynamic. Each restriction or addition of rights is applied as soon as the database syncs, which is every ten seconds by default for access rights. Fast enough for you? If not, consider that NT requires you to log out and log in again to receive the new rights additions or restrictions via its 15-year-old LANMAN access token technology.

The information about who can access object properties is stored in the object itself in a property known as the access control list (ACL). Please see Chapter 8 in my *NetWare Administration* book for more—much more.

2.12.1   NDS object rights

NDS object rights include the following:

- *Supervisor (S):* This is the sum of all other rights. Unlike the supervisor right in the file system, the supervisor NDS object right can be blocked through an IRF. Granting this right implies granting the same supervisor right to all NDS properties.

- *Browse (B):* The browse right allows trustees of the object(s) to search the tree in NWAdmin and through the NLIST and CX commands.

- *Create (C):* This right, available only on container objects, allows an object trustee to create objects in and below the container.

- *Delete (D):* This right permits the removal of objects from the NDS tree.

- *Rename (R):* This right grants the object trustee the ability to change the object's name.

- *Inheritable (I):* Only available in NetWare 5, this right allows assigned object rights to be inherited. Unchecking this feature on a container object will restrict inheritance by making the administrator explicitly grant object trustee rights to the container.

2.12.2   NDS property rights

Users have more than 55 property rights (or attributes); groups have more than 20. This level of granularity is ideal for security in NetWare administration.

NDS property rights include the following:

- *Supervisor (S):* This right is the sum of all other rights.

- *Read (R):* This right provides the ability to see or read the attributes, or properties, of an object.

- *Compare (C):* The compare right works in tandem with the read right and is used to query any property, returning only a true or false response.

- *Write (W):* This right automatically includes the add/remove self right. You can modify, `add`, `change`, and `delete` property values. This right, granted to the object trustee ACL property of any object, effectively gives supervisor access.

- *Add/Remove Self (A):* An object trustee can add or remove itself as a value of the `object` property.

- *Inheritable (I):* Only available with NetWare 5.x and above and used only at the container level, this right enables the inheritance of property rights from a container.

Warning: Rights granted through selected properties overwrite property rights granted through the All Properties radio button.

ACLs

An NDS object's trustee is an NDS object that is placed in the `Object Trustees ACL` property of another object. To change the trustee's access to an object, change the trustee's entry in the object's ACL: `Right-click an object→trustees of this object`. Only trustees with the write right for the `ACL` property may change the trustee assignments or the inherited rights filter (IRF). Every object listed in an ACL may have separate or different rights to an object's properties. Granting property rights to an object allows a user to see or edit the trustees of the object.

ACL list property

An object trustees control list holds information about who (which NDS objects) may access the object properties stored in the object itself, specifically in the property known as the ACL. An object's ACL will display all objects that are explicit trustees of the object. The ACL property also stores the object's IRF.

2.12.3   Default NDS rights

Default NDS rights include the following:

- Rights granted to the (public) object are passed to everything connected to the network—connected, not authenticated;

- (Public) receives the read right to the messaging server;

- Admin receives the supervisor and inheritable rights to ROOT;

- Users inherit the rights of their containers, which are read property rights to the login script and read to the print job (non-NDPS) configuration;

- Users are granted the read right to the ROOT properties of network address and group membership, read to the default server property of (public), read and write to the user's own login script property and print job configuration property, and, finally, read to all of the user's property rights;

- The supervisor right to the server object is given to any user who installs a server into the NDS tree;

- A server receives the supervisor object right to itself, permitting the server to modify the parameters of its own object.

NetWare 5 includes security features not found in earlier versions, such as the following:

- Increased granular controls within NDS for better control over who can perform specific administrative functions within the NDS environment.

- Inherited Rights check box within NetWare Administrator to allow (default) or disallow NDS object and/or property rights to flow down the OU (the inheritable check box is checked by default if All Properties is selected for the property rights).

- A helpdesk-enabled password management feature, which provides a specific attribute within an OU, allowing an Admin-assigned user object the ability to change user passwords without granting full permissions to `user object` attributes. Password administration can be done in mixed NetWare 4.x and 5 environments, but your primary connection must be to a NetWare 5 server with a replica on it, or the Change Password button may be grayed out. On the client, right-click the small red N in the `systray→NetWare connections→` to verify that your primary connection is to a NetWare 5 server (the primary connection has an asterisk by it).

■ Security Equal to Me tab within the NetWare Administrator lists all objects that are equivalent to a given object so that the system administrator knows who is granted effective rights to any object within the NDS environment. Security equal to permissions are not transitive. In other words, you cannot assume Admin security equivalence by making your security equal to another user who has the Admin equivalence. You will only gain equivalence to the explicit rights that the user possesses.

■ Replacement of the lock monitor console, in MONITOR.NLM with a screen saver NLM—SCRSAVER.NLM—that you can make require NDS authentication to obtain access to the server console. Additionally, access at the server console can be limited based on the system administrator's access rights. This is utilized to help separate duties between various types of system administrators, such as backup operators and NDS administrators.

■ PKI; integration of SSLv3 and LDAP into NDS; enhanced cryptographic services, Novell Modular Authentication Service (NMAS), which includes support for Smart cards, tokens, biometric authentication, and other secure authentication services.

2.12.4   NDS

NDS has to be the most important piece of NetWare security. Without a valid login, you cannot access files on the server. A login to the network invokes the first step in user object security. A login attempt first verifies that the input name is a valid user name in the context. If so, NDS checks for account restrictions. If the user object has passed the first two requirements, the input password is hashed against an RSA public encrypted key. The key is an algorithm applied against the password, and a mathematical value is calculated. The encrypted mathematical value, and only the derived value, is sent over the wire. The password never leaves the workstation. The mathematical value arrives at the preferred login server and is checked against the stored password encrypted in NDS. NDS must do the same mathematical public key algorithm calculation against the NDS stored password to authenticate and permit network access.

Realize that you can attach to the server without authenticating to it. Therefore, information can be revealed to a hacker without him or her ever logging in. Shareware and Novell tools such as nlist, cx, bindery, bindin, finger, userdump, and userinfo can be used to collect information.

2.12.5   NDS security recommendations

My recommendations for NDS security include the following:

- Disable users who have not logged in for the past *x* (a number you determine) months. Allow for remote users who sometimes are not connected to your network for an extended period of time. Delete them if they do not call about being disabled on the network.

- Use a very long 18-character password for Admin and secure it in a safe place—not on a sticky note.

- Use a null character somewhere in the Admin password. (e.g., ALT+0255). This way, if a hacker could ever see the Admin password, for whatever reason, he or she would see a blank where the null character exists.

- Limit the number of people who know the Admin password to four or fewer. Severely limit the number of people who have security equal to Admin.

- Keep the Admin object in a container that contains no other users.

- Rename the Admin account immediately. Use an underline in the name.

- Do not let anyone use the Admin account. Grant the Admin security equivalence to separate user objects. This enables auditing based on individual user objects, not an Admin object that may have had many people using it.

- Administrators should have two accounts: one to provide security equivalence needed to perform various Admin duties, the other to provide a generic end-user equivalent account for most of their work. This may be an inconvenience but will help alleviate potential accidents.

■ Implement a policy to manage user passwords. Require a minimum password length of at least seven characters. Refer to suggestions made in my other Digital Press book, *NetWare Administration,* for password management suggestions.

Warning: CHECKNULL is a freeware hack utility that checks NDS user accounts for passwords and shows accounts that do not have passwords. This utility is handy for admins/consultants to use to verify that users do have passwords.

■ Enable intruder detection on every OU, which is turned off by default. Right-click on OU→Detail→Intrusion Detection→. Select Detect Intruders. Enable it on the O, too; but be careful, since the Admin object exists under the O by default, and it is possible to lock the Admin out if someone attempts to guess the Admin password.

Warning: If Intruder Detection is off, you can use a "brute-force" password cracker; therefore, turn it on.

■ Enforce the connection limit for users. Two is sufficient for everyone other than Admin—one for access, one for messaging broadcasts. If you are using ZENworks, you may need another granted connection per user. Give Admin several to unlimited, but monitor the Admin connections, too.

■ Use the expiration date property for contractors. Allow access based on their contracted time limit. Some organizations use this for everyone. They put a one-year expiration date after the user object is created. This is a great idea for lazy administrators but would not work well in a large environment.

■ I do not see many shops that use the time restriction options in NDS, but they add an additional layer of security. Be careful: You do not want to get calls at 11:30 P.M. for access by the payroll department making a late check run.

■ I rarely see network address restrictions used. Many times the automated login name and password give more rights than are given a normal user. For that reason, configure the login name to only use that specific MAC or IP address (other address restriction options are available). This is especially helpful for older applications logging in to the server on a dedicated workstation with a "known" user name. Look for and protect user object accounts, such as the following:

- PRINTER
- LASER
- HPLASER
- BACKUP
- MAIL
- POST
- FAXUSER

- Use the MAP ROOT command to map to a "fake" ROOT. This will hide directories from the end-user's view.

- Use an IRF to prohibit global access to files or directories. Be careful when using them, since they are hard to keep track of. Without a third-party utility to show IRFs (such as Bindview), you are condemned to remember all of the IRFs you and previous Admins used throughout the tree. IRFs are appropriate for the following directories:

- SYS:PUBLIC\DNSDHCP
- SYS:PUBLIC\JRE
- SYS:PUBLIC\MGMT
- SYS:PUBLIC\NLS
- SYS:PUBLIC\SWLC
- SYS:PUBLIC\WIN32
- SYS:PUBLIC\WIN95
- SYS:PUBLIC\WINNT

- For groups, OUs, or individual users, grant explicit rights to a file or NDS object by trustee assignments. This will replace any previous inherited rights.

- Use OUs, when possible, to form natural groups in your network. A user object is security equivalent to the OU that it is in. That means that any rights you assign an OU flow down to every user under the OU. Use containers to assign rights to network resources.

- Uncheck the Inheritable attribute on each OU that you want separated from support by other administrators.

- Prohibit/restrict guest and anonymous account access.

- Helpdesk functions can be enumerated with the granular nature of NDS. I go into more detail in my other Digital Press book, *NetWare Administration*.

- Protect the backup account objects. Backup programs often use Admin equivalence, which is a security hole. Use network address restrictions in the objects' properties for the backup node, if possible.

- Check to see if your USER_TEMPLATE object has a password. If not, it is possible for someone to clone a user object with the template.

Note: Backdoors are not always evil. Giving yourself a backdoor—as an administrator—provides a safety net. Consider the tradeoff—tight security versus practicality.

To gain Admin privileges, the hacker needs access to the server, either by authenticating as a user or by having physical access to the server console. Once a hacker has security equivalence to Admin, he or she wants to hide his or her tracks. A common backdoor is to create an OU with a single user object in the OU. The hacker would then give the user object explicit trustee rights to the user object and the new OU, then take away the browse rights to the OU from the rest of the tree by removing the public object's browsing rights.

You can use Bindview or a freeware utility, HOBJLOC.NLM, to find these hidden OUs and users. The HOBJLOC.NLM is found on Novell's Web site or at http://www.netwarefiles.com. Load the HOBJLOC.NLM like any other .NLM and use an Admin password to start the utility.

Note: Once I found that someone had hidden a user object with Admin rights in a tree. The name of the user object, you ask? GOD, of course.

Auditing NDS

The following programs can audit NDS:

- ManageWise (I like ManageWise, although it has no upgrade path that I know of);

- Novell's Auditcon (it is kludgy and complex);

■ Blue Lance LT Auditor;

■ Bindview.

2.13   Login script variables

2.13.1   Login script property

It may seem unusual to put all of the login commands in this NDS chapter. Login scripts, though, are NDS properties of the user, container, and profile objects. The following is a list of login script commands to customize your end-user's experience. Most clients use little more than simple MAP commands.

Login script

This property is displayed under the Login Script page. The Login Script page lists commands that are executed to customize the user environment after the user authenticates to NDS. Giving property rights to this object will allow the user to see and edit the login script. The Login Script property replaces the system login script from the NetWare 2.x and 3.x days. When a user logs in, the LOGIN.EXE utility searches one level above (to either the Organization or Organizational Unit) and runs that script (if any), and then runs the user's login script.

Mobile users seem to cause problems for administrators, since they do not want to flood the dialup line with unnecessary updates and traffic. Use the %NETWORK login script variable, which tells you the network segment being used to access the network. Read about it in the July 1994 AppNote, *Configuring NetWare 4 for the Mobile User,* written by none other than Marcus Williamson.

Login scripts are available via the following:

■ *Container:* Use as a system login script.

■ *Profile:* Use when you have a group of users in a container that need additional customization; only one profile login script is assignable per user.

■ *User:* Use sparingly, since this is administratively heavy.

■ *Default:* Use only when no other login scripts are assigned. This provides a simple search mapping to the SYS:PUBLIC directory.

Login script variables are listed on Novell's Web site.

2.14 NDS tuning and optimization

Tuning the database is like tuning your car. You cannot get to work without either. Keep the database healthy and up-to-date with the following recommendations.

Some of the most common culprits of NDS errors are:

- Corrupted packets—physical layer errors;
- Differing versions of DS.NLM;
- Lack of SLP infrastructure;
- LAN/WAN connectivity problems;
- Obituary problems in the DS.NLM code;
- Schema not synchronized throughout the tree;
- Having NetWare server(s) in the NDS database but not in the NDS tree;
- Mixed (NetWare 4.x and NetWare 5.x) trees;
- IP-preferred connections on NetWare 5 servers timing out when talking to IPX-preferred connection NetWare 4 servers;
- Improperly designed trees;
- TIMESYNC.NLM problems;
- Lack of space on SYS; NDS crashes.

2.14.1 Tuning the directory—Novell's recommendations

It would not be unusual for a piece of directory information to be read thousands more times than it is written. It would, therefore, behoove you to tune a heavily used NDS NetWare server to support more reads than writes.

Best Practice: Compaq allows this ability within the RAID array card. Set it to 75 percent read, 25 percent write on dedicated DS servers. Check with your vendor's support to see if you can tune your RAID card.

By default, NDS never uses more than 8 MB of RAM cache. This may seem odd, but NDS is made to run on small servers. I have seen trees with over 40,000 objects have their ROOT partition on a server with 64 MB of RAM. The access speed of RAM is almost instantaneous—100 times faster than a request from the hard drive. Therefore, on larger trees, Novell gives you the opportunity to cache as much of the NDSv8 database as you would like. Since RAM is cheap, and login times are the standard measure for how your end users view the network, I would recommend reserving as much RAM as possible for NDS. Cache the whole database if you can. In NDS 8 you can set the cache size for NDS on a server by typing :SET DSTRACE=!mb[bytes]. Realize that the number is bytes, not kilobytes or megabytes. Novell says that the smallest tested size is zero bytes and the largest tested size is 2 GB. NDS will run on either. To increase the amount of memory available to the NDS, use SET DSTRACE=!MB (memory in bytes), where the number of bytes in a megabyte is 1,000,000 (1 million): SET DSTRACE=!MB55000000. In this example I allocate 55 MB of memory to DS caching.

Novell makes the following recommendations:

1. Look up TIDs to do an NDS health check and follow them.

2. Use the DSTRACE commands and filters to view NDS synchronizations. Document all error codes and troubleshoot them. Use the TIDs.

3. For servers used for applications, assign up to 40 percent of the memory for DS cache.

4. For servers used for dedicated NDS fault tolerance, assign up to 80 percent of the memory for DS cache. (ArcServe sometimes gets errors if set at 80 percent; if you are using ArcServe, assign no more than 60 percent.)

5. Sufficient memory should remain for file caching, backups, and mounting the volumes. Existing documented recommendations should be followed for these settings to avoid problems.

It is possible to set a zero cache size, but it is a bad idea. Make sure that the syntax is correct when entering the SET statement. There is a SET parameter, which allows a HEX value to be used, but if it is not used correctly, the cache will be set to zero. The best way to set the cache is to use the decimal SET parameter shown. Check the cache setting after changing it to check that the cache is not zero:

```
SET DSTRACE=OFF
SET DSTRACE=ON
SET DSTRACE=*P
```

Toggle to the DSTRACE debug screen and check the SMI Max cache setting.

The DS cache setting is automatically stored in SYS:_NETWARE\ _NDSDB.INI; therefore, it is not necessary to place it in the AUTO-EXEC.NCF.

Best Practice: See my other Digital Press book, *NetWare Administration*, for information on tuning the NetWare OS and client tuning recommendations.

Products that leverage NDS, such as NDS for NT, Border Manager, ZEN, the login process, and bindery support (not only bindery emulation) can double the number of NDS object entries in the database, which places a heavier load on everything that relies on NDS.

Warning: Do not assign more memory to DS than is actually available, or the server will run out of available memory and freeze up.

Configuring the NDS cache size

Although the following parameters are available, I have only seen the !mb used:

- !me#: Entries to cache per thread;

- !mp#: Partitions to cache per thread;

- !ma#: Attribute overflow objects to cache per thread;

- !mb#: Bytes of RAM memory to cache;

- !m#: KB of RAM memory in HEX to cache.

2.14.2   Tuning the directory—my recommendations

My recommendations are based upon much experience and talking to people who have seen or worked on Novell's NDS source code.

- Use 256 MB RAM as a minimum for NDS servers.

- If using NDSv8 or above, cache the entire NDS database in RAM.

- Use a RAID5 configuration with a hot, swappable spare.

- Use SCSI hard drives (for the best I/O). Remember that NetWare is I/O and RAM intensive, not so much processor intensive.

- Use the same NDS version throughout your entire tree and upgrade within a replica ring before moving on to the next replica ring.

- Use the same DSREPAIR version within replica rings.

- Never upgrade LOW PRIORITY THREADS (a server SET command).

- Patch your current NDS and NetWare version.

- Keep the SYS volume free of print queues, applications, user home directories, and so on. Dedicate the SYS volume to NDS and the OS installed utilities.

- Remove the Java SWAP file from the SYS volume. You can use the following server console commands: :SWAP ADD VOL1, then :SWAP DELETE SYS.

- Up the MINIMUM PACKET RECEIVE BUFFERS in SERVMAN (4.x) or MONITOR (5.x). Check your available free buffer space first (you cannot do this tuning on a 48-MB RAM machine). I like to use 3,000 as my minimum, 10,000 as my maximum.

- Set the minimum service processes to 1,000, or three per connection—not per user, per connection.

  - NDS will take this last number (Minimum Service Processes) and divide it by two and limit its authentication buffers to this limit. Thus, this number needs to be ≤2 multiplied by the MAXIMUM number of simultaneous expected concurrent logins.

  - Also, set the new service process wait time to 0.3: MONITOR→ SERVER PARAMETERS→MISCELLANEOUS.

- Also, make sure you do not share interrupts on your hot cards (LAN, disk, etc.). Always use BUSMASTER cards to offload work.

- Realize that a bottleneck in medium to large sites may be due to network traffic. Use more than one network card and use specialized network cards in your server. For example, companies such as Alaritech (http://www.alacritech.com) make a network adapter that offloads CPU processing to a LAN card chipset. Alaritech brags of an average performance gain of 238 percent over Intel's PRO/1000 Gigabit Ethernet adapter, with non-Gigabit tests running at more than a 400 percent improvement.

- Intel and Cisco have teamed up for a proprietary solution. You can also look for 3Com and other major NIC vendors to have load-balancing solutions.

2.15   Tools for NDS

Many clients ask me for NDS tools and recommendations. There can never be too many tools for such an important database. In the following sections I outline my most important tools and advice. Most of these freeware tools can be downloaded at http://www.novell.com/coolsolutions/freetools.html.

2.15.1   NDS aware RCONSOLE

Freeware. A very cool tool, RCONSOLE is normally a service a NetWare server advertised with a type 107 SAP. You can let router boy filter the SAP and still connect to every server in your enterprise via the type 4 (NetWare server) SAP. Do not be without this tool.

2.15.2   REMADR.EXE

Freeware. Advertised for NetWare 4.10, which might experience problems with concurrent connection restrictions on users where the simultaneous user connection property has been limited. This utility clears out the `net-work address` attribute on a per-user basis. Read the documentation for more information.

2.15.3   (NDS) Report Generator

Freeware. This tool generates complete documentation reports from Net-Ware 4.x (and 2.x/3.x) servers.

2.15.4   DS Designer

If you have a large tree, you can hardly do without this utility. DS Designer is an excellent third-party utility for modeling and recording your NDS tree, partitions, and replica rings. It is very useful for proactive modeling and current documentation. The utility is cheap and should be in every shop with over 25 servers, as well as in the toolbox of every consultant who consults on NDS tree designs. You can use DS Designer to run a schema comparison. The program uses SCHCMP.EXE to do the schema comparison for you and analyzes the report file. You can use it for NDS health checks, too (http://dsdesigner.hypermart.net).

2.15.5   SAP Snoop

Freeware. Find all of the SAPs on the network. This is not purely an NDS utility, but it is worth mentioning.

2.15.6   Script

Freeware. This allows you to import and export login scripts.

2.15.7   Sync scrsav pwd AOT

This tool uses a ZENworks AOT file to set the workstation screensaver to the NDS password. The marquee is the NDS user name.

2.15.8   SCANTREE

Novell's SCANTREE utility can analyze the NDS tree to provide essential information—number of levels of NDS, types of leaf objects, and so on. SCANDS.EXE is available from http://support.novell.com.

2.15.9   Schemax

Schemax is a free NDS tool to extend the schema. It should now be integrated into ConsoleOne. Novell has been talking about doing this for some time. If not, it is a free download.

2.15.10   TREEINT.NLM

This is a freeware NDS tree integration utility buried on Novell's developer site. It merges a one-server tree into any other size tree and is great for new server rollouts. Search for it at http://developer.novell.com.

2.15.11   NDS aware TIMESYNC

TIMESYNC is an NDS module/NLM that provides uniform time between NetWare servers. TIMESYNC.NLM is dependent upon SAP type 26B. The NDS Aware TIMESYNC uses full NDS names to locate other NetWare time servers. It sort of piggybacks on top of the NetWare server SAP type 4, thereby allowing router boy to filter SAP 26B. Similar to DSTRACE, this version uses color to highlight critical information. This utility is backward compatible with previous versions.

2.15.12 DreamLAN

DreamLAN Consulting publishes some great NDS tools (http://www.dreamlan.com).

2.15.13 DSDIAG.NLM

DSDIAG is available for free download from Novell or comes with NetWare 5.1. This is a multipurpose C-worthy utility used to run reports on NDS. For example, you could run a schema comparison report with DSDIAG.NLM using the -DA switch, then run the List Schema report. You will then be able to identify schema inconsistencies. This utility is also used to run reports to import into the third-party software DSDesigner.

Check the Novell TIDs to explain the functionality of this module. Information gathered by DSDIAG.NLM includes the following:

- Detailed diagnostic information on the NDS tree partitions and replica rings;

- Partition status;

- Number of readable rings;

- Documents replica rings;

- Subordinate references in each ring (important);

- Version and server name;

- Address of NDS—the DS.NLM;

- Replica depth of network;

- Consistency check;

- Location of partition roots by NDS or by servers;

- Unreachable partition reports;

- Isolates duplicate IPX internal addresses.

    This is not a very intuitive tool.

2.15.14 CRON.NLM

Just about any server task can be automated with CRON. CRON.NLM is an unsupported administrator tool used to schedule command-line tasks. This is a great utility to automate mundane tasks.

Some best practices are to use CRON jobs to do the following:

- Back up NDS; save .DIB sets daily;

- Run the CONFIG.NLM;

- PURGE volumes; use a CRON job to purge your SYS volumes monthly.

Warning: I see many shops using STUFFKEY.NLM to run DSREPAIRs. Do not. DSREPAIR can error out or ask for additional keystrokes, which can keep the database locked. Use CRON.NLM and the provided switches to run DSREPAIRs.

2.15.15 Backing up the NDS Database

Back up your NDS database nightly. Of course, your backup software can and should do this. You would be wise to make a .DIB set of the database too. A .DIB is a proprietary copy of the database dumped to the SYS:SYSTEM directory. The .DIB set can only be restored by Novell's technical support; therefore, do not substitute it as a backup in place of the nightly NDS backup with your regular backup software.

Best Practice: Use a CRON job to do a DSREPAIR -RC nightly.

2.15.16 NetPro

NetPro (http://www.netpro.com) is one of my favorite third-party tools. Two of the NetPro line of Novell-supported products include DS Expert and DS Analyzer.

DS Expert version 3.2 for NDS

(Sister product would be Directory Analyzer for AD.)

DS Expert is an NDS monitoring utility. Do an NDS health check from one tool—no going from server to server. Multiserver trace features can set up multiple DSTRACE screens together. Monitor and report NDS schema inconsistencies or stuck obits—probably the two most problematic NDS issues.

NetPro's DS Expert monitors over 30 conditions in real time. Alerts are sent via SNMP, so any application or alerting system that supports SNMP will page, e-mail, call, or alert in whatever manner is supported. Other features include the following:

■ The application is event driven (real time)—versus using a less efficient polling interval.

■ Health check information is presented 24-7 in real time.

■ The admin can get an at-a-glance view of the tree and partition view of the NDS database. You can decide how you want to view the information. You set thresholds and decide whether, when there is an event, the agents alert by e-mail, pager, or another SNMP-enabled device.

■ DS Expert focuses on the infrastructure of NDS. It does not report on locked-out users, attribute changes, and so on. It supports NDS versions 6, 7, and 8.

■ It will integrate with MangeWise.

■ There are 37 different alert events; most are DS or low SYS space.

■ It has a 600 K minimum RAM footprint.

■ It has a three-tiered architecture.

■ It stores log files and communicates with all agents.

■ Alert logs displayed in GUI may be viewed by Novell's portal Por-tal→NDS Management.

■ The DS Commands page allows DSTRACE commands to be executed on the server, which gives you the chance to correct many replication problems. It is protocol NCP dependant.

■ DS Analyzer monitors and will send alerts about agents not loaded on servers.

DS Analyzer 2.0

DS Analyzer is NetPro's look inside NDS from a network traffic view—a protocol-independent NDS sniffer. (See Figure 2.3.) The product includes the following:

■ Sports a distributed architecture;

■ Uses two NLMs that do not poll;

Figure 2.3
*NetPro's
DS Analyzer
version 2.0.*

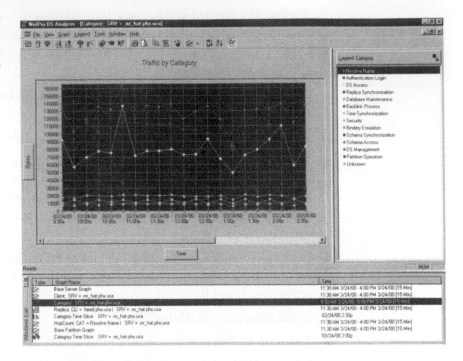

- Has a 2-MB RAM minimum footprint (16-MB RAM was once reported based on a box of 133 replicas and a DIB set of over 600) and a 2 percent to 16 percent utilization hit on server CPU;

- Agent is distributed on each server;

- Uses a proprietary database;

- Admin can trend information;

- Admin can see the effects of a ZEN for Desktops, DCHP, or other directory-enabled applications in the NDS tree, and background processes are identified;

- Saves info for 30 days (configurable) in DB by default or by size of the DB (up to 1 GB);

- Is server specific—even the servers without replicas;

- Specific information—for example, can see how many hops a client uses to log in;

- Relies on the administrator to make a change to NDS—the program does not make changes;

- Runs on NetWare 4.11 up to current eDirectory;

- Displays background processes associated with NDS—tree walking, schema, synchronization;

- Client specifies a time range to poll information and unicast it back to the client;

- Knowledge base in the product with possible causes, NDS resolution items, and corresponding NDS error codes;

- Knowledge-based information written by former Novell NDS gurus.

Best Practice: Make an NDS change, then validate your change with before-and-after graphs using DS Analyzer. This can help you make your tree more efficient.

2.15.17 Visio

Now owned by Microsoft, Visio is an impressive utility. It is supposed to auto-discover your network, although I have never gotten this part to work very well (in older versions).

It can discover your entire NDS tree, but I would prefer to use this utility for design purposes. I like DS Designer better for NDS design purposes.

2.15.18 DSBROWSE.NLM

The DSBROWSE.NLM allows you to view a NetWare 5.x .DIB file. It has functionality similar to the DSVIEW for NetWare 4.x, but better. This is for advanced administrators.

2.15.19 NDS links

http://www.netwarefiles.com

http://www.novellfans.com

http://www.novellshareware.com

http://www.novell.com/coolsolutions/freetools.html

http://www.visualclick.com

http://www.netwarefiles.com

http://www.novellshareware.com

http://www.novell.com/coolsolutions

http://developer.novell.com

http://developer.novell.com/research

http://www.connectotel.com

http://www.dreamlan.com

http://www.netadmincentral.com

There are more, although most are linked from within these main sites.

3

Standards-Based Directory Services
by Bob Johnson

3.1   Introduction

This section talks about the three standards-based directory technologies—
X.500, the Lightweight Directory Access Protocol (LDAP), and the
Domain Name Service (DNS). During the early to mid-1990s, the trade
magazines were rich with articles about X.500 directory products, implementation stories, and lessons learned. The question arose: When all the
computers are connected, how in the world can you find anything? Directories were one of the technologies that offered great potential in unlocking
the power of the Internet.

Then came the World Wide Web (the Web)—we used to call it the
World Wide Wait—and suddenly electronic directories were just not interesting anymore. Almost overnight, articles about directories disappeared
from the trade journals. Everything was being put onto the Web, and everyone in the world had just gotten his or her very own Uniform Resource
Locator (URL). And again the question arose: When everything is put onto
the Web, how in the world can you find anything?

3.1.1   A short digression

This takes us to a very interesting distinction between electric directories
and the Web. When you search the Web, you are often looking for specific
information about tires, fishing rods, mortgage rates, and so on. Web search
engines such as Yahoo!, Excite, and Google (my personal favorite) allow you
to enter keywords, then dredge through a huge pile of words extracted from
hundreds of millions of Web pages and kick back all the entries that match
your query. The more words you enter, the closer the match. But how useful
is it when you enter the word "mortgage" and get back the message "found
1,263 categories and 3,764 sites" (Yahoo!), "2,144,230 found" (Excite), or

"about 2,010,000" (Google)? If you are looking to refinance a home in Columbus, Ohio, how useful is it to have 2 million sites to choose from? Even if you enter "mortgage, Columbus, Ohio," you get "about 26,400" responses (Google).

Electronic directories offer more structure in searching. A directory allows you to use some information you do have to find the information you do not have. Consider the white pages in your phone book. You use the information you know (a name) to find information you do not know (a phone number). The information is already filtered in that you only have the names from your city, not the entire civilized world, to search through. Yellow pages work in the same fashion. You know the subject you are looking for, in this case mortgages. The entries are already filtered, so you are only searching through entries in your area. Additional information, such as addresses or display ads, is presented to help you make your selection.

Electronic directories were originally designed to replace their paper predecessors. The telephone companies envisioned a huge, global electronic directory service that could replace the individual printed versions maintained by every phone company in the world. When e-mail became popular, electronic directories were created that allowed you to look up users by name in order to obtain their e-mail address. Public key infrastructures (PKIs), quickly becoming the current rage, also require electronic directories to find encryption certificates and to obtain the information needed to verify digital signatures (e.g., signing certificates to perform certificate validation and certificate revocation lists to ensure the signing certificates are still valid).

3.1.2   An unofficial history

Beginning in the 1970s, the International Telecommunications Union (ITU)—formerly the CCITT—created a series of specifications for networking and data communications. You may have heard of (or used) X.25 for creating wide area networks. You may also have heard of the X.400 messaging specifications, created in 1984 and revised in 1988. The specification for the X.500 directory service was originally ratified in 1998, and subsequently revised in 1993, 1997, and 2001. The X.500 standard is several hundred pages long, and includes (among other things) the X.509 specification that defines how public key certificates are stored and used within electronic directory services.

Early work on implementation of the CCITT standards was primarily performed in various universities throughout the world. Significant work on X.500 was performed at the University College London in the late 1980s and early 1990s. Two projects born there were the thorne directory (an early RDBMS-based version) and the quipu directory (a memory-mapped version). A few directory products eventually evolved from the work done on the thorne directory.

The ISODE consortium, a nonprofit organization, was formed with the purpose of providing and maintaining source code for CCITT software technology, including X.500. The X.500 technology selected was the quipu version mentioned above. This version of the directory was made widely available to universities and corporations throughout the world and became the basis for several early commercial products.

The CCITT specifications were built on the Open Systems Interconnection (OSI) seven-layer stack, which was a good concept but required computers with significant memory and processing capability. Remember that the cutting-edge technology of the day was the 50-Mhz 386-based system, and it had not been long since personal computers (PCs) were limited to a maximum of 64 K of memory. Directory clients were required to use the Directory Access Protocol (DAP) to gain access to the X.500 directory. Desktop computers of the day simply could not handle the processing load required. Hence, the LDAP was born.

LDAP was originally designed as a very "thin" text-based protocol that would allow PC-based software applications to talk to X.500 directory services. It was designed by W. Yeong, Tim Howes, and Steve Kille. Version 1 (Request for Comments [RFC] 1487) was implemented by Colin Robbins at UCL in the early 1990s. A subsequent revision (v2, RFCs 1777 and 1778) added more functionality and fixed a few shortcomings.

For many years, LDAP remained an access protocol (as the name implies). It presumed that the X.500 directory server was running on some big UNIX platform out in the corporate network. A front-end or gateway process was responsible for accepting the LDAP queries, converting them to X.500 requests, sending them to the directory service, and converting the directory responses back to LDAP replies. In 1997, LDAP was again revised to add more functionality (RFC 2251). Before version 3, LDAP was always a lightweight method for accessing traditional X.500 directories. The following clause in the version 3 specification, excerpted from RFC 2251, however, has been universally interpreted to mean that the directory service accessed no longer need be an X.500 directory server:

Relationship to X.500

This document defines LDAP in terms of X.500 as an X.500 access mechanism. An LDAP server MUST act in accordance with the X.500 (1993) series of ITU recommendations when providing the service. However, it is not required that an LDAP server make use of any X.500 protocols in providing this service, e.g., LDAP can be mapped onto any other directory system so long as the X.500 data and service model as used in LDAP is not violated in the LDAP interface.

With the advent of the LDAPv3, several major vendors (who will remain nameless) joined together in press announcements and at trade conferences to pronounce the death of X.500 and the rise of LDAPv3 as the new global directory service. Unfortunately, an access protocol does not a full directory service make. Several years later, folks, LDAPv3 is still being extended to add functionality such as access control, distributed operations, replication, and security—functionality that X.500 had provided nearly a decade before. Although many LDAPv3 proponents denounce the complexity of X.500, the total page count of the LDAPv3 specifications is already significantly greater than that of X.500—and still growing.

By now, you may be wondering where the DNS fits into all of this. DNS predates both X.500 or LDAP, and every Internet-connected computer system in the world uses it. Its main purpose is to find the actual Internet Protocol (IP) address for a specific computer system. A computer might have an Internet Fully Qualified Domain Name (FQDN), such as sales.somecorp.com. When you send an e-mail to fred@sales.somecorp.com, your computer has to look up the dotted numeric IP address for the recipient's e-mail service. To do this, your computer queries DNS for the address of sales.somecorp.com and receives a number such as 123.93.228.16, which is the actual IP numeric address where your computer will send your e-mail. When you consider that the Internet is composed of millions of individual computers, the fact that you may not have heard of DNS is a testament to its strength and robustness. It does its job very, very well.

3.1.3 The problem with open standards

X.500, LDAP, and DNS are all touted as open standards, meaning that the specifications are readily available to anyone who wants to design a compatible product. In the 1980s and 1990s, we thought this was a pretty good idea. We believed that open standards would foster the development of compatible and interoperable products, leading to competition and the general betterment of all the products.

We were partially right. Open standards did foster competition between vendors of interoperable products. Instead of the entire industry benefiting, however, two disturbing things happened. First, the market was fragmented into products from several small vendors who had great difficulty garnering sufficient sales volume to grow and evolve them. The big vendors—Novell, Microsoft, and Lotus—stayed out of the fray. So did their huge, loyal customer base. Second, vendors began to create proprietary extensions to the standards. This became a bit of an embarrassment as the Web evolved and new features implemented by one vendor regularly "broke" the other vendors' products. This "one-upsmanship" has started to surface again in LDAPv3 extensions. Let us take a closer look at how this works (without naming names or pointing fingers).

Let us say that your company builds desktop client and server products. Your goal is to provide the client products to as many people as possible, as cheaply as possible—maybe even for free or bundled into the operating system. The hope is that everyone will want to buy your expensive server products because they already possess the client products. If you support truly open standards between your client and server products, your clients would be able to work with any vendor's server products that supported the same standards. Ergo, your servers are interchangeable and the customer has no particular reason to prefer your server products. Worse still, your competition can undercut your price in order to attract more customers. If you respond by matching or undercutting your competitor's price, a price war develops and your profitability goes out the window (along with your customers); and that is bad for business.

How, then, do you respond? By offering the customer more! In addition to the strict open standard, you offer advanced functionality that is not described by any standard. If your client products are connected to your servers, the user will have the use of these advanced features. If they were connected to your competition's servers, they would have only basic functionality. You might even decide to leave the missing functions on the drop-down menus, but gray them out so they cannot be selected. Hopefully, your customers will think these proprietary extensions are worth the price you charge for your servers. In marketing parlance, this is known as *customer capture*.

If you do not think this is happening every day, watch the tug of war over Instant Messaging or the struggle between ActiveX and JavaBeans, or check out some of the vendor-specific extensions to the LDAPv3 standard.

3.2   ITU X.500

The X.500 specification describes a network of directory systems that would be owned and operated by individual organizations but could cooperate and function as a seamless global directory. X.500 is a very powerful and mature directory technology. Its specifications were originally ratified in 1988 and subsequently revised in 1993, 1997, and 2001. The X.500 Recommendations (e.g., the ITU-T standard) consists of several sections, which are listed in Table 3.1. These documents are available (for a fee) from http://www.itu.int.

Table 3.1   *X.500 Standards Documents.*

Recommendation	Description
X.500	Overview of Concepts, Models, and Services
X.501	Models
X.509	Authentication Framework
X.511	Abstract Service Definition
X.518	Procedures for Distributed Operations
X.519	Protocol Specifications
X.520	Selected Attribute Types
X.521	Selected Object Classes
X.525	Replication
X.530	Use of Systems Management for Administration of the Directory
X.581	Directory Access Protocol—Protocol Implementation Conformance Statement (PICS) Proforma (1993 version)
X.582	Directory System Protocol—PICS Proforma (1993 version)
X.583	PICS Proforma for the Directory Access Protocol
X.584	PICS Proforma for the Directory System Protocol
X.585	PICS Proforma for the Directory Operational Binding Management Protocol
X.586	PICS Proforma for the Directory Information Shadowing Protocol

3.2.1   The X.500 information model

The X.500 standard can be roughly divided into three pieces: the information model, the protocols, and the security model. The information model describes the structure of the X.500 database, including the organization, naming conventions, and the schema. LDAP follows the X.500 information model but not the X.500 protocols or schema.

Tree structure

The global directory described by X.500 is a huge inverted tree. At the top of the tree would be country-level directory servers. Below each country-level would exist companies, government agencies, states, and other national entities. Responsibility for directory information can be delegated downward. For instance, the operator of a national directory service can delegate responsibility for operation of a state-level directory server. Further, the state-level directory service could then delegate responsibility for townships, state agencies, and organizations that were registered for operation within that state. Townships would be able to further delegate responsibility for directory services to city-level organizations, such as city planning, traffic, police, or maintenance organizations. A company could also be registered at the national level and would be free to subdivide its internal directory and delegate responsibility as it saw fit to various divisions within the company. Figure 3.1 shows a conceptual view of this global X.500 directory service.

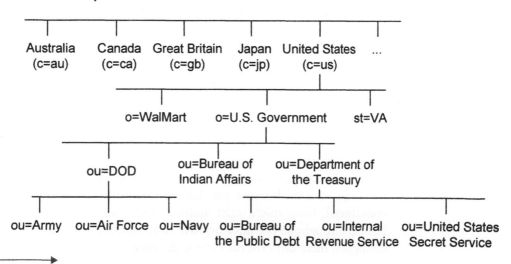

Figure 3.1   *The global X.500 service.*

In X.500 terminology, each level of the directory is called a *node* (referred to as *containers* in several of the LDAP directory products). For instance, in Figure 3.1, the c=US, st=VA, and o=U.S. Government levels are all nodes. The relationships between nodes of the X.500 directory are described by knowledge references and referrals. A knowledge reference is a pointer to another level or part of the directory. X.500 directory servers follow these pointers to perform chained operations (discussed in detail below). Referrals point to another directory server that handles a specific portion of the directory tree. The directory client is responsible for locating, contacting, and querying the identified directory server.

Knowledge references come in three flavors: superior, subordinate, and peer. A superior reference points to the node's parent, subordinate references point to a node's children, and peer references point to another directory server that handles a specific subtree of the directory (similar to a referral). Again, refer to the o=U.S. Government node in Figure 3.1. The node has a superior reference to c=US and subordinate references to ou=Bureau of Indian Affairs and ou=Department of Defense. The ou=Department of Defense has a peer reference to the ou=General Services Administration node. The ou=Bureau of Indian Affairs level contains referrals to the c=US, o=U.S. Government, ou=Department of Defense, and c=CA (Canada).

Since LDAP was originally designed as a lightweight method of accessing X.500 directory services, it naturally inherited the X.500 information model. The tree structure described by the X.500 standard is also used by LDAP. The concept of chaining and referrals will occur again in the discussion of X.500 distributed operations and in the section on LDAP.

Distinguished names and relative distinguished names

Each object stored in the directory is identified by a Relative Distinguished Name (RDN). The RDN is the value that uniquely identifies an entry within the current node, or container, of the directory. For instance, if the RDN is a person's full name (e.g., the person's commonName or cn), each directory entry within a specific level will have a unique RDN. At a given level of the directory, there can exist only one, single entry with an RDN of cn=John Smith. Because the directory contains several levels (nodes or containers), there might exist multiple nodes with an RDN of cn=John Smith throughout the directory tree. But within each individual node or container, there can exist only one such entry.

An entry in the directory is specified by its full Distinguished Name (DN), which is composed of all the RDNs starting with the top of the tree and moving downward to the specific entry. In the original X.500 syntax, the RDNs that composed a full DN were separated from each other by an @ sign and listed beginning at the top of the tree. The full DN would look like the following:

```
c=US@o=U.S. Government@ou=General Services
Administration@cn=John Smith
```

LDAP typically reverses the order and uses commas rather than @ signs, as follows:

```
cn=John Smith, ou=General Services Administration, o=U.S.
Government, c=US
```

Functionally, both DNs are the same.

Schema: syntaxes, objects, and attributes

All of the stuff that goes into a directory is described by the directory's schema. According to the Merriam-Webster online dictionary (http://www.m-w.com), *schema* is defined as "a diagrammatic presentation; broadly: a structured framework or plan." In other words, a schema defines the types of information that can be stored in the directory and also provides information that directory clients use in order to present that information in human-readable form. An X.500 schema has three major types of components: syntaxes, objects, and attributes.

A *syntax* is a definition of the kind of information that can be stored in the directory. It can include parameters such as minimum or maximum length, allowable characters, and format (for information such as phone numbers, U.S. Social Security numbers, or zip and postal codes). A syntax can define the kind of information that can be stored in many different attributes in the directory. For instance, the syntax generalText defines the type of information that can be stored in many, many attributes within the directory.

An *attribute* is a specific component of information, such as country, state, phone number, last name, zip code, public key certificate, and so on. In the directory, an attribute is composed of the attribute type and the attribute value and looks like commonName: Fred G. Smith. In this example, commonName is the attribute type, and Fred G. Smith is the value. If you are familiar with relational databases, you could envision each attribute as a column. The attribute type would be the label at the top of the column, and each row could have a different attribute value. Each column would be a different attribute. All of the attribute values across a row would constitute a complete entry.

It is rare that the objects in a directory would contain only a single attribute. An entry for a person would contain several attributes defining that person's name, address, phone number, and so on. These attributes can all be grouped into an object class called `person`. An entry in the directory can then specify the `person` object class, making available all the attributes defined therein. Several object classes can be combined to describe an entry in the directory. For instance, you might desire to combine information about mailing, account balance, credit limits, PKI credentials, and shipping information in a directory entry called `customerAccount`. If those object classes have already been defined before, you can combine them to create your new directory object.

The attributes defined within an object class are inherited by all objects that include that object class. As an example, the `inetOrgPerson` object class includes the `organizationalPerson` object class and, therefore, inherits all of the attributes defined in `organizationalPerson`. The `organizationalPerson` object class includes the `person` object class and inherits all the attributes defined in the `person` object class. Since the attributes defined in `person` are inherited by the `organizationalPerson` object class, they are further inherited by the `inetOrgPerson` object class.

Putting the pieces together: inetOrgPerson

Let us take a quick look under the hood (or "bonnet") at the `inetOrgPer`-son object class, which is defined in *RFC 2798: Definition of the inetOrgPerson LDAP Object Class*. Figure 3.2 shows the schema definition.

Let us break this down a bit. The `2.16.840.1.113730.3.2.2` is this Object Identifier (OID) for this object class. Its name is `inetOrgPerson`. It inherits the attributes from the object class `organizationalPerson`. It "MAY" contain the list of attributes shown (staring with `audio`, `business`-

Figure 3.2
*inetOrgPerson
object class
definition from
RFC 2798.*

```
( 2.16.840.1.113730.3.2.2
  NAME 'inetOrgPerson'
  SUP organizationalPerson
  STRUCTURAL
  MAY (
      audio $ businessCategory $ carLicense $ departmentNumber $
      displayName $ employeeNumber $ employeeType $ givenName $
      homePhone $ homePostalAddress $ initials $ jpegPhoto $
      labeledURI $ mail $ manager $ mobile $ o $ pager $
      photo $ roomNumber $ secretary $ uid $ userCertificate $
      x500uniqueIdentifier $ preferredLanguage $
      userSMIMECertificate $ userPKCS12
  )
)
```

```
( 2.5.6.7
   NAME 'organizationalPerson'
   SUP person
   STRUCTURAL
   MAY (
      title $ x121Address $ registeredAddress $ destinationIndicator $
      preferredDeliveryMethod $ telexNumber $ teletexTerminalIdentifier $
      telephoneNumber $ internationaliSDNNumber $
      facsimileTelephoneNumber $ street $ postOfficeBox $
      postalCode $ postalAddress $ physicalDeliveryOfficeName $ ou $ st $ l
   )
)
```

Figure 3.3   *organizationalPerson object class definition from RFC 2256.*

Category, carLicence, etc.). Note that there is no "MUST" section in this definition. None of the attributes shown are mandatory. It might inherit some mandatory attributes from the organizationalPerson object class. RFC 2798 says we can find the definition of organization-alPerson in *RFC 2256: A Summary of the X.500(96) User Schema for Use with LDAPv3*. Figure 3.3 shows the organizationalPerson object class definition found in RFC 2256. The object class is OID 2.5.6.7, has no mandatory attributes, and has several optional attributes starting with title, x121Address, registeredAddress, and so on. Note that it, in turn, inherits the attributes defined in the person object class, which can also be found in RFC 2256 (Figure 3.4).

A couple of attributes are listed under "MUST." The person object class requires that the sn (surname) and cn (commonName) attributes be populated. The other attributes are optional. Remember, these attributes are inherited by all the object classes that reference person. That means that the sn and cn attributes are inherited by organizationalPerson and inetOrgPerson and therefore become mandatory attributes in those two object classes as well. We will not dwell on the definitions for each attribute in these three object classes, but Figure 3.5 provides a single example for

Figure 3.4
person object class definition from RFC 2256.

```
( 2.5.6.6
   NAME 'person'
   SUP top
   STRUCTURAL
   MUST (
      sn $ cn
   )
   MAY (
      userPassword $ telephoneNumber $ seeAlso $ description
   )
)
```

Figure 3.5
telephoneNumber
attribute definition
from RFC 2256.

```
( 2.5.4.20
  NAME 'telephoneNumber'
  EQUALITY telephoneNumberMatch
  SUBSTR telephoneNumberSubstringsMatch
  SYNTAX 1.3.6.1.4.1.1466.115.121.1.50{32}
)
```

your enjoyment. The EQUALITY and SUBSTR values specify the rules to be used during searches. The long numeric value by SYNTAX is the OID of the syntax that defines the information that can be put into this attribute.

A note about OIDs

An OID is a string of numbers that uniquely identifies an object. They are allocated hierarchically and form a "tree," somewhat like an X.500 directory. The sequence of numbers that composes an OID is sometimes referred to as a *registration arc*. At the top level of the OID registration tree are the numbers 0, 1, and 2, which mean ITU-T assigned, ISO assigned, and Joint ISO/ITU-T assigned, respectively.

Under each of these three "root" numbers can be any number of other numbers. The sequence of numbers describes a path through the OID tree. Once a number has been assigned to an organization, that organization is free to assign any numbers that it sees fit within its registration arc. For example, when an organization receives the number "1.2.3," that organization is the only one that can say what "1.2.3.4" means. It is free to create any number of levels underneath its arc and could define an OID of "1.2.3.4.5.6.7.8.9." OIDs are defined in Chapter 28 of X.208 (which also defines Abstract Syntax Notation—ASN.1, which is much more than you probably ever want or need to know). X.208 can be obtained from the ITU at http://www.itu.net. Have your checkbook or charge card ready.

To give you a quick idea about how OIDs work, let us break down a few that you have already seen. There is no known official registry of OIDs. At the time this book was written, the biggest and best volunteer effort is maintained by Harald Tveit Alvestrand and can be found at http://www.alvestrand.no/objectid. Figure 3.6 lists information taken from that site.

You can also take an OID and use it to determine the object it represents. Remember the SYNTAX OID in the object telephoneNumber? Figure 3.7 breaks it down. If you are paying attention, you may notice a few surprises here. First, you might not know that 1.3.6.1 is the "official" Internet OID arc. Even if you do, however, did you know that it was registered

```
organizationalPerson (OID = 2.5.6.7)
   2 = Joint ISO/ITU-T assignment
      5 = Directory (X.500)
         6 = X.500 standard object classes
            7 = id-oc-organizationalPerson

inetOrgPerson (OID = 2.16.840.1.113730.3.2.2)
   2 = Joint ISO/ITU-T assignment
      16 = Country assignments
         840 = USA
            1 = US company arc
               113730 = Netscape Communications Corp.
                  3 = Netscape LDAP
                     2 = Netscape LDAP object classes
                        2 = (not listed, presumed to be id-oc-inetOrgPerson)

telephoneNumber (OID = 2.5.4.20)
   2 = Joint ISO/ITU-T assignment
      5 = Directory (X.500)
         4 = X.500 attribute types
            20 = id-at-telephoneNumber
```

Figure 3.6   *Some common OIDs.*

under the Unites States Department of Defense? By the way, Critical Angle is no longer in existence, having been bought out some time back.

You may well be asking yourself, why bother with OIDs if they are this complicated? Because they uniquely identify a syntax, object, attribute, policy extension, matching rule, or just about anything else you want to use them for. If you are creating a directory for a single company that will not ever connect to anything else in the world, you may never need to assign an OID. Even if you do, you could pick something from thin air and nobody would be the wiser. However, when you want to interoperate with other companies or government bodies, the proper use of OIDs will ensure that your objects can never be confused with those issued by another party. In reality, if you need to create your own schema extensions, you would be well advised to hire a consultant who understands OIDs. At any rate, even if you never have to assign a new OID, perhaps this has helped you to understand them a little bit better.

3.2.2   X.500 directory operations

Figure 3.8 shows a conceptual model of an X.500 directory service. In this example, the X.500 Directory Information Tree (DIT) is actually shared among several different Directory Service Agents (DSAs). Each DSA masters the information stored in its local Directory Information Base (DIB).

Figure 3.7

*Breaking down the
telephoneNumber
syntax OID.*

```
OID = 1.3.6.1.4.1.1466.115.121.1.50
    1 = ISO assigned
      3 = ISO Identified Organization
        6 = US Department of Defense
          1 = OID assignments for the Internet
            4 = Private
              1 = Enterprises
                1466 = Mark Wahl (Critical Angle)
                  115 = LDAPv3 Schema Framework
                    121 = LDAPv3 Syntaxes
                      1 = LDAPv3 Syntaxes (?)
                        50 = Telephone number syntax
```

The individual DIBs connect to each other by means of knowledge references. The operations performed by an X.500 directory can be roughly divided into four groups—client access, distributed operations, replication, and referrals.

Client access

In the original X.500 model, Directory User Agents (DUAs) communicated with X.500 DSAs by use of the DAP. Using DAP, the DUA contacts a local DSA and binds (creates an association) with it. You can think of this bind or association as being sort of a virtual pipe. Once it's established, any number of transactions can flow back and forth between the DUA and DSA. The association can be dropped whenever the DUA and DSA complete a set of transactions, or it can be held active for a defined length of time in the event that another directory operation might be needed.

Figure 3.8

*The X.500
directory model.*

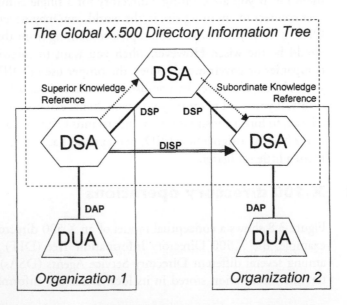

Today, almost all directory access operations (both X.500 and LDAP) are performed using LDAP. When clients connect to an X.500 directory using LDAP, they are actually connecting to an LDAP server process that acts as an LDAP-to-DAP gateway into the X.500 directory system (Figure 3.1). The LDAP-based queries from the client are essentially converted into DAP and provided to the local DSA. The responses provided by the local DSA are converted back into LDAP responses and sent back to the client.

Distributed operations

If the local DSA does not hold the requested information, it will try to send the query to other DSAs using the Directory Service Protocol (DSP). This is called *chaining*, because the query will be routed from one DSA to another until it reaches the DSA that holds the information. The local DSA that launches the chained request is called the *submitting* DSA, and the DSA that performs the requested operation is called the *performing* DSA.

The performing DSA chains the result of the directory operation back to the submitting DSA, who sends it to the DUA. Refer to Figure 3.8, and let us track an example of a chained operation. Let's say that a user in the Air Force wants to look up an e-mail address for a user in the Bureau of Indian Affairs (BIA). The user enters the search request into the DUA, which submits the request to the Air Force DSA. The Air Force DSA does not hold a copy of the BIA information, so it routes the query to its parent, the Department of Defense (DoD) DSA. Since the DoD DSA does not hold the needed information, it routes the query to the BIA DSA, which performs the query. The result is routed from the BIA DSA to the U.S. Government DSA, then to the Department of Defense DSA, then to the Air Force DSA, and finally back to the user's DUA. All of this was invisible to the user, who simply requested the information and eventually received the answer.

Shadowing (replication)

In real life, large organizations have locations scattered across the country or around the world. Consider a hypothetical company, MegaCorp, which has locations in Singapore and Paris and head offices in Chicago (Figure 3.9). Assume for a moment that each location maintains its own directory information and that all the local directories are connected into a distributed X.500 directory information tree. If a user in Singapore needs to find an address for an employee in the Paris office, the directory query would be routed from Singapore to Chicago, then to Paris. The response would come back along the same path. There may be many reasons why this sort of direc-

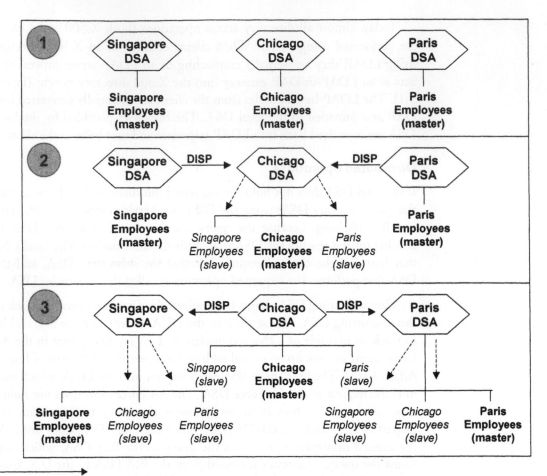

Figure 3.9   *X.500 directory shadowing.*

tory search would be unreliable. It depends upon international communications (probably satellite). There will be a noticeable lag in response time due to the processing that has to occur on three different DSAs and the transmission of data halfway around the world and back again—some tens of thousands of miles. If any portion of the global corporate network or any of the DSAs is down or unavailable, the search will fail. And maintaining a high-speed network between all of these locations may be cost prohibitive.

If we could put a copy of the Paris user information in Singapore, the search request could be answered immediately from that local copy. There would be no need to chain the query across two oceans and three continents. X.500 can perform this sort of directory data replication using the Directory Information Shadowing Protocol (DISP).

DISP provides a master-slave shadowing capability. Directory information is owned, or mastered, by a single DSA. In the X.500 directory model, information can only be modified by the DSA that masters that specific directory data. Any number of slave DSAs, or replicants, can be set up to receive a copy of the directory data from a master DSA. DISP shadowing agreements can be set to perform replication at specific times, or incrementally as changes occur. Only the information that was changed is sent from the master DSA to the slave DSAs. Slave DSAs can also send updated information to subordinate DSAs, allowing a company to set up multitiered replication strategies.

In Figure 3.9, MegaCorp uses DISP to provide shadow copies of employee information to all locations. In this example, the corporate offices in Chicago serve as a replication hub. Both Paris and Singapore shadow employee data changes to the Chicago office. This allows the Chicago office to have a complete version of all employee information. The Chicago DSA then shadows the changes it receives to the other office. In this example, when a new user is added in Paris, a copy of the data is shadowed to the Chicago DSA. The Chicago DSA then shadows a copy to the Singapore DSA. The data were mastered in Paris, but both Chicago and Singapore have received shadowed copies of the information.

Referrals

In addition to chained operations and shadowing, X.500 provides another means of finding information, called *referrals*. In the referral model, the local DSA knows the identity of a DSA that might contain the requested information, but no agreement exists for use of DSP between the DSAs. Therefore, the local DSA cannot chain the request onward. Instead, the local DSA returns a referral to the DUA. It then becomes the DUA's responsibility to disconnect from the local DSA and connect to the DSA listed in the referral. This is the query model used by LDAP. When using referrals, the responsibility for finding the requested information is placed onto the DUA. The DUA could theoretically follow any number of referrals, connecting over and over to different DSAs until it found the information for which it was searching.

3.2.3   X.500 security model

X.500 provides a very mature security model designed to ensure that information is only created, modified, removed, and accessed by individuals with the appropriate rights to do so. The X.500 security model is based on the concept of mapping the requester's identity against access controls that specify who is allowed to create, change, search, list, and delete directory data. In X.500 each operation (whether performed locally or chained) carries the requester's identity. Each object and attribute stored in the X.500 directory can contain access control lists that specify who can perform various sorts of operations. The performing DSA checks the user's identity in the request to ensure that they are allowed to perform the requested operation. This is a key difference between X.500 and LDAP. The LDAP security model is discussed at length later.

Anonymous, simple, and strong authentication

X.500 understands three basic levels of authentication:

- *Anonymous access* means that any user is allowed to perform an operation.

- *Simple authentication* means that the DSA will request and validate a password before the user is allowed to perform the operation.

- *Strong authentication* requires that the user possess cryptographic credentials that can be used to positively prove the user's identity. Most likely, these credentials will be a Private Key Token and a matching X.509 Public Key Certificate. The X.500 standard defines various possible means of proving identity, but most PKI products implement a bidirectional digital signature exchange to prove a user's identity. An explanation of public key cryptography is outside the scope of this book, but there are many good texts available on the subject.

X.509 certificates

The X.509 specification (which is part of the X.500 standard) defines how trusted certificates containing public keys can be created and stored in an X.500 directory and how those certificates (and their corresponding private keys) can be used to perform authentication of users and other entities. Although the X.500 directory standard has lost in popularity, the X.509 specification has become the de facto industry standard and is used by nearly every commercial PKI system. Even though the X.509 specification is relatively mature and stable, PKI products from various vendors are rarely interoperable.

Signed binds

The process of creating a DUA-DSA or DSA-DSA connection (e.g., an "association") is called a *bind*. X.500 directory components can require that digital signatures be exchanged to prove the identity of the directory components before the association is allowed. Although this level of assurance is defined, many products do not fully support it and few (if any) real-world directory services require it.

In order to support signed binds, each DSA and DUA must possess cryptographic credentials and must be able to create and validate digital signatures based on those credentials. Normally, the DUA will assume the identity of the user and will utilize the user's credentials to create its digital signature. Providing the DSA with its own identity and credentials in order to support a digital signature exchange is more difficult.

Signed binds only provide a marginal level of protection from spoofing and various sorts of denial of service attacks. If a bad actor wants to stage a denial of service attack, it is much easier to attack the system hosting the DSA than to create a bogus DAP or DSP session.

Signed operations and access control

Access Control Information (ACI) can be defined for every piece of information stored within an X.500 directory. ACI can be used to restrict access to that particular piece of data, even down to the attribute level. ACI can define whether a specific user (or group of users) can create, modify, or delete a piece of information. Multiple ACIs can be applied to a piece of information such that different people or groups have different rights.

As an example, consider the e-mail address attribute within a user's entry. The directory administrator would be allowed to create, modify, or delete the attribute. An e-mail administrator might be allowed to modify the value but not create or delete it. Access could also be restricted such that only users in the same organization could read the e-mail address.

Each X.500 directory operation carries the DN of the requester. It can also carry an optional digital signature, to further prove the identity of the requester. Since the requester's identity accompanies each operation request, the performing DSA is always able to validate whether the user is authorized to perform the requested operation.

Border and sacrificial DSAs

It's a pretty good bet that all the information in your directory is not suitable for full public view. As an example, you'll probably want to keep some (or most) of the information about your employees restricted from open access. More than one headhunter has used a company's corporate white pages service as a list of prospective clients. The three basic methods of protecting your company's information are:

- Employ access controls on the information held by your directory, and treat all queries from outside your organization as anonymous;

- Funnel all directory operations between yourself and the outside world through a Border DSA, which acts as an application-level firewall for your directory and usually contains a replica of the information you want to share with the outside world; or

- Place a Sacrificial DSA outside your corporate infrastructure and "push" a sanitized copy of the public information outward to it.

Access controls are critically important to restrict unauthorized access to directory information, but they may not provide sufficient protection. For instance, you may be relying on the user's Distinguished Name in the directory request and allowing organizational users to list and read all the information in the directory. If a bad player can create a bad directory request with a name that you trust, he or she can gain access to directory information. That request can come from anywhere on the Internet, so most organizations believe that it's a good idea to protect their directory from outside access by one or more of these three techniques. Access controls were discussed earlier, so we'll just examine Border and Sacrificial DSAs in this section.

A Border DSA serves as an application-level firewall that sits between your directory and the outside world (see Figure 3.10). Typically, a Border DSA sits just inside the corporate firewall or possibly in a DMZ (demilitarized zone) network segment with your e-mail and Web servers. All outside directory requests are received by this DSA, who either returns information based on the DIT that it holds (or a replicant of your other directory information) or chains the query inward. A couple of specialized Border DSA products used by the military have the ability to completely hide any information about your internal directory, to the extent of modifying the `masterDSA` attribute or removing it entirely, and removing any trace information that may accompany the response to a query. They can typically also act as a blind directory proxy, applying a fictitious user identity to outbound queries, mapping the responses to the original requests, and chaining the responses off to the originating user with the organization. Needless to say, these "militarized" Border DSAs are rather specialized. You, however, can use just about any X.500 product to create an effective Border DSA if you are not quite that paranoid. Simply replicate information into the Border DSA, and do not configure it to chain queries inward. It will

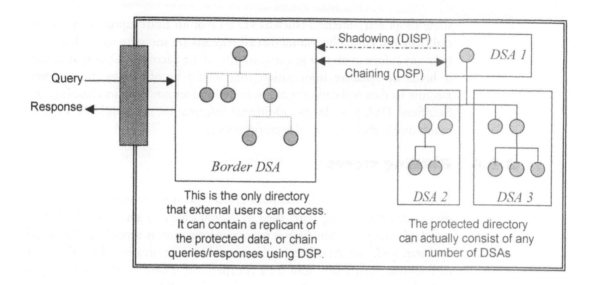

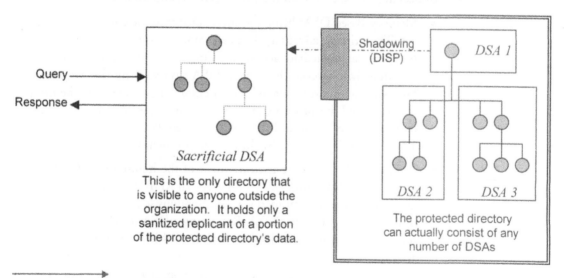

Figure 3.10   *X.500 Border DSA and Sacrificial DSA.*

enforce access control information on the replicated entries and return any applicable information from the replicant that it holds. The Border DSA should not master any part of the DIT.

Sacrificial DSAs (also in Figure 3.10) are nearly the same as Border DSAs, except for two regards. First, they almost always exist outside the corporate firewall, albeit perhaps within a DMZ. Second, they usually receive a refresh of the replicant data that they hold on a regular basis, usually by some proprietary method (such as via FTP or an LDIF update). A Sacrificial DSA will normally assume that all requests are anonymous, and will not hold any information of a sensitive nature. If the Sacrificial DSA is attacked, it holds no sensitive information that would be of use to the attacker. Because its data replication is one-way and it does not support chaining, the Sacrificial DSA provides no additional information that could be used to compromise the corporate directory service.

3.2.4   Backing stores

Much noise and little light has been given regarding the database technologies (called the *backing store*) used by X.500 directory services. The X.500 standard does not define how directory information is actually to be stored and retrieved, and therefore vendors use this as an area in which they can differentiate themselves from their competition. There are three basic types of backing stores, each with their own benefits and limitations.

- Memory-Based DSAs bring the entire DIB into the computer's memory. The primary advantage is speed. Since everything is in memory, the DSA has immediate access and can return this information very, very quickly. However, this type of DSA has two main disadvantages. First, the data must be loaded into memory anew each time the DSA is started, and this process can take a long time (several minutes). Second, the size of the local DIB and replicated data that can be held by a single DSA is restricted by the amount of memory available.

- Relational Databases are used by most of the high-end X.500 directory servers. When properly configured, an RDBMS can provide very good performance combined with tremendous scalability—up to tens of millions of entries per DSA. Restarting a DSA usually takes only a few seconds because the database isn't loaded into memory. The disadvantages are that RDMS-based systems can require very large amounts of disk storage, and can be very poor performers if not properly configured and indexed.

- Object-Oriented Databases may offer a good compromise between memory-mapped and RDBMS-based systems. They offer the speed and scalability of RDBMS systems but are more efficient in their use of memory and disk resources. They may not operate as quickly as memory-based systems but will be nearly as fast as the best RDBMS systems. Although object-oriented database technology is extremely interesting, few vendors have implemented these systems to date.

Another point to understand is that the database underneath a DSA is usually dedicated to the use of the DSA and is not accessible for use as a general-purpose database tool. Although full database systems provide technology such as journaling, check pointing, replication, and two-phase commits, you should not assume that a particular product provides this functionality unless the documentation specifically addresses it.

3.2.5   Application Program Interfaces

Several years ago, the X/Open group developed an Application Programming Interface (API) that could be used to make applications "directory aware" by allowing them to use the DAP protocol in order to access X.500 directories. This API did not evolve as newer versions of the X.500 standard were developed and implemented and is no longer interesting except as a historical footnote. Some directory vendors provide APIs or tool kits, but they are generally useful only with that particular vendor's products.

Almost without exception, directory users and applications use LDAP to access directories—whether native X.500 or not. APIs will be discussed later, in Section 3.3.4.

3.2.6   Strengths and weaknesses of X.500

Your organization will have to weigh the strengths and weaknesses of X.500 when making a decision whether to implement X.500, LDAP, or some other directory technology. X.500's benefits include:

- *Maturity.* X.500 has evolved over nearly two decades. Many international organizations and governments have worked to identify and correct weaknesses and technical problems. Many organizations have built very large multinational directory services based on X.500.

- *Distributed architecture.* Its distributed nature allows local organizations to maintain ownership and control of their own data, yet cooperate in a larger directory structure. X.500 provides distributed operations that include chaining and replication.

- *Strong security model.* It has a strong security model, allowing for identification and authentication of remote users. Most PKI security products rely on the X.509 specification for security certificates—part of the X.500 recommendations.

Unfortunately, X.500s drawbacks have overshadowed its technical strengths. Although products have been available for a decade, X.500 has not been widely accepted by the commercial market or the major software vendors such as Microsoft, Lotus, Novell, and Netscape. There are many reasons for this, including:

- *Lack of a global directory tree.* An international directory tree would require international cooperation and coordination between country-level DSAs, which would require that country-level DSAs actually exist in each country. Only a handful of countries have implemented a production X.500 directory service.

- *No registration authorities.* Registration of national level DSAs has never been agreed upon. This would be necessary to allow users in one country to obtain directory information from other countries. Only a very few nations have set up a formal registration authority for the purpose of registering states/provinces and organizations within their country. Although the American National Standards Institute (ANSI) is the official ITU-T registration authority for the United States, it has never created a policy or process for officially registering an X.500 name under the c=US level of the directory. Authority to operate lower-level directory services and perform registration at those levels has been delegated to states and to the U.S. government by ANSI. However, to date no states are known to have implemented a formal X.500 registration process. The General Services Administration is responsible for registration of government agencies under o=U.S. Government, but there is no office within GSA that handles that responsibility at this time.

- *No service providers.* Originally, the ITU believed that the telephone companies and government PTAs of the world would create and run the global X.500 directory infrastructure. However, these service providers could never develop a business model that they believed would be profitable. They also feared that registration of their customers in a global directory would create unlimited competition between service providers, because it would allow competing companies to gain information about their customers.

- *Complexity.* X.500 is quite complex, and few people understand it well. This overall lack of expertise makes organizations fearful of relying on a technology that may not be supportable in the long run. Some organizations that have implemented X.500 infrastructures have had trouble keeping technical staff once they are trained.

- *Technical shortcomings.* For all its power and maturity, X.500 is lacking in a few areas. Opponents of X.500 technology have pointed to these shortcomings as reasons that companies should choose a different directory technology. X.500 does not have a good way of storing multinational and global organizations such as NATO or the United Nations. It offers no encryption of data traveling between DSAs and is, therefore, susceptible to snooping. And it does not offer multimastering, multilevel security, or selective attribute replication.

- *Time synchronization.* X.500 operations bear a time stamp, and DSAs can be configured to ignore operations after a defined time limit. This would normally be done for performance or security reasons. However, this requires that all of the DSA systems' clocks be set within a few seconds of each other. If a DSA's clock is out of synch it will ignore all operations, thinking that they have timed out.

3.3 LDAP

As stated earlier, in Section 3.1.2, it was noted that LDAP was originally created to help underpowered "PC" desktop computer systems talk to X.500 directory services. Originally designed by W. Yeong, Tim Howes, and Steve Kille in RFC 1487 (and updated as version 2 in RFC 1777) LDAP didn't really hit its stride until 1997 when LDAPv3 was defined in RFC 2251. Since that time, LDAP has become the standard method for applications to access directories, and several vendors have introduced robust directory servers that are specifically designed for large, enterprise-level directory services. Even though X.500 isn't quite dead, its offspring—LDAP—is most certainly alive and kicking.

3.3.1 The Internet standards process

It might be helpful to understand the difference between the ITU standards process and the Internet standards process. In the ITU process, the standards are agreed to and committed to paper during a long process of coordination and discussion between technologists from around the world. Once consensus is reached, a draft standard is created and then examined in great detail. Eventually, the official standard is published. The X.500 standard is available from www.itu.net—and will cost you a good chunk of change.

Once an ITU standard is published, implementation specifics must be coordinated and documented through International Standardized Profiles (ISPs) or industry-specific profiles. Once this is accomplished, vendors can create products based on the standard. If problems are found, deficiency reports are submitted for inclusion in the next version of the standard. This process takes a good while. The X.500 directory standard was created in 1988, and updates have been issued in 1993, 1997, and 2001.

In stark contrast, the Internet standards process starts with an Internet Engineering Task Force (IETF) working group consisting of any number of interested technologists. They develop a working draft document for discussion, and this document is kicked back and forth via e-mail and quarterly meetings. At some point, it is submitted to the Internet Activity Board (IAB) as a proposed standard. If accepted, it is published as an RFC document via the Internet—for free. At this point, it has made the first stage in its life and has become a Proposed Standard.

The next stage in an Internet standard's life comes when three or more groups (vendors, developers, or experimenters) actually implement and test the proposed standard. Their input will be integrated into the proposed standard, and it will be reissued as a Draft Standard. From this point, there is a window of time during which comments and objections to the draft standard can be submitted. At the end of this time, the IAB can elect to make the RFC an Internet Standard. Only then does it become an official standard that is not subject to revision.

To recap, the life cycle of an Internet standard is working group draft, to proposed standard, to draft standard, to Internet standard. The status of all published RFCs is noted in the RFC-INDEX, which is updated every time a new RFC is published or a status changes.

You should also be aware that three other types of RFCs exist. Informational RFCs can be published by anyone, for any reason. Normally, they contain informed opinion, best practices, or general discontent with some situation regarding the Internet. The second type is actually a special subset of the informational RFC, which appears every year on April 1, such as the RFC describing the Internet Coffee Pot Protocol. The third type is the Experimental RFC, which describes something of great interest to a specific technical group but probably will never be a standard. All RFCs are not standards, and, in fact, many of them never will be.

3.3.2   The LDAPv3 standard

Now back to LDAP. The only Internet directory standard is RFC 2251, LDAPv3. Even this RFC was given special dispensation because of its importance (the RFC contains a note to this effect). All of the prior LDAP RFCs were informational, proposed standards, and draft standards.

As mentioned earlier, LDAP is the Lightweight Directory Access Protocol. It is a standardized, extensible protocol that applications can use to get information from a directory service. Because it is a standardized protocol, client and server software from different vendors can interoperate. In fact, LDAP is quickly becoming the de facto directory protocol and a great many commercial software products (including most PKI clients) can use LDAP to retrieve needed information. LDAP runs over Transmission Control Protocol/Internet Protocol (TCP/IP) (e.g., the Internet software that is shipped included with nearly every computer built today).

The four LDAP models

The proposed LDAPv3 standards define four models that describe areas of LDAP functionality:

- The Information Model, based on X.500, defines the types of information you can store in the directory. A note of caution: Nodes of the directory are often called *containers* in LDAP implementations. Administrative domains are usually called something else in LDAP implementations, such as subtrees, vertices, or contexts.

- The Naming Model, also based on X.500, defines how that information is stored, organized, and retrieved from the directory.

- The Functional Model, based only roughly on X.500, defines how information in the directory is maintained and accessed.

- The Security Model, which is significantly different from X.500, defines how information in the directory is protected from unauthorized modification or access.

The Information and Naming Models in LDAP are essentially the same as for the X.500 directory and were discussed in some detail earlier in this chapter. We'll talk a bit about the Functional Model, and examine the differences between the X.500 and LDAP Security Models a little later.

The core protocol

LDAP is a client/server protocol. This means that the client program (an application such as e-mail or perhaps a directory browser) runs on one computer, and the actual directory server is normally running on a different computer. LDAP defines how requests for information are formed by the directory client and how responses are returned to the client by the directory server. This type of architecture allows the bulk of the work to be centralized on a larger computer—the server—while a minimum amount of processing has to be done by each client system (usually a personal computer). With today's computers, this allows the client system to be optimized for the type of work done by the end users (e.g., color screens, printers, etc.) while the server system will usually be a much larger and faster system with a lot of memory and disk storage.

LDAP defines the communication between client and server as a series of messages. The client sends a message that contains a request for information to the server. The server processes the request and sends a message, or messages, containing the result (or error condition) back to the client. A single request can generate multiple response messages from the server. One message is returned for each entry that matches the request, followed by a message containing the result code. Each request contains a unique message identifier, and the results returned contain the same identifier. This allows the client to associate responses with specific requests. It is actually allowable for the LDAP client to issue multiple requests at the same time, each with a unique identifier. The message identifiers in the responses allow the client to sort out the different responses to different requests, and to handle responses that might be arriving out of order. The LDAP client is responsible for handling these details so that the directory user or application will not be aware of them.

The LDAPv3 Functional Model defines three categories of operations and a total of nine different operations. These are:

- Update operations include add, delete, modify, and modify DN (e.g., rename) and are used to create and maintain the information in the directory.

- Interrogation operations include search and compare and are used to request information from the directory.

- Control and authentication operations include bind, unbind, and abandon and are used by a directory client to set up and terminate a directory session (the abandon operation tells the server to quit processing a specific request).

Extensibility

One of the major advantages of LDAPv3 over its predecessors is extensibility. LDAPv3 can be extended to include new functions and capabilities. If a new function is required to support a particular product or capability, it can be defined and standardized without causing changes to the underlying LDAPv3 protocol. For instance, additional functions for distributed operations and security are currently being developed as additions to LDAPv3.

The extended capabilities supported by any given LDAP server are listed in a special directory entry called the *root DSE*. It contains attributes that describe the configuration and capabilities of that particular LDAP server.

Encoding rules

X.500 defines two different ways that information can be encoded—Basic Encoding Rules (BER) and Distinguished Encoding Rules (DER). BER is the simpler of the two, and LDAP uses a subset of the X.500 BER capability—sometimes referred to as Lightweight BER (LBER). LBER represents the basic types of information, such as number and strings, as simple sequences of text. These sequences contain encoded information rather than plain human-readable text. Even with a "sniffer," you would probably need a protocol analyzer to decode the messages flowing back and forth between client and server.

A potential difficulty exists with the storage and retrieval of binary information, such as images and sound clips. Not all directory products encode and decode these objects in exactly the same fashion, so be prepared to test any proposed directory product if this is a requirement for your organization.

Lightweight Directory Interchange Format

The Lightweight Directory Interchange Format (LDIF) is a standard method of representing directory data in a text form. LDIF is primarily used as a bulk-loading protocol, to export data from and import data into an LDAP server. LDIF files can be created and edited with traditional text editing tools. There are actually two types of LDIF files. The first type contains a series of directory entries composed of a series of lines, with the first containing the full DN of that entry. After this line come the attributes, one per line. There is no set order for attributes, but generally the `objectclass` attributes are listed first, right after the `dn`. An LDIF entry might look something like that shown in Figure 3.11.

Figure 3.11
A typical LDIF data entry.

```
dn: uid=ssmith, dc=megacorp, dc=com
objectClass: top
objectClass: person
objectClass: organizationalPerson
objectClass: inetOrgPerson
cn: Samuel Smith
cn: Sam Smith
sn: Smith
mail: ssmith@megacorp.com
telephoneNumber: +1 202 555 1212
description: Number Uno Big Kahuna
```

Figure 3.12
*A typical LDIF
update entry.*

```
dn: uid=ssmith, dc=megacorp, dc=com
changetype: modify
replace: telephoneNumber
telephoneNumber: +1 203 555 1213
replace: description
description: Pacific Regional Sales Manager
```

Figure 3.12
*A typical LDIF
update entry.*

The second type contains a series of LDIF update statements, which are to be applied to directory entries. Normally, this file serves as an input to an automated update utility for bulk updating of directory entries. A typical use for this file would be to synchronize data in the directory with another data source, such as an e-mail product's address book. The entries in this file are also text and look something like Figure 3.12.

The entry starts with the DN of the directory entry to be updated. Then follows a `changetype` instruction, such as add, delete, replace, or rename. Next come a series of entries that specify the attribute to be updated and the attribute value (if the `changetype` is add or replace).

LDIF files can contain binary data, but these data must be converted to a format called *base 64*, in which the data are represented by a series of printable (e.g., 7-bit) characters. Complete information about LDIF can be found on the IETF Web site (http://www.ietf.org) or in any of the several good books currently available on LDAPv3.

3.3.3   The LDAP security model

LDAP is a connection-oriented client/server protocol. Once an LDAP client binds to an LDAP server, any number of operations can be performed during that particular session. In order to secure these operations, the LDAP security model provides for three types of functionality:

- *Authentication.* LDAP users can be required to provide proof of identify before they are allowed to connect to the directory and perform various operations.

- *Access Control.* Based on the authenticated identity of a user, access controls determine the operations that a user is allowed to perform on information held within that specific directory server.

- *Transport Security.* Authentication information, operational requests, and directory data flowing between the LDAP server and client can be encrypted to prevent unauthorized disclosure.

Used together, these three functions provide for a fairly substantial security capability. However, LDAP also has some security shortcomings, which will be discussed below.

Authentication

Authentication is the process of presenting the user's identity to the LDAP server. The server may allow anonymous access, or it may require a password or some sort of strong credentials, such as a digital signature. The LDAP server is responsible for verifying the information presented by the user. Verification may be as simple as matching the password provided against the userpassword attribute stored in the user's entry within the directory. It may also be as complicated as validating a digital signature by checking the trust path and certificate revocation status of the public key credentials used for authentication. If the user's identity can be validated, the client is allowed to bind to the LDAP server with that identity. Otherwise, the user is only allowed to bind to the directory anonymously.

The original LDAPv3 specification was lacking in any formal definition of security services. To fill this gap, the Simple Authentication and Security Layer (SASL) was defined by John Myers in RFC 2222. SASL is a method for adding authentication support to connection-based protocols (including LDAP). In an SASL-protected session, the client issues an authentication command that includes an SASL mechanism name. Every SASL mechanism name must be registered with the Internet Assigned Numbers Authority (IANA), whose Web site can be found at http://www.iana.org; RFC 2222 gives instructions for registering new authentication mechanisms with IANA. If the server supports the requested SASL mechanism, it initiates an authentication protocol exchange—a series of server challenges and client responses specific to that particular security mechanism. During this authentication protocol exchange, the client transmits the user's identity and negotiates for the use of a mechanism-specific security "layer."

The transmitted authorization identity may actually be different from the client's identity, to permit agents such as proxy servers to authenticate using their own credentials, followed by requesting access privileges belonging to the identity for which they are proxying.

If a security layer is requested/negotiated, it is used to protect all subsequent data sent between client and server. The security layer is generally used to implement data-level encryption in order to prevent unauthorized disclosure due to snooping or packet inspection.

Access control

The LDAPv3 core standard provides for no access control capability. However, most vendor products offer some sort of access control—usually a subset or variant of the X.500-style ACI functionality. When selecting an

LDAP server, you should ensure that you understand the method by which access control is implemented in the product you are considering.

Most LDAP servers implement an inherited access control model. When access controls are implemented on a container, any objects further down in the directory tree will typically inherit the higher-level access controls. As an example, if you apply a policy that any anonymous user can read objects in the `o=Megacorp.com, c=us` directory, all objects within this entire subtree will normally inherit this access control. It can be overridden further down the directory tree if needed. For instance, you might want to severely restrict access to the `ou=Personnel, o=Megacorp.com, c=us` level of the directory. An access control statement applied to that container would override the inherited access control definition set higher in the directory tree. Some LDAP servers ship with default access controls already defined, while others will require you to define all your own access control information.

Replication brings another set of problems with regard to inherited access controls. Since inherited access controls flow downward from higher levels of the directory, some of the applicable access control information may not exist in the portion of the directory that you want to replicate. The method employed to sort out this dilemma will differ between products—caveat emptor. If you wish to use LDAP-based products to build a distributed directory service, you must test the products before deployment to ensure that they are capable of meeting your requirements. You will not have a clue from reading the directory vendor's product data sheets.

Another issue to be aware of is the difference between the way that X.500 and LDAP check user identity. This is important, because access controls are applied based on the user's identity. If you cannot be sure of a user's identity, the directory server cannot accurately enforce access controls.

SSL and TLS

Secure Socket Layers (SSL) and Transport Layer Security (TLS) are two methods of encrypting information flowing between two Internet-based computer systems. SSL is the older of the two and is used extensively in securing access to sites on the Web and in electronic commerce applications. SSL encrypts the data carried within the "packets" flowing between the two computers. Any stream of information flowing across the Internet is actually busted into little chunks, called packets. These packets flow independently from the sending computer to the receiving computer. The receiving computer stores up the packets and reassembles the data stream—all without the user's knowledge. The information carried in these packets (such as LDAP queries, responses, and passwords) is text and can easily be viewed by many hardware and software tools known as "sniffers"—hence the term "packet-sniffing." SSL encrypts the information contained within the packets so that only the receiver can decode it.

TLS is a relatively recent standard, and as of this writing has not been implemented in a great many products. It provides functionality similar to SSL but at the transport layer rather than the packet layer. In other words, the data stream itself is encrypted in TLS before being broken into packets, whereas SSL breaks up the data stream first and then encrypts each packet.

Both SSL and TLS allow mutual authentication using strong authentication and can use X.509-based certificates issued by commercial PKI systems. The LDAPS protocol uses SSL to provide authentication and protection of information. Future implementations of LDAPv3 clients will use TLS to provide the same services.

LDAP and firewalls

LDAP presents significant challenges when securing the corporate network, because it does not (yet) implement any sort of chaining. Users from all over the world may expect to be able to directly contact your LDAP-based directory. If that directory exists within your corporate network, you will have to open your firewalls to allow this access. Most firewalls are not able to act as an application-level LDAP gateway. The only thing you could do to restrict access is to deny connectivity to all systems inside your organization except the LDAP server, and restrict access such that only LDAP operations and results can be passed between the LDAP server and users across the Internet. However, this configuration is still extremely worrisome to most security administrators, especially since most (or all) external LDAP access will be anonymous.

A new technology, the reverse proxy server, addresses a great deal of LDAP's security concern in this type of environment (Figure 3.13). For a traditional service such as Web access, a proxy server will sit inside the corporate firewall. Users are not allowed to access the Internet, but they can connect to the proxy server. The proxy server is allowed to connect to Web servers outside the corporate networks on behalf of the user. Responses come back to the proxy server, which then forwards them to the appropriate user. A reverse proxy places the proxy server backwards, outside the corporate firewall. In the event of a reverse LDAP proxy, such as the iPlanet Directory Access Router (IDAR), any user from the Internet can connect to the IDAR. A single hole through the corporate firewall allows the IDAR to connect to the corporate LDAP server to send LDAP operation requests and receive results.

Figure 3.13
*LDAP reverse
proxy server.*

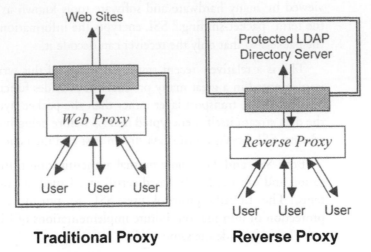

Traditional Proxy   **Reverse Proxy**

3.3.4 LDAP APIs

Today, it seems that nearly every application in the world is LDAP-enabled. The Directory Enabled Network (DEN) specification, proposed by a consortium led by Cisco and Microsoft, proposes a method where firewalls and routers can be configured and managed with information kept in an LDAP directory. But, what about all those "home-grown" applications that your business relies on? How can you retrofit them to take advantage of directories for functions such as identification and authentication? Also, how can new applications being developed work with your organizational directory?

You need a good API or Software Developer's Kit (SDK)—a tool kit that provides a simplified set of functions to access and utilize directories. Fortunately, the developers of LDAP have always seemed to understand the importance of creating directory-enabled applications, and you have a choice of several LDAP APIs. The original University of Michigan LDAP distribution included a C programming library for directory access—the LDAP C API (documented in RFC 1823). A proposed update for this API is currently being drafted by an IETF working group (http://www.ietf.org). The source code for the original U-Mich C API is available from http://www.umich.edu/~dirsvcs/ldap. Netscape provides an updated C SDK that supports both LDAPv2 and LDAPv3 at http://developer.netscape.com and http://www.mozilla.org.. Netscape also provides an LDAPv2/v3 Java API, available from http://developer.netscape.com (with source code at http://www.mozilla.org), and a draft Java API specification is currently in draft form, available from http://www.ietf.org. Perl LDAP is also available from Netscape for LDAP-enabling Perl applications.

The Java Naming and Directory Interface (JNDI) from JavaSoft is an API/SDK that can allow Java applications and applets to access directory systems. Each type of directory, such as X.500 or LDAP, requires a service provider interface (SPI), a software module that plugs into JNDI. Information about JNDI is available from http://www.javasoft.com or from Sun at http://java.sun.com/products/jndi.

3.3.5 Differences between X.500 and LDAP

Although LDAP is based on the X.500 information model, significant differences between LDAP and X.500 have been identified in the sections above. To recap, the major differences are highlighted again here.

Client access

X.500 requires DUAs to use the DAP, which provides a very robust interface protocol with good security functionality. Unfortunately, very few X.500 DUAs were ever built, and few (if any) APIs exist for adding DAP support to existing applications.

LDAP, on the other hand, is somewhat insecure, but easy to deal with, and there are many APIs and SDKs that can be used to add LDAP support to applications. Therefore, almost all directory user agents and applications available today use LDAP to access directory services. Without exception, X.500 directory products provide support for access by LDAP clients.

Distributed operations

In X.500, each directory request carries the Distinguished Name of the user making the request and can optionally carry a digital signature. This request flows from DSA to DSA until it arrives at the performing DSA that masters ("owns") the requested information, a process known as chaining. The performing DSA checks the user's identity in the request against the access control information that applies to the requested information to determine whether the user is allowed to perform the requested operation. Since the performing DSA may not be the DSA that the user originally sent the request to, the identity in the request is the performing DSA's only means of identifying the user.

Since LDAP does not support chaining or distributed operations, the original DSA that a user contacts must also be the performing DSA. If that DSA does not contain the requested information, it can only return a referral pointing to another DSA that might contain the requested information. Therefore, LDAP authenticates the user when it first binds to the server.

From that point, as long as the session is active, the server uses the logon identity in order to enforce access controls (if implemented). Some LDAP servers have implemented SASL in order to provide for a strong (credentialed) authentication when users connect to the directory. SASL security implementations are likely to be proprietary to a specific vendor. In other words, you will probably have to use that vendor's client products and server products together to obtain the SASL security. Another vendor's client products may not work with the vendor's specific SASL implementation.

Access controls

X.500 provides access controls that can restrict access based on the operation requested versus the identity of the user. These are discussed in depth in Section 3.2. The LDAP standard provides no access control, but many LDAP vendors implement access controls based (to varying degrees) on the X.500 methodology.

Transport-level security

X.500 was designed to use the OSI protocol "stack," which includes the X.200 specification for creating OSI networks. Unfortunately, there are few (if any) OSI networks in existence. Therefore, RFC 1006 proposed a method of substituting the Internet protocols for the OSI network layer and has become the de facto standard for running X.500 directory products across the Internet. X.500 provides no encryption capability to protect information as it flows across the Internet between DSAs or between a DSA and directory user. Queries and responses can be intercepted and viewed by third parties without your knowledge. A very few X.500 products have the ability to use SSL to protect information flowing between DSAs, and may implement TLS security in the future. These implementations are product-specific and will not be interoperable between products from different vendors.

LDAP has no inherent transport protection, but a great many LDAP servers implement SSL to encrypt the data flowing between the client and server. In the near future, many LDAP products will also implement TLS for protecting this information.

Replication

X.500 produces the DISP for replicating information between servers. DISP works well but requires a bit of experience to set up and tune properly. LDAP has no inherent replication capability. The LDIF specifies a file-based format, which many LDAP products can use for bulk loading or for simple replication between LDAP servers. Some LDAP vendors also provide a product-specific replication capability. An Internet Engineering Task Force working group is working on a draft standard for LDAP-based replication as of this writing.

3.4   Domain Name Server (DNS)

The Internet Domain Name Server (DNS) is the protocol that all Internet-based computers use to find each other's IP addresses. An Internet e-mail address looks something like user@mycorp.com. The user name is to the left of the @ sign, and the name of the computer that handles the e-mail is on the right. In order to send an e-mail message, however, your computer must know the target computer's dotted numeric IP address. DNS provides a global directory service designed to find the IP address that belongs to a specific Internet host name.

Since most users are familiar with Internet-style e-mail addresses, many organizations are considering organizing their directory service in a structure similar to their Internet domain name. With X.500, a Distinguished Name might look like c=us, o=Mycorp, ou=Sales, cn=Fred Smith, but an Internet-style name might look like pn=fsmith, dc=sales, dc=mycorp, dc=com. The idea is that this would make it easier for people outside your company to find information in your directory, because Fred's e-mail address would probably be fsmith@sales.mycorp.com.

3.4.1   Representing DNS within X.500 and LDAP directories

X.500 is a completely separate directory system from DNS. However, a proposed Internet Standard, as described in RFC 2247 and RFC 2377, provides a method of representing Domain Name System domain components using the X.500 information model. This allows both X.500- and LDAP-based directory services to store information in a structure familiar to Internet-literate users.

RFC 2247 defines an attribute, DomainComponent (dc), which can be used to store a domain component such as "gov." It also defines two objects, domain and dcObject. The dcObject object can be added to existing objects so that they can contain a dc attribute. The domain object allows the addition of new entries that contain a dc attribute. RFC 2247 is a proposed Internet standard. It is, therefore, fairly stable and not subject to major changes. However, it may not be widely implemented in applications and commercial software products yet.

Using `domain` objects, it is possible to represent the DNS "tree" within an X.500 or LDAP directory service accurately. Searching based on DNS-style naming can be very intuitive to users who are familiar with Internet e-mail addresses. The `dcObject` object can allow for construction of DNs that look very much like X.500 but are actually composed of `Domain-Component` attributes. This sort of DN would look like: `pn=john.smith, dc=irs, dc=treas, dc=U.S. Government, dc=us`. This style of naming similarity to pure X.500 naming could cause significant confusion. Because it does not map to the Internet-style e-mail addresses, it is not intuitive to use and, therefore, provides very little benefit. As the Internet and DNS evolve in the future, country-based naming may come into use. If so, this decision will be revisited at that time.

3.5   X.500-based directories

As noted earlier, X.500 has been around for more than a decade, and X.500-based directory services have found a strong niche in the market as metadirectories within large organizations. Metadirectory is a fancy name for a centralized directory that can accept information from a variety of other sources, including other directory technologies, legacy systems, databases, and just about any other authoritative source. Some X.500 products are sold as metadirectory products, while others have a base X.500 product and a higher-level product that includes the metadirectory functionality.

Many organizations distribute the ownership and maintenance of corporate directory information to the division, region, or even office level. The X.500 access control model provides good functionality in this arena, allowing administrators to create or delete entries, users to modify specific portions of their entries, and only authorized personnel to see specific bits of that information. The X.500 shadowing protocol provides replication that places replicas of directory information throughout the organization in order to protect against network and equipment failures.

Because of the potential size of organizational databases, almost all directory products today use some sort of database technology for data storage. Some use an indexed file system utility (a rudimentary database specifically designed for quick storage and retrieval of data), while others rely upon commercial database offerings. At least one uses a commercial object-oriented database. The discussion of object-oriented versus relational databases is outside the scope of this chapter. Be assured, however, that every vendor has marketing literature proclaiming the virtues of its solution and casting shadows on all other products. Caveat emptor—make vendors prove their claims in the lab before you believe the marketing literature.

A couple of X.500 directory products have come to be used as the preferred storage technology for some very large public key infrastructures. This makes sense, because the X.509 specification for public key certificates is part of the X.500 standard. There is a subtle catch, however. Any directory product (or Web server or database for that matter) can store and retrieve X.509 certificates. Not many directory products know how to use X.509 certificates in order to establish the identity of a directory user or administrator. Those that are capable of using X.509 certificates are almost guaranteed not to be interoperable with any other vendor's products (at least the security functionality). If a public key infrastructure is in your future, plan on picking and living with a single vendor's products—at least for the foreseeable future.

Last, but certainly not least, every X.500 directory server product provides support for LDAPv2 and LDAPv3 clients. Some fully implement the LDAP security models; others do not. X.500 vendors provide varying levels of completeness and interoperability with LDAPv3 clients. With only a couple of exceptions, every X.500 directory system in the world is accessed using the LDAP protocols. To this end, at least, X.500 directories can support darn near any sort of directory-enabled application (at least those that can speak LDAP).

In the interest of full disclosure, I should probably admit that I was employed by NEXOR for nearly three years and by Control Data (now Syntegra) for over eight years before that. I am fairly familiar with the directory offerings from both companies. I have been accused, jokingly I hope, of being an X.500 bigot. Although I will try my best to provide a level and coherent view of each vendor's offering, you may want to take this into consideration.

3.5.1   Computer Associates: eTrust Directory

Originally developed in Australia by DataCraft, Ltd., this X.500 directory (after being purchased a couple of times) has ended up as part of the Computer Associates eTrust Security products family. From the beginning, the eTrust directory was designed for speed and scalability. It was probably the first commercial directory product to demonstrate subsecond response times with a million entries at trade shows.

The eTrust directory (http://www3.ca.com/Solutions/Product.asp?ID=160 or http://www.ca.com/eTrust) has evolved to become a very, very scalable and robust directory service that is used within several international organizations worldwide. It was recently selected to be the standard electronic directory technology used in the U.S. Internal Revenue Service, primarily due to its scalability and security capabilities.

eTrust Directory relies upon the Ingres database engine for its datastore and claims to be "the only directory solution to deliver high performance, scalability, and reliability through the use of an embedded, commercial RDBMS." This may be partially true, because most products use an indexed filing system rather than a commercial RDBMS. However, at least two other directory products (Oracle and NEXOR) use commercial database products. Reliance on a commercial RDBMS is actually a good thing, because it provides great performance and scalability; the potential to access information via SQL legacy systems; and the traditional database strengths of locking, logging, journaling, two-phase commits, and backup and recovery.

eTrust Directory uses a proprietary method to index every attribute stored in the directory, providing astonishing performance—but at the cost of significant disk real estate. To support a large directory, plan on spending a good chunk of change to buy some serious computer hardware. eTrust Directory is not cheap, and it may require a significant amount of horsepower to get the level of performance needed to support a large organizational directory service.

Because of the large organizational directories that use the eTrust Directory, it has evolved a bit more than its competition in the arena of distributed operations. In addition to supporting the standard DSP protocol for chaining, the eTrust Directory can be instructed to use load balancing between multiple directory servers. It can also be architected with directory "routers" at the top of your organizational hierarchy. These directory routers are special-purpose instances of the directory server that only contain knowledge references to the information kept in various portions of the organizational directory. They have the ability to apply a sort of "shortest path" routing to ensure that directory queries are sent to the closest directory server.

eTrust Directory is not positioned as a metadirectory, per se. However, the DXlink module provides a method whereby the eTrust Directory can connect to existing LDAP directory servers within the organization. The LDAP directory appears to be a normal part of the X.500 DIT to any chained query. The eTrust Directory is available for Sun Solaris and Windows NT.

3.5.2   Critical Path: InJoin Directory and Metadirectory

The InJoin Directory Server and Metadirectory (http://www.cp.net/products/injoin_index.html) products are based on a merging of the PeerLogic LiveContent and ISOCOR Global Directory Server technologies, which were both acquired by Critical Path (http://www.cp.net). Both products had a heritage in ICL's i500 directory.

The InJoin directory provides speed and scalability similar to Computer Associate's eTrust product. It utilizes a disk-based database and claims to "scale to 20 million entries and deliver millisecond response times to hundreds of queries per second." It uses a proprietary database management system, and offers quality of service functionality that includes two-phase commits, roll-forward and roll-back, and incremental "hot" backup capability (backups that do not require taking the DSA out of service).

The ICL i500 directory was the main directory sold in support of Entrust's Public Key Infrastructure products and had evolved to provide a very good set of security features. Many very large organizations, including several bank systems, use this directory service in combination with Entrust PKI systems. Owing to this heritage, InJoin's security features include the following:

- Schema support for X.509v3 certificates, certificate revocation lists, and other PKI-related objects and attributes;

- SSL support for protecting client access and protecting DSP chaining between directory servers;

- SASL support;

- Strong authentication of users and administrators using X.509v3 certificates;

- Password encryption to prevent snooping or unauthorized disclosure.

Because of the nature of PKI-enabled applications, the directory service providing the PKI support must be highly survivable, and PKI information is usually replicated so that it may be close to the end-user's location. In addition to the X.525-based DISP, the InJoin directory offers several advanced (albeit proprietary) replication capabilities, including the following:

- *Selected object classes and attribute replication, allowing only specific attributes within specific objects to be replicated.* Most directory products only replicate entire subtrees, administrative domains, or naming contexts. Using selective attribute replication, an organization can "push" a very limited set of objects and attributes outward into a Border or Sacrificial DSA using DISP.

- *Single replication agreements can include multiple naming contexts (subtrees or administrative domains).* If an organizational DSA held several nodes of the directory tree, traditional DISP shadowing would normally require that a shadowing agreement be created for a node or subtree.

- *Fast bulk shadowing for initial data loads or data refresh and recovery.* Note that this is a proprietary method provided in addition to the DISP shadowing protocol support.

Critical Path's InJoin directory server is available for Windows NT 4/Intel, Microsoft Windows 2000, Sun Solaris, HP/UX, IBM AIX 4.3, and Silicon Graphics IRIX 6.5.

3.5.3   Data Connections Ltd: DC-Directory and DC-MetaLink

You may not have heard of Data Connections Ltd's (DCL) DC-Directory (http://www.dataconnection.com/dirs/diridx.htm), because DCL prefers to license its product as supporting software within other vendors' products or systems and licenses its metadirectory offering, DC-MetaLink, in the same fashion. DCL also sells both products into the high-end service providers market. DCL is primarily a software engineering firm, rather than a product reseller, and has developed a reputation for providing strong software that can be customized to meet specific programmatic and network requirements.

DCL claims that the DC-Directory product can support up to 5 million directory entries on a single server and that the directory's multithreaded, nonblocking architecture is optimized for real-world performance. It is supposedly architected to take advantage of additional processors in multi-CPU servers. According to DCL, "typical" usage and hardware "can result in between 10s and 100s of operations per second, but all such benchmark numbers are misleading without a discussion of specific requirements and usage scenarios." In other words, your mileage may vary.

DC-Directory is licensed as a base product with a series of option packs, including the following:

- Access (Web client);

- Distributed (distributed operation);

- MetaLink (metadirectory support);

- Custom (schema customization);

- Secure (security features);

- SDK (developer APIs).

In addition to X.500 protocols, DC-Directory supports access by LDAPv2/v3 clients. Security support for LDAP includes SASL authentication, TLS/SSL, DIGEST-MD5, and the GSSAPI over Kerberos v5 (Secure option pack). Security for X.5000 can include certificate-based strong authentication in conjunction with third-party PKI solutions, including X.509-based PKI, Entrust (DC-Directory is Entrust Ready), RSA Keon (DC-Directory is RSA Keon Ready), Entegrity SDP, and Spyrus/Fortezza.

In the Software Developer Kit option pack, DCL provides the Java LDAP APIs, a C-language LDAP Hooks API, the X/Open XDS API (for X.500 DAP access), and the T-XDS API (a text-token version of the XDS API).

The DCL distributed option pack includes support for chained operations using the DSP and replication using the DISP. Replication can be performed as supplier- ("push") or consumer- ("pull") initiated and can occur periodically, when changes to data occur, or immediately. Information to be replicated can be restricted to specific subtrees, specific attributes, or entries that contain a specific attribute value. Replication based on specific attribute value is very interesting for secure applications, such as populating a sacrificial DSA. For example, a supplier-initiated shadow could be configured to push only those employee entries that contained an attribute called publicInformation with a value of Yes.

DC-Directory also provides a bulk import/export facility that understands various flat-file formats and LDIF. Exported data can be selected based on type of entry and attribute filtering, similar to the replication capabilities noted earlier. The datastore behind DC-directory was developed by DCL and optimized for directory operations (write once, read often). This datastore incorporates journalizing, replay, and rollback capabilities. Each directory update is recorded as a single atomic operation in the journal file. DC-Directory provides online (real-time) backup capabilities, plus the ability to restore from a previous backup set.

DCL's metadirectory functionality is sold separately as the MetaLink option package. DCL's approach to directory synchronization is a bit different from that of most products. MetaLink provides a directory synchronization server that is closely integrated with the core DC-directory product and data store. MetaLink can provide live, real-time synchronization with several directory technologies, such as LDAP, Netscape/iPlanet Directory Server, Microsoft Active Directory, Novell NDS eDirectory, Relational Databases (over ODBC), SQL Server, Oracle, Informix, Microsoft Exchange, and Lotus Notes. Configuration of synchronization has the same general level of control as DC-Directory's shadowing capability.

MetaLink also has the ability to import and export data with files and claims to support "a rich grammar for configuring mapping rules, which means that most mappings do not require any plug-ins or script development." (From experience, the most complex and labor-intensive portion of any metadirectory project is usually development and testing of the directory synchronization mappings and scripts.) File types supported include LDIF, Microsoft MS Mail File Sync (import only), Lotus cc:Mail File Sync (import only), and Comma-Separated-Value (CSV) format. MetaLink also provides a Java API that provides persistent triggers, which fire when changes are made to specified data records, and an SDK that allows for the development of custom connector modules.

DC-Directory is available for the following platforms: Windows NTv4 with SP5 or higher, Windows 2000, Solaris (SPARC), Red Hat Linux, HP-UX, and IBM AIX.

3.5.4   NEXOR

The NEXOR Directory (http://www.nexor.com/products/diry.htm) server has its heritage in quipu, one of the first operational directory servers created in the late 1980s at University College London and the directory used by the ISODE Consortium to create the Paradise project—the world's first distributed global X.500 directory service (although it was primarily used by university researchers). The NEXOR Directory has continued to evolve from those early steps into a robust and scalable object-oriented X.500 directory server used within major corporations, service providers, and several international military organizations. Two offshoots of this product are NEXOR Directory Guardian, a high-assurance application-level firewall product that isolates and protects directory enclaves from outside attack, and NEXOR Directory Boundary Agent, an LDAP high-assurance application-level proxy firewall for Internet directories.

Because of its heritage, NEXOR directory has been involved in conformance and interoperability testing by several organizations. This testing has occurred through formal bodies such as EuroSInet and through industry initiatives such as the World Electronic Messaging Association (WEMA)

Directory Challenge, the European Electronic Messaging Association (EEMA) Interoperability Demonstration, and the Paradise-NameFLOW Project. It is the reference implementation used by international conformance testing bodies.

Although several directory vendors have adopted the "object-oriented" mantra of late, I believe that NEXOR was the first to market with a truly scalable, object-oriented X.500 directory server designed to store 20 million objects on a single directory server. NEXOR Directory uses the commercial Versant object-oriented database as its backing store, providing all the benefits of object-oriented technology in addition to commercial database functionality, such as journaling and distributed storage. The number of concurrent users is limited only by the capability of the host server running the Directory.

NEXOR Directory provides full support for 1993 X.500 distributed operations, including replication using DISP. It also provides a bulk-loading capability that connects directly to the datastore, allowing for very fast data loading from LDIF and flat files. This loading capability has been tested to support data loading at a rate of 250,000 entries per hour. Extraction of existing directory data into flat or LDIF format files can occur at an even faster rate.

NEXOR Directory has a few features that have grown from the demanding mission-critical requirements of service providers and military organizations. A proprietary method of replication allows shadowing at a much faster rate than native DISP. It has the ability to switch rapidly between master and shadow servers in the event of network failures, and any shadow system can instantly take over from the master server. NEXOR Directory also supports strong authentication using X.509v3 certificates. NEXOR Directory is available for Windows NT and Sun Solaris.

3.5.5 Syntegra

A couple of years ago, Syntegra (the consulting services arm of British Telecom) purchased Control Data Systems, Inc. In addition to the Control Data's professional services staff, they inherited the Global Directory Server product. Surprisingly, Syntegra has kept the product alive and has even extended it, creating the Global Directory/Meta Edition (http://www.syntegra.com/what_we_do/directories/), the Aphelion Directory (an extremely scalable, high-volume directory), and Directory Sentinel (a Border directory product).

The Syntegra Global Directory product is used by more than 400 companies, service providers, and government agencies worldwide. In addition to private industry, you will find this product inside the U.S. Department of Transportation, NASA, the National Oceanic and Atmospheric Administration (NOAA), and several state governments. It is a very solid and mature implementation of X.500 and LDAPv3. It is also at the heart of the Syntegra Mail*Hub and Intrastore products.

The Global Directory/Meta Edition adds metadirectory functionality to the Global Directory product. The Meta Edition includes directory synchronization tools that can be used to import, merge, and export directory data with any number of external directory services and data sources. It also includes the WebLink 500 Web service, which is essentially a customizable set of CGI scripts with which an organization can customize a Web-based directory access capability.

Meta Edition also includes the LDAP MetaConnector, which is a sort of DSP-to-LDAP converter. With MetaConnector, an organization's LDAP directory servers appear to be subtrees within the organization's X.500 directory. Naming contexts and access control information is mapped, such that directory users can seamlessly browse and update information in either system and never be aware that they have crossed the boundary between X.500 and LDAP directory servers.

The Aphelion Directory server is a top-end directory server designed to handle "hundreds of millions of entries—on a single server or multiple servers—that can be spread over multiple disks and scaled linearly over multiple CPUs." The Aphelion Directory has been optimized to provide fast startup times and implements advanced searching and indexing techniques to further improve performance. It has a fully multithreaded architecture, allowing it to take full advantage of large, multiprocessor servers. The optional Distributed LDAP Service Module (DSLM) allows a set of separate directory servers to appear as a single directory, accessible through one LDAP-based interface. The Global Directory product family runs on Sun Solaris, Hewlett-Packard HP/UX, IBM AIX, and Microsoft Windows NT.

3.5.6   Siemens DirX

Siemens is yet another vendor that has been providing X.500 directory technology for a number of years. The Siemens DirX directory family (http://www.siemens.com/directory) includes the following components:

- DirX Server is the basic X.500/LDAPv3 directory server product.

- DirXmetahub is the synchronization engine designed to work with the DirX server and provides automated bidirectional synchronization with all connected directories.

- DirXweb provides access to Internet LDAP directories via Web browsers.

- DirXdiscover is a high-end, Windows-based directory user agent (client) that uses LDAP to access directory services.

DirX is an LDAPv3 and X.500 DSA, and the NT version has received the Microsoft-Designed-for-BackOffice certification. Its multithreaded, robust design supports symmetrical multiprocessor (SMP) servers. Intelligent query routing and load balancing ensure that queries are routed to the server that offers the best performance. A proprietary caching methodology improves throughput rates (the X.500 directory standard does not provide for caching, forcing queries to be returned from disk storage rather than cached). DirX provides Secure Socket Layer/Transport Layer Security (SSL/TLS) protection for LDAP servers and clients. It also provides secure management of X.509 public key certificates and has been tested with products from Baltimore Technologies, Entrust Technologies, VeriSign, Xcert, and SmarTrust, among others.

The DirXmetahub component is a bidirectional directory synchronization engine that facilitates the merging ("joining") of information from various directory sources into a single metadirectory database. Directory information formats supported include LDAP; X.500; Microsoft Windows NT; Microsoft Active Directory; e-mail systems, such as Microsoft Exchange and Lotus Notes; IBM RACF; Siebel CRM; human resources, such as SAP R/3 and PeopleSoft HR; ODBC; and structured files in a variety of formats, such as Extensible Markup Language (XML), LDIF, and CSV. Each of these data types is handled by a specific predefined "meta-agent." An interesting feature of the DirXmetahub is the ability to perform direct synchronization from one connected directory to another one, storing the data in the metadirectory datastore. An SDK enables users to develop customized metaagents.

DirXweb, based on a Java servlet implementation, provides simple access from a Web browser to any LDAP or X.500 directory using LDAP. Standard HTML and Java development tools can be used to create HTML pages, and the DirXweb Script Language can be used to implement dynamic directory access from HTML pages.

3.6   LDAP-based directories

We can expect a great number of vendors to come up with Internet Directory or LDAP Directory offerings in the next couple of years. Early entries into this market segment have already been gobbled up by larger companies, and more companies seem to wade into the battle each and every month. One difference between LDAP-based directories and X.500 products lies in the level of Web-based support. Evaluation copies of several of the products noted in this section are available for free from the vendors' Web sites, and a large amount of product documentation is also available for download. You can begin to work with most of these products without signing nondisclosure agreements, purchasing a limited-use version, or even dealing with a salesperson. Who says the Web has not changed the way we do business?

3.6.1   IBM SecureWay

The IBM SecureWay Directory (http://www.ibm.com/software/secureway/directory) is billed as a highly scalable, cross-platform LDAPv2 and LDAPv3 directory server that runs on IBM AIX, OS/400, OS/390, Sun Solaris, and Windows NT. IBM claims that it "can support millions of entries and thousands of LDAP clients." This may be more than just brag, because it uses IBM's DB2 Universal Database as its backing store.

The DB2 Universal Database is a well-known and widely used relational database implementation, used by organizations worldwide. It is extremely scalable and can support databases that are terabytes in size. Given the right hardware, the size of the database and number of concurrent users is, for all practical purposes, unlimited. The SecureWay Directory takes advantage of the underlying DB2 database, providing such features as automatic failover, journaling, and two-phase commits.

Each LDAP operation is treated as a separate database transaction that consists of a start command, a number of individual attribute updates, and an end command. The update is not applied to the database until a "commit" end command is received. If part of the update fails, the entire transaction is rolled back, ensuring that full consistency is retained. Information about updates to the directory is journaled and can be rolled back. Update information is also written to a change log, which can be used by metadirectory products or by applications that cache data (allowing them to determine whether cached data are still current or have been modified).

The SecureWay Directory is standards based and complies not only with the Internet Engineering Task Force (IETF, http://www.ietf.org) LDAP RFCs (1777, 1778, 1779, 1959, 1960, 2251, 2252, 2253, 2254, 2255, and 2256), but also with the Network Application Consortium's (NAC, http://www.netapps.org) Lightweight Internet Person Schema (LIPS) and the Management Task Force (DMTF, http://www.dmtf.org) Common Information Model (CIM) schema, which incorporates the Directory Enabled Networks (DEN) schema.

The SecureWay Directory allows access controls to be defined down to the individual attribute level. Security capabilities include weak authentication (passwords) and strong authentication (crypto-token) support, Secure Socket Layer (SSL) support using X.509v3 certificates, Simple Authentication and Security Layer (SASL) support, and Kerberos 5 authentication with client- and server-side plug-ins that support the GSSAPI SASL mechanism. A security audit function can log LDAP operations, including client IP addresses and the DN associated with each directory bind. The SecureWay Directory is Tivoli-enabled, allowing the SecureWay directory configuration and database to be managed as part of a Tivoli-based organizational network management architecture. The SecureWay Directory Client SDK includes the JNDI API, and an extensible server architecture allows implementers to write server plug-ins (dynamic link libraries or shared objects) that follow the plug-in APIs published by Netscape (making these plug-ins compatible with the iPlanet Directory Server).

As part of the SecureWay Directory solution, the IBM Application Framework for e-business provides a set of metadirectory functions. In this architecture, the SecureWay directory becomes a master directory that contains a superset (e.g., a "join") of all the information in the organization's directories (referred to as "slave" directories). The attributes for an object in the master SecureWay Directory would contain all the attributes for that object in each slave directory.

The synchronization process can be event driven, activated when an object is modified or is added to or deleted from a slave directory. A secondary replication can be set up to propagate this information from the master directory down into all the other slave directories. This secondary replication can be event driven or triggered by a scheduled update.

LDIF data files can be loaded into the SecureWay Directory by two methods. The ldif2db tool provides a Web-based administrative interface for loading and creating LDIF files. For much faster data loading, the bulk-load tool allows the loading of large amounts of LDIF data directly, bypassing many of the directory's data-checking and fault-tolerance features. The bulkload tool does offer a "SCHEMACHECK" option, which can be used to check for schema problems in the data without actually attempting to load the data. IBM recommends that "updates and administration of directory contents occur at the master directory," and notes that "the synchronization function from slaves to the master is provided for the cases when an administrator for one of the slave directories does not have access to the master directory administration tools, or when a slave directory allows its users to update their personal data (such as personal phone number) in that directory." The primary benefit of the SecureWay dirEctory is likely to be found by organizations with expertise with DB2 or with the requirement to support LDAP directories on IBM systems.

3.6.2   iPlanet

iPlanet is a cooperative arrangement between Sun Microsystems and Netscape (now AOL, er, I mean AOL/Time Warner—hard to keep track). Both companies contribute technical expertise and financial support. iPlanet Directory Server (http://www.iplanet.com/directory) used to be the Netscape directory and has its heritage in the LDAP work done at the University of Michigan. iPlanet claims that Directory v5.0 can handle over 50 million entries per server, can import over 1 million entries per hour (bulk loading), and has achieved a query rate of 5,000 queries per second. As iPlanet likes to point out, this directory is the one that runs inside of AOL, handling approximately 30 million users on a 24-7 basis. Whether or not you subscribe to AOL, that's a pretty compelling endorsement of the scalability and reliability of this product. What iPlanet does not tell you is that architecting a directory service like that is no walk in the park. It uses a lot of horsepower and some pretty interesting failover capabilities, but nobody can deny that it gets the job done.

iPlanet Directory is part of the iPlanet family, a group of enterprise-level server products. The other members of the iPlanet family (Enterprise Server, Messaging Server, Calendaring Server, Web Proxy Server, and Certificate Management System) can use the iPlanet Directory to authenticate users, determine group memberships, store user certificates and related information, route mail and other information, and maintain distribution lists.

iPlanet Directory v5.0 is the successor to Netscape Directory v4.0 and has developed the reputation of being a very solid LDAP directory server and is currently used by many international companies and several U.S. government agencies, including the U.S. Department of Defense. iPlanet

Directory v5.0, however, provides even more scalability and several advanced features not available in the Netscape directory offering. iPlanet Directory v5.0 adds the ability to use multiple database back ends, multi-mastering, and chained operations to the Netscape directory product. iPlanet uses a file-based DBMS, which has been highly optimized for directory operations as the backing store, providing the ability to provide impressive performance against very, very large directory databases. It provides the ability to have a single directory server handle several individual directory databases, providing significant improvements in flexibility of indexing and replication. This ability to segment the directory tree into multiple databases permits different subtrees to be defined as individual databases, having different indexes and cache settings. This allows you to fine tune the directory performance and can provide significant improvement in directory updating, replication, and indexing times as compared with the earlier Netscape v4.0 directory.

iPlanet Directory supports both incremental replication and high-speed bulk loading from LDIF files. Schema and access control information are transferred as part of the replication process, ensuring the consistency of replicant directory servers. Version 5.0 adds multimastering, an important capability for creating survivable, distributed directory services. In a multi-mastered architecture, a subtree can be mastered by more than one iPlanet Directory Server. Changes to the individual directory attributes in that subtree are logged along with a Change Sequence Number (CSN). This information is propagated to any other directory servers that either master the same subtree or hold a replica of the subtree (the replication mechanism is the same for both). Changes are posted from this log to the other master. Since only the modified attributes are sent, only those changes are posted. The other attributes in the directory entry remain unchanged. This mechanism can also be used to ensure that the directory service is survivable and can accept updates, even if one particular directory server goes out of service. Updates would be posted against one or more of the other master directory servers, and the downed system would simply recover from the replication log when it comes back online.

It seems, however, that every benefit also brings one or more drawbacks. The new multimastering means that the v5.0 database is incompatible with earlier versions. iPlanet provides a migration tool to aid in moving v4.0 data to the new databases. Also, v4.0 supported both supplier-initiated and consumer-initiated replication. Version 5.0 only supports supplier-initiated replication. A replicant can no longer request changes since the last replication update—it must be able to receive the replication when the master is ready to send it. Also, it becomes critically important that the time clocks on all directory servers be synchronized. Otherwise, updates may fail or give unpredictable results because the CSN values are inconsistent.

Another new feature of v5.0 is a proprietary method of directory chaining. Queries and responses can be passed between iPlanet Directory servers, rather than using referrals to force the user to disconnect and reconnect to another server. This reduces network traffic somewhat but is also much kinder to an organization's security architecture. Corporate firewalls can be configured to allow chained LDAP operations but block direct queries by users. A word of caution is in order, however. Since LDAP performs client/ server authentication and does not provide X.500-based strong authentication (credentials being rechecked by the performing DSA), you should treat any such chained LDAP operations as being anonymous. But I digress; that discussion could be fodder for many, many security discussions (and perhaps another book).

Two additional features new with v5.0 are roles and class of service. Roles is a mechanism that "unifies the static and dynamic group concept supported by previous versions of the iPlanet Directory Server." Typically, roles are used to determine whether a user is of a particular type and can be used to enforce access controls or other authentication decisions. For instance, a role might be "Directory Administrator" or "Help Desk." Class of service allows sharing attributes between entries. These attribute values are not stored with each entry, but they appear as if they were populated within each entry. An example might be "Omaha Office"—each user with that class could appear to have the same office mailing address, street address, helpdesk number, and so on, even though those values were actually part of the class and not present as attributes within each user's entry. Also, you only have to change common information in a single location, rather than tracking down every user who works in Omaha.

A great number of development tools and much information are available for use with the iPlanet Directory. Software Developer's Kits are available for Java, C, and C++. An LDAP-enabled version of Perl is available from Mozilla (http://www.mozilla.org), along with a lot of tutorial information, source code, examples, and other developer resources. An XML gateway (XMLDAP) provides Web developers with the ability to present directory data in multiple formats, such as XML, HTML, WML, DSML, and VXML.

Security functionality includes the ability to define access controls down to the access-control level (based on user name, IP address, or Internet domain name), to support x.509v3-based authentication and to use SSL to encrypt both client/server and server-to-server communications. iPlanet Directory also provides RSA PKCS#11 support for hardware-accelerated SSL, MD5 authentication, and password policy management (min/max, history). iPlanet Directory v5 implements LDAPv2 and v3 RFCs, including 1274, 1558, 1777, 1778, 1959, 2195, 2222, 2247, 2251, 2252, 2253, 2254, 2256, 2279, 2307, and 2377. It is available for Sun Solaris 2.6 and 8, HP/UX 11.0, IBM AIX 4.3.3, Microsoft NT 4 Service Pack 6, and Microsoft 2000 Server Service Pack 1 and Advanced Server Service Pack 1.

IDAR, a companion product, is a reverse-proxy LDAP firewall. IDAR proxies directory queries from multiple users and communicates with a protected iPlanet Directory Server through a single connection. This allows a corporate firewall to restrict access to corporate directory services from the outside world. IDAR has the ability to perform failover between multiple directory servers, should one be unavailable. It also has the ability to perform load balancing between multiple directory servers in high-throughput environments. The iPlanet Directory Server Integration Edition provides additional metadirectory functionality. Changes made to information in other applications are sent to the iPlanet Directory, and modifications to directory information can be propagated back to those and other connected applications.

3.6.3 OpenLDAP

The OpenLDAP Foundation (http://www.openldap.org), established in August 1998, is working to create and promote an open-source LDAP directory server. It is affiliated with the Open Source Initiative, a nonprofit corporation dedicated to promoting open source definition through the OSI Certified Open Source Software certification mark and program. The basic idea behind open source is that programmers will read, redistribute, modify, and debug the source code. This is basically the process by which the Linux operating system has grown so rapidly in capability and gained widespread acceptance. OpenLDAP defines itself as "an open implementation of the Lightweight Directory Access Protocol." The IETF RFCs defining LDAP are obviously freely available. A good deal of the source code for the project appears to be derived from work done at the University of Michigan, including SLAPD and SLURPD (the LDAP directory and update daemons). I personally know of people who have done significant testing and prototyping work using these products. However, I know of nobody who has yet trusted them to support his or her business applications. Bot-

tom line: If you want to play with compiling and modifying your own
LDAP server, this is a good place to start.

3.6.4   Oracle Internet Directory

Oracle Internet Directory (OID, http://www.oracle.com/ip/integrate/oid/
index.html) is Oracle's LDAP-based directory server (what else?). If your
company has Oracle expertise, this is a product that you will probably want
to become familiar with. OID is an LDAPv3 directory service available
with the Oracle9i Application Server. OID supports very high levels of scalability, both in terms of number of entries in the directory and the number
of concurrent users. The underlying Oracle9i database is capable of supporting a datastore of over 1 terabyte, which would translate to storing
somewhere around half a billion (500 million) directory entries—probably
more than most organizations need at present. OID takes advantage of the
tools and services provided by Oracle9i, such as a bulk loading utility based
on Oracle's SQL*loader.

The LDAP servers in OID are multithreaded, using a technology called
"connection pooling"—sharing a common pool of persistent database connections. According to Oracle, this technology "prevents running into
resource limitations as the number of simultaneous LDAP client connections increase." The OID architecture also allows running multiple LDAP
servers on a single Oracle Internet Directory server node, allowing OID to
take good advantage of multiprocessor platforms. In other words, each OID
can support multiple LDAP servers, each supporting a large number of
individual users.

Oracle Internet Directory is designed to take advantage of the high availability features of the underlying database technology. For instance, OID
takes advantage of the Oracle Advanced Symmetric Replication Services
(OASRS) to support a multimastering capability. Change information
within each OID server is recorded in a change log, which is replicated by
OASRS to other OID servers in the community. When an offline server
comes back online, the change log provides the information required to
resynchronize that server with the rest of the community. Administrators
can even add and remove OID servers within the replicated community
without loss of availability or bringing down existing servers. Other features
used by OID include the ability to perform hot backups, to recover quickly
from server failures, and to use such options as Oracle Parallel Server.

Oracle Internet Directory supports simple (password) authentication
and certificate-based authentication through SSL. Access control can be

defined down to the attribute level. OID is part of Oracle's enterprise security strategy. Information, such as user identities, remote user "wallets," and role information, is stored in the OID. When users log into an Oracle database server, the server can connect to the OID to retrieve user configuration and role information in order to set the security context of that user. Using the directory in this fashion permits centralized administration of database user roles and privileges, making it easy to allow or disable access to all systems—for example, when a new employee is hired or when one leaves the company.

3.6.5 Radiant Logic

The RadiantOne Virtual Directory Server (VDS, http://www.radiant-logic.com) is billed as "the New Generation Directory Engine for LDAPv3 directories." You may wonder what sets this product apart from the pack. VDS is not actually a directory server in that it does not store any directory data itself. Rather, it is a sort of a reference engine, storing pointers to data stored in your LDAP directory servers and relational databases. Requests received by the VDS are passed on to the data source hosting the data. So what sets VDS apart from a regular LDAP directory doing referrals?

In addition to LDAP referrals, VDS can pass the query along to a relational database that supports OLE DB, ODBC, or JDBC access. A utility called Intelligent Object Mapping and Cache (IOMC) is used to extract schema and build LDAP namespace hierarchies from relational databases. Essentially, VDC can provide an LDAP-enabled layer that provides a consistent view of an organization's data, whether these data are stored in LDAP-enabled servers or databases. Why is this better than using an LDAP-enabled RDBMS, such as the Oracle Internet Directory or IBM SecureWay?

Ignoring Radiant Logic's advertising claims, the real reason is that most companies have great difficulty creating a single organizational directory— LDAP, X.500, or otherwise. A typical company will have dozens of different "authoritative sources" of data. Technological issues aside, experience has proven (repeatedly) that data ownership and maintenance should be left in the hands of the organization that creates the data. In other words, either copy the data into a metadirectory or maintain a pointer to their native location. VDS does the latter.

The Virtual Directory Server includes a virtual LDAP directory "proxy" to various databases, a Schema Manager tool, the IOMC schema extractor, the DirectoryView Designer Tool, a point-and-click LDAP namespace designer, SmartBrowser, and a Web client. VDS also has a plug-in capability for Sun/Netscape iPlanet and IBM SecureWay Directories. It is available only for the Windows NT, 98, and 2000 operating systems.

3.7   A note on quotations

In the earlier sections on X.500 and LDAP server products, you may have noticed several passages where product capabilities such as scalability and performance were quoted—something like ". . . the ABC directory has the ability to support 'fourteen quadrillion entries and provide nanosecond response times for up to 86 million concurrent users'."

Obviously, I didn't have time to set up each product and empirically test them to verify their performance figures. Any time you see quoted passages as above, I pulled them directly out of the vendors' own product advertising literature or whitepapers. All of the sources used are available electronically on the various vendors' Web sites. If performance figures aren't shown as quotations, then I have had some real-world experience with the product and am fairly confident of the information provided.

4

Migrations, Upgrades, Metadirectories, and Case Studies

by Curtis M. Sawyer and Bob Johnson

4.1   Deployment and legacy system integration strategies

Implementing a corporate directory service is rarely as simple as buying a new product, testing it a little bit, and then rolling it out. All the old stuff tends to get in the way. That old stuff is likely to include every e-mail system, directory service, and legacy application in your organization. You can not throw it away and start over, so you have to deal with it. This chapter discusses directory deployment and the integration of legacy systems, as well as the issues an organization must consider when evaluating approaches to enterprise directory services.

4.1.1   One directory service or many?

Organizations typically have many separate, but related, directories. They also typically have different requirements that each of these directories is attempting to meet. Organizations usually want to create an internal directory service that would aggregate information from several sources and make it available to organizational users and applications. Organizations also typically want to make some data available publicly or to a select number of "trading partners."

This situation raises a question: Are these separate directory services, or are they one? They contain different groups of directory information, with separate users, operational and access requirements, and security issues. The final determination depends on many factors, such as existing architectures, sunk costs, and security requirements. Metadirectory vendors these days are not consolidating disparate directories into a single, physical directory, but rather they are synchronizing directories into a single, logical directory.

4.1.2   Buy or "roll your own"?

Some organizations have significant internal development expertise, including experience with very large databases and with the organizations' specific directory server products. Other organizations have little directory experience and currently outsource. This consideration is really twofold:

1.   Does the organization purchase a metadirectory product or build one?

2.   Does the organization rely on internal staff or external resources to build, configure, and run the metadirectory?

First, because building a custom solution is a significant development effort, and because the metadirectory market has finally matured, commercial products provide a better solution. They can be upgraded as technology evolves, and vendors can provide technical support rather than requiring internal staff support. Second, metadirectory products still require a level of customization that almost requires external resources, either from the product vendor or a contractor familiar with metadirectories.

4.1.3   A multivendor integration project

Depending on the directories being synchronized, it may be the case that no single software vendor will be able to provide all the required product functionality. Regardless, significant effort will be required to interface the new directory service with existing systems. The target solution could potentially be composed of products from several vendors and would require the services of an integrator who has demonstrated experience in building multivendor enterprise directory systems.

4.1.4   X.500 information model

Even with the proliferation of LDAP, many factors have resulted in the X.500 information model remaining the preferred information model. This model includes X.500 directory server products and LDAPv3-based products, which are compliant with the X.500 information model. These factors include a requirement to support Public Key Infrastructure (PKI) products (based on the X.509 standard), interoperability with many existing directory service capabilities, a mature security model including identity-based access controls, and an extensible schema to allow future enhancement.

4.1.5   Replication to border DSAs

To facilitate public access to those directories that require it, and to enhance the security architecture of such an arrangement, a potential solution is a "Border" directory service agent (DSA) or directory. To accommodate public access to the directory, external users should never actually access the directory servers that master directory data. Directory information should be published from the central directory service, located in a secure demilitarized zone (DMZ) usually outside the corporate firewall, into Border DSAs. Users would access these Border DSAs to obtain directory information. This architecture provides significant protection, should one or more Border DSAs become compromised. A reliable method of publishing information to the Border DSAs should be implemented. If the Border directory supports it, the X.500 Directory Information Shadowing Protocol (DISP) can provide this functionality.

4.1.6   LDAP access

The market is clearly moving to the Lightweight Directory Access Protocol (LDAP) for information retrieval. This situation presents a challenge, because the LDAP security model is rather immature and is not compatible with the pure X.500 security model. Many functions provided by X.500, such as identity-based access control and chained operations, are not yet provided in LDAP-based directory products. LDAP started as an access mechanism and does not define either the information repository or the communication protocols between repositories.

4.1.7   PKIs

PKI technologies are becoming critical to organizations' business operations. PKI products are almost universally based on the X.509 standard and use the X.500 information model. An organization cannot have a PKI without a directory to hold the certificates. People connect to this directory in order to retrieve an individual's public certificate so that they can encrypt or decrypt mail to or from that individual. To ensure that the particular "John Smith" in the directory is the correct individual, organizations would like to have additional information in the directory, such as office phone number, title, or postal address. This information certainly exists elsewhere in the organization and would need to be synchronized with the PKI directory.

4.1.8   Access controls

Some organizations will require a compartmentalization strategy to protect directory data from unauthorized disclosure. Specific groups would be allowed to access specific portions of the information held by the directory but restricted from other areas by compartmentalization. The issue with this strategy is that it places a heavy burden on the directory administrators to maintain these access control lists (ACLs) for each directory entry. The easier method administratively would be either to rely on existing access controls for the disparate directories logically combined into an enterprise directory or to use the Border DSA approach. With the Border directory, a very limited set of the directory information can be presented to the public through a directory that is synchronized from the main directory with only those data required by the public. Read access to that information can, therefore, be essentially unrestricted (anonymous).

4.2   Addressing design and implementation issues

The first steps in building a directory services organization are to implement the directory steering groups, as discussed in this chapter, and apply other organizational and political lessons learned from the case studies. Other issues, detailed in the following sections, must be resolved.

4.2.1   Political issues

Internal politics are the most challenging aspect of major projects such as this one. There are many stakeholders, influencers, and contributors. Each enters into the project with his or her own agenda, concerns, and issues. These will range from business, operational, and funding issues to private agenda items relating to enhancing personal power and control. The working group leaders must work to identify and fully address the common issues, to identify and take into account specific issues related to individual suborganizations, and to uncover and remove hidden organizational and personal agenda items. In this way, the leader builds consensus and achieves buy-in from all the stakeholders.

4.2.2   Technical issues

Technical issues can be grouped into three rough categories: coordination, implementation, and evolution.

Coordination issues include the following:

- Developing a consistent enterprise-wide directory schema;
- Connectivity to all infrastructure, existing and legacy services, and directory users;
- Registration and coordination of addressing and naming information.

Implementation issues include the following:

- System architecture and functionality;
- Identification and mapping of data sources;
- Selection and application of appropriate management and migration tools;
- Service-level agreements, both with service providers and with client communities.

Evolutionary issues include the following:

- Maintenance and troubleshooting of the directory service;
- Piloting, testing, and integrating new functionality;
- Upgrading or replacing outdated components;
- Following emerging standards;
- Revising and validating the architecture based on technical advances and new standards.

4.2.3 Business issues

Business issues will relate to the funding, procurement, and operations of an enterprise-wide directory service and would include the following:

- Developing a service and cost model (e.g., enterprise-owned versus outsourced);
- Identification of funding sources;
- Procurement strategy or identification of available contracting vehicles;
- Contracting for a pilot of the proposed solution prior to committing major funding;
- Reuse of existing assets.

4.2.4 Security issues

An enterprise-wide directory would contain information that supports many different business applications within the enterprise. Even though these applications may not be considered mission critical, the aggregate loss of all these applications due to a directory outage may cause significant operational difficulty. Therefore, an organization-wide directory service will quite likely be viewed as a mission-critical asset that must be protected by adequate security measures. Security must be defined centrally, as an enterprise-wide set of issues; however, it must be implemented locally.

Security issues will include the following:

- Creation of security policies and recommendations;

- Validation and approval of proposed security architectures;

- Identification of security risks and mitigation/protection strategies;

- Privacy and appropriate use policies.

4.2.5 Critical infrastructure protection

As mentioned above, an enterprise-wide directory will support many applications and would, therefore, be considered mission critical. Thus, the directory service must be included in any sort of risk analysis and mitigation strategy. The directory must also be survivable to ensure that this information is available at all times.

4.2.6 Operational issues

There are several operational issues an organization must consider. Time synchronization, DAP and LDAP differences, and performance concerns are all documented in the *EMA Challenge '97 Technical Report* and are discussed here since they are still relevant. Readers interested in more detail are urged to contact the EMA for the full report (http://www.ema.org).

Time synchronization

It is important to synchronize network times in a widely distributed global directory services environment. Time synchronization is essential in an X.500 environment. The X.500 protocol is designed such that the clocks of all servers (DSAs) must be in sync to within a very few seconds, but it does not impose any synchronization requirements on the clients (DUAs). Since timing is critical to DSA operations, all administrators for a specific DIT must synchronize their DSAs to the same time. If there is even a small difference in the universal time on the clocks of the systems involved, the consequences are significant. If the originating DSA stamps an operation at 16:00:00 and has set a 15-second time-out, and the receiving DSA thinks the time is 16:00:20, the operation will experience "communications time-out value exceeded" upon reaching the target DSA, even if the communication path is instantaneous, which is unlikely.

The solution is for all the universal clocks in the distributed computers to have the same time values. Accomplishing this solution depends on the directory platforms and the degree of connectivity with other organizations. For a mix of UNIX and NT workstations, the Network Time Protocol (NTP) can set a single system time for all interconnected DSAs across the world. NTP now ships as part of the Sun Solaris operating system. This Internet standard method of ensuring equal clock values and free NTP software is available on the Internet at http://www.eecis.udel.edu/~ntp/ (for UNIX systems) and ftp://ftp.drcoffsite.com (for Windows NT). For NT systems, other time synchronization products are available as well.

DAP and LDAP differences

There is an important difference between the way X.500 DAP and versions of LDAP process certain directory operations. A DUA that uses the DAP protocol performs an X.500 LIST operation by retrieving the Distinguished Names of the immediate subordinates from the knowledge references held by the target DSA. In performing this LIST, the DSA should contact all subordinate DSAs to check each entry's access controls. If a subordinate DSA is unavailable or a response is delayed, then a referral is returned. (Note that some DSAs do not always contact subordinate DSAs during a one-level LIST.) Thus, a DAP LIST inquiry directed at the c=US DSA by DAP DUAs should always return the known subordinates. The LDAP protocol substitutes a SEARCH operation in an attempt to accomplish the same result as a LIST. The LDAP implementations actually search the directory for the subordinate entries themselves in order to construct the response to the inquiry. If a given subordinate DSA is disconnected from the infrastructure or temporarily unavailable, the LDAP DUA does not "find" it and, thus, does not return its entry, because LDAP does not return referrals. Users and administrators should be aware of this important difference between DAP and LDAP DUAs. To ensure reliable results in an LDAP environment, administrators might try replicating organization entries to their parents. This fact is important should the organization use X.500 protocols to connect to a parent organization. In that event, a problem with the superior DSA could impact the performance of the subordinate DSA.

LDAP and X.500 DSAs and DUAs do not always handle errors the same way. Since LDAP does not follow DSA referrals and DAP does, different DUAs can respond with different results from the same search. DUAs can automatically follow a referral, query the user before following a referral, or produce an error. This difference means that LDAP DUAs may return a reduced picture of the DIT. Additionally, DSAs and DUAs also handle actual errors quite differently. While no DUA or DSA should crash or cause a crash, this behavior has occurred in our experience. Beta and untested products contributed to some problems, but X.500/LDAP interoperability is an area the vendors will continue to work on to improve.

Performance concerns

Network problems and delays, coupled with system outages, can cause disruptions in directory service and variable results. The Internet is inherently unreliable. Performance is variable and outages do occur. Whether a link is quick or slow can determine if a time limit is exceeded or not for a particular query. The load on a DSA can also cause exceeded time limits. Users and administrators should remember that performance is dependent on multiple factors and will vary. Some directory features mitigate such problems (e.g., shadowing and alternatives in references).

Again, close coordination by the administrators of interconnected systems is essential to performance, as well as to providing relevant, timely data. Any change in a supplying, receiving, or interconnected system can cause performance problems in the synchronization or response processes.

4.3   Directory migration

Several different groups within any organization maintain portions of the information about a single entity. A person within the organization may have a network login, an e-mail account, a telephone number, a street address, and human resources information. But, different pieces (e-mail address, employee number, telephone number) are administered by different people, probably in different locations. The concept of collecting data from these various sources into a single directory is referred to as a meta-directory.

4.3.1   The metadirectory concept

The original metadirectory concept paper by the Gartner Group described an idealized service that would allow information to be maintained locally by the original data owners but that would provide access to this information from anywhere in the enterprise. This approach resembles most document archiving and knowledge management systems. The underlying concept is to leave the information where it is created and provide a means to allow other parties to access that information securely.

The Gartner paper put forth the concept of a directory "join" drawn from database technology. The concept is similar to a relational database "join," where fields from multiple databases are combined to create a new view. In the idealized "join," all of this information would appear to exist within one single directory entry but would, in reality, comprise portions of multiple data sources. The concept is similar to a relational database "join," where fields from multiple databases are combined to create a new view.

In databases, common ("key") information is used to obtain the records from multiple files, and a new "view" (or "join") is constructed. The common "keys" (e.g., employee numbers, state codes, zip codes, part numbers, invoice numbers) between databases provide the means of connecting ("joining") these disparate records together into a new record ("view"). Figure 4.1 illustrates this concept.

When implementing this concept with directories, an organization will encounter one major issue. It is difficult to design a join of multiple, disparate data sources "after the fact." The key values necessary for joining data are defined when a database is originally designed, not after the pieces have been in service for several years. It is quite difficult to establish common keys between the various data sources that could make up a metadirectory. In the example above, a common key exists in the telephone system, the e-mail system, and human resources. There is, however, often no common key between the various data sources. Even the employee name cannot be guaranteed to be consistent between data sources. For instance, you may have several "John Smith" entries, all referring the same person. A person may be listed as "John Smith," "John Q. Smith," "John Quincy Smith," and "J. Q. Smith" in various data sources. Alternatively, two employees may have the same name across multiple directories. The process of identifying key fields and structuring "joined" databases is known as "normalizing" the database.

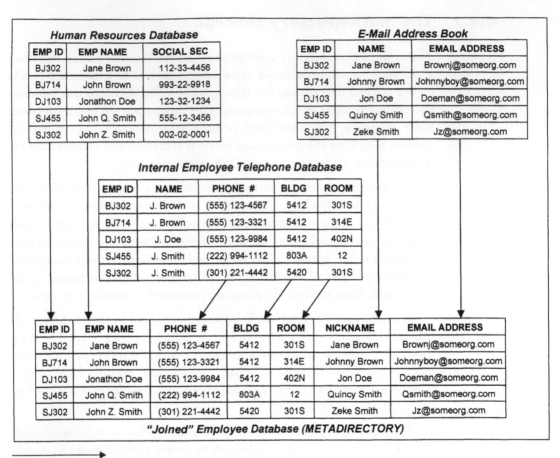

Figure 4.1   *Metadirectory join concept.*

In order to implement a full metadirectory capability, you would need to do the following:

- Identify all the data sources to be combined into the directory.

- Establish a single, authoritative source for each piece of information, such that only one administrator can create that information, and all other parties must use that specific value in their own data repositories (e.g., one person can assign an e-mail account, name, or employee number).

- Establish a registration procedure to ensure that all data sources are created essentially at the same time and that any significant changes are coordinated between the various data sources.

- "Clean" any existing data sources by modifying the data within them to conform to the new process, ensuring that "key" fields are consistent and unique.

Select a metadirectory product that can support incremental "joins" of information, or use a relational database to create a joined view (assuming you can either migrate the data sources to a relational database or import the source data into a database using a technology such as SQL or LDIF).

4.3.2   Metadirectory architectures

The metadirectory architecture the vendors have now embraced involves using connectors to join data from multiple, disparate directories, while leaving the data in the original system. This solution has the following advantages:

- Not introducing yet another repository to be the enterprise directory;

- Maintaining legacy systems that may have a specialized reason for existing;

- Enhancing buy-in from the data owners if their systems are not being replaced;

- Reducing the amount of work required to achieve a consolidated view.

If an organization has a limited number of directories, it may still decide that a consolidated approach is better. The real solution probably entails a combination of directory consolidation, retirement, and synchronization. Determining the solution requires taking the standard steps: performing a requirements analysis, conducting a system survey, and developing a detailed design.

4.3.3   Migration strategy

As elimination of a current directory may be difficult or impossible, organizations should pursue a policy of only allowing replacements that are compliant with the enterprise-wide directory policy and guidance.

In any migration, user buy-in is essential. The political hurdles are far higher than the technological ones. It is critical that users perceive management as helping the organization meet business requirements rather than simply mandating change. By allowing working groups and steering committees to set policy, users will not perceive management as being the insti-gator of this process. The peer review that these working groups provide will also act to increase buy-in.

The following tactics will also aid in obtaining user buy-in:

- *Inventory systems and stakeholders.* Create a fairly comprehensive list of existing and planned directory projects. Use this list as the starting point for identifying the working group participants.

- *Establish information sharing mechanisms.* Conduct as much business as possible electronically to reduce travel expense and interruption to business operations. Create an electronic e-mail distribution list for discussions and a Web-based document-archive site for sharing information.

- *Stimulate initial discussion.* Start generating a groundswell of interest and identifing influencers and stakeholders. Place any available information on the Web server. Send a letter to all interested parties and stakeholders inviting them to join the e-mail discussion group. Assign a moderator from the Chief Information Officer's (CIO) office to conduct the discussion group.

- *Create a steering committee.* The creation of an enterprise directory will require a centralized oversight and coordination capability. We recommend that a steering committee, two working groups, and a directory infrastructure management office be created (Figure 4.2). This division of responsibility better gains buy-in from the various stakeholders and manages the complexity of the project. There is likely to be a certain amount of crossover between the working groups. The primary purpose of the division is to define three major types of issues: business issues, technical issues, and security issues. The goal is to reduce distractions and keep the groups focused on their immediate tasks, rather than engaging in tangential discussions. For instance, the security working group should not be overly concerned with the procurement process or with the directory architecture and operation. Each group should refer issues outside its "charter" to whichever group has a charter to work that particular issue.

- *Create a vision statement and charters for the working groups.* Create initial drafts of policy and appropriate use statements.

- *Create a security working group.* Identify stakeholders and other technical representatives to participate in the security working group.

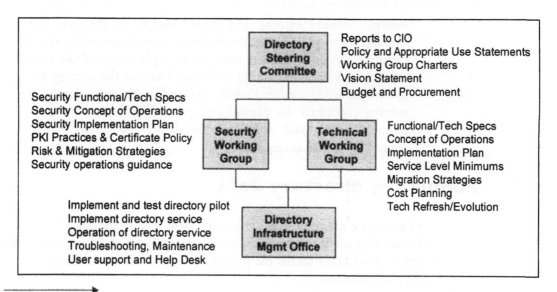

Figure 4.2   *Recommended directory oversight organizational structure.*

Create an e-mail distribution list just for security working group discussions. Identify mission-critical directory-based information and the applications that rely on it and ensure that they are addressed in the critical infrastructure protection plan. Create a security functional and technical specification and concept of operations. Work with the steering committee on an acceptable use policy and security issues. Identify PKI requirements and create a statement of certificate policy and practices. Create a security implementation plan and a security architectures and protections guidance (e.g., for firewalls, guards, and access control). Coordinate with other working groups as needed. Sample plans are sometimes available from the vendor or trade organizations, such as the Electronic Messaging Association. Other organizations may be willing to share their plans, and these types of contacts can be made at trade organization conferences. Organizations may be hesitant to share some plans, however, such as security-related documentation. A vendor or a consultant can provide this type of planning assistance.

■ *Create a technical working group.* Identify stakeholders and other technical representatives to participate in the technical working group. Create an e-mail distribution list just for technical working group discussions.

■ *Create functional and technical specifications and a concept of operations.* Create a target directory architecture. Create an implementation strategy. Identify existing and future sources of directory data. Develop a strategy and guidance for integrating these sources into the directory. Develop migration strategies for replacement of older technologies and reuse of existing resources. Develop the strategy for a directory hosting service. Provide cost and architecture data to the steering committee for planning purposes. Develop a strategy for technical refresh and evolution. Coordinate with other working groups and parties as required.

4.4   Populating directory data

An enterprise directory needs to be populated. If directories are being synchronized purely through the use of connectors, parts of this section do not apply. This section details the process involved when some directories are being consolidated.

4.4.1 Sources of directory data

The most important aspect of defining the sources of information is to locate the authoritative source of all data. For an employee name, it may be a form completed upon hire within the human resources department. For a phone number, it may be the telephone switch software. Determining the authoritative source is essential (regardless of a synchronization or consolidation architecture), because it ensures that the data in an enterprise directory are accurate.

4.4.2 Directory synchronization process

The major components of the directory synchronization process are shown in Figure 4.3. This synchronization process does not assume that connectors are providing one logical view, but rather that directory data are being uploaded to a consolidation directory at some regular interval.

As Figure 4.3 shows, there are two primary methods for using directory synchronization or consolidation utilities to load data into a directory. These methods include the following:

- Extracting the updates from transactional data, such as a log or audit file;

- Obtaining a full dump of the database and comparing it with an earlier version to identify changes.

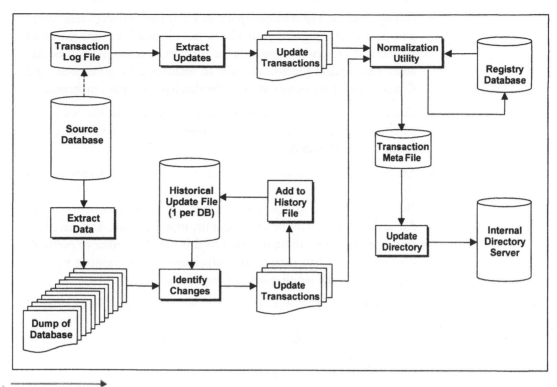

Figure 4.3   *Directory synchronization overview.*

In the first instance, a utility program will extract directory-related transactions from a source's transaction file or audit log. These transaction updates will be provided to the normalization utility (see below), which converts them to a standardized format that will then be provided to the Update Directory function. The Update Directory function applies the transaction updates to the enterprise directory and writes the directory transaction and status to an audit log file.

In the second instance, a complete dump of the source database is compared with a previous version of the same database. The list of changes will be provided to the normalization utility, which converts them to a standardized form that will then be provided to the Update Directory Function.

The main components of the Directory Synchronization Process and their functions include the following:

- *Extract data:* This component will extract a dump of the source database. This extraction will likely be a full dump into a large text file, probably in Comma-Separated Value (CSV) format.

- *Identify changes:* The data dump obtained by the "Extract Data" component will be compared with a historical file of all the data extracted before, and a file containing only the differences (changes) will be created. This update file will contain all additions, modifications, and deletions that have occurred since the database was last synchronized.

- *Add to history file:* These changes will be applied to the historical file. This strategy will keep them from being identified as changes in future synchronizations.

- *Extract updates:* It may be possible to extract information about changes directly from a transaction history or log file, bypassing the "Identify Changes" component entirely. The result will be the same. An update file containing all additions, modifications, and deletions since a given time will be included in this file. A number of methods could be utilized to extract this information from existing sources, depending on the requirements of the data source:

  - X.500 DAP or DSP (Directory Access Protocol or Directory Service Protocol);
  - LDAP (Lightweight Directory Access Protocol);
  - ODBC (Open Database Connect);
  - ODSI (Open Directory System Interface);
  - SQL (Structured Query Language);
  - Proprietary methods.

- *Normalization utility:* The normalization utility will receive update files from each data source, convert the data to a single common format, and create a single transaction metafile containing all updates that need to be applied to the directory.

- *Update directory:* The directory's administrative directory user agent (ADUA) will receive the transaction metafile and apply these updates to the directory. The ADUA will be responsible for logging all transactions and maintaining an audit trail. If the update is interrupted for any reason (e.g., power loss or system failure), the ADUA will be responsible for restarting the update and ensuring that it is fully applied. If specific transactions cannot be posted or if the update process encounters an unrecoverable error, the ADUA will notify the directory administrator of the problem.

4.4.3   Data cleansing and initial load

Data sources are combined ("joined") to form a single metadirectory that contains a consolidated view of information from all three sources. The following two aspects may not be readily apparent, but they are critical to this application:

1.   *Common key:* Each record should have a readily identifiable, unique "key" value. This value is common between all the data sources and becomes the primary key for the join operation.

2.   *Authoritative sources:* Each field or column ("tuple" in relational terms) in the joined metadirectory view is drawn from a specific column in only one database. The source database that provides this field is defined as the authoritative source for that piece of information. An authoritative source must be defined for each data item.

While reviewing the data sources for most organizations, two problems become quite apparent. First, there is no single key value present within all the data sources. Usually there is no single data item, such as an employee ID number, that would be a likely candidate for this common key value. Often, the employee's name appears to be the only common piece of information between databases.

The second problem is that the employee names are not consistent between databases. This inconsistency means the joining of these disparate data sources into a metadirectory cannot be automated. The data values are not consistent and, therefore, cannot be processed programmatically. At this point, human intervention will be required in order to accomplish joining data together into a metadirectory.

Before the directory can be created, several tasks must be accomplished. All authoritative sources of data will be "cleansed." This cleansing will include the following:

- Redundant and expired entries must be removed.

- Each data item for which a database is an authoritative source must be audited and corrected. For example, if the database is an authoritative source for the employee's name, all the names must be examined to ensure that they are correct and complete.

- A common key value will be established in order to facilitate the join. This common key value must be present in all information that is to be synchronized into the directory. Otherwise, there is no means of matching and joining the information. You cannot create a new "view" of data unless there is a common key within each table or database to be joined. This value will be present in the extracted data provided to the normalization process. This decision means that the value will either exist in the source database, or it will be added as a function of the extraction process. We highly recommend that the unique value be added to the source databases. This field can be accommodated by one of the following:

- The preferred solution for any given database will be to add a new field to each data record. Data sources that are based on relational database technology, X.500 or LDAP, should accept this change with little difficulty.
- If unused data fields already exist within the data source, it may be possible to use one of them to contain the unique value. Care must be exercised to ensure that the unique value is not accidentally overwritten or modified, once established.
- The unique value could also be concatenated to a field that already exists in the source data. The extraction process would separate that field into its component values before sending the data to the normalization process.
- If none of these three approaches are viable, the only remaining possibility will be to create a separate database or table that maps unique values to records extracted from the data source. There are many problems inherent to this approach. In order to accomplish the join operation that marries the unique ID to the extracted records, each record must have a unique key field that is unchangeable. This key field could be the employee's name or even a record number within the source database. The data source does not have to be authoritative for this field. It would only be used to look up the correct unique ID value when extracting records for directory synchronization. Maintenance of this unique ID table or database would almost certainly be a manual process.

- The authoritative source for the unique ID data element will establish a unique ID for each entry maintained by it, and this item will be the initial data feed into the directory synchronization process. This strategy will cause the data items from that source to be added to the enterprise directory. Data from other authoritative sources will only be added after those sources have added the unique ID field and have cleansed their databases. These other authoritative sources will be added singly, verifying operation of the directory synchronization process for each source. When all authoritative sources have been added, population of the enterprise directory will be complete.

■ After the enterprise directory is established, the unique ID value will be included in all new entries created in the various authoritative data sources. The process that originally creates an entry that appears within the directory will be the only authoritative source for the unique ID value. The act of creating a new entry will cause the directory synchronization process to add the new entry to the enterprise directory. As information is created within the various other authoritative data sources, each will reference the enterprise directory in order to obtain the correct unique ID value for inclusion within the new entry. In this manner, all new entries within the authoritative sources will be populated with the correct unique ID value for that entry. Therefore, the directory synchronization process will have the information needed to perform the join between the various authoritative data sources.

■ Once the enterprise directory has been completed, we recommend that the various consumers of the data within the enterprise directory also begin cleansing their databases. This cleansing would consist of updating all the nonauthoritative data items within the various data sources and consumers so that they align with the data values held within the enterprise directory.

4.4.4   Initial entry application

While it is a laudable goal, there is usually no single system that can provide an initial entry point for creation of entries for the directory. Hiring a new employee, bringing on a contractor, or allowing an external customer access to directory systems all begin as manual paper processes. This information is entered somewhat asynchronously into various systems. Synchronization connectors must bear the burden of consolidating information in this case.

4.5   Politics and religion: who owns the data?

The seven-level ISO "stack" provides a model for describing communication systems, starting at the bottom with a physical layer, and moving upward to data link, network, transport, session, presentation, and application layers. A standing joke states that the most problematic layers of this seven-level stack are levels eight and nine, politics and religion. Regardless of the technical merits of the proposed solution, levels eight and nine can kill a project. If you cannot gain control of the political and ownership (religion) issues, your directory project is headed toward serious difficulty. More directory projects have failed and more money has been wasted as a result of political infighting and turf battles than any other single cause—perhaps more than all other causes combined.

4.5.1   Reality of politics

In an organizational directory project, there is rarely (if ever) a single person or position that controls the technical specifications, business requirements, budget, cost/profit accountability, implementation, user applications, and support staff. Yet, all of these functions must cooperate in order for a complex directory implementation to be truly successful.

Organizational structure

Most large organizations in the world today did not emerge fully grown. Rather, they evolved over time, growing, capturing, and integrating other organizations into the larger whole. Today's global corporation is actually a conglomeration of smaller, often very independent, business units. For example, General Motors sells cars, trucks, recreational vehicles, parts, service, financial services, and many other related products. Each segment of a large corporation is usually a separate business unto itself, with separate management and information systems. The business and information systems used by each business unit evolved to support that particular business unit and are probably not the same as, or interoperable with, similar systems in the other business units.

Typically, there are two groups within the organization that manage the interface between the various business units: corporate accounting and corporate information systems. More often than not, the centralized corporate information systems division is involved in an ongoing turf battle over control of the information systems used within the various business units. Directories are often seen as a means of sharing information between the business units of a large organization. In many organizations, a cross-functional working group already exists to study and iron out problems arising from the tug of war between the organization's desire for free flow of information and cost reduction, and the individual business units' desire to control their own systems, information, and business practices. Needless to say, the results obtained by such cross-functional working groups vary greatly because of the politics involved. Before implementing your organizational directory service, it is very possible that you will be required to build your business case, present it to a similar working group, and justify it to all the various business units before receiving funding and permission to proceed. Be prepared.

Roles and stakeholders

Half of the battle in approaching the politics within any organization is to identify all the stakeholders in the project. Understanding the roles, responsibilities, and motivations of these people can help you identify and manage the politics of the projects. Some of the roles you will encounter include the following:

- *Recommenders.* Recommenders learn the issues, perform a reality check, and pass their approval or disapproval to those who are managing the project. The recommender is one of the most influential and important people to work with, because he or she can kill the project before it ever gets started. If you are reading this book, chances are very high that you are a recommender.

- *Seymours.* Seymours are a special class of techie. They claim to be recommenders, but in reality they just like to play with cool stuff and learn new things. Typically, management does not have high confidence in the recommendations of Seymours because they tend to like fancy, high-tech solutions to problems that can be solved by more pragmatic, cost-effective means. These people are called Seymours because regardless of how much information the vendor provides, they always want to "see more." They are the ones who like to get every product from every vendor on a free trial basis and set up a lab to "investigate the issues and compare available products."

- *Tirekickers.* Tirekickers are a subclass of Seymours. They simply want to be involved. It does not matter what the topic is. If there is a meeting being held, they want to be part of it. They can pull a meeting or an entire project off track because they do not really have a stake in its success. If it fails, there are plenty of other meetings to attend and "contribute to."

- *Project managers.* Project managers are the first tier of management that will be held accountable for the success or failure of the project. They will likely be technically oriented, but will not have the time required to understand all the nuances of every product. They are responsible for obtaining budgets and approval to proceed. They rely heavily on the recommenders.

- *Approvers, budget authorities, and final authorities.* These roles can be filled by separate people, or they can be shared between people depending on an organization's size and structure. If the approver and budget authority is not the same person, you may have to prove your business case twice in order to get the "go ahead." The final authority is typically top management, who is quite likely to be involved in approving the project because of its magnitude, either in cost or in impact to multiple business units. Often, the final authority relies on recommendations from the manager and budget authority. Some- times, however, this person will ask very difficult questions and will not want a drawn-out discussion of the technical merits. He or she will just want to know how a project will improve business operations and impact the bottom line.

- *Users.* Users are the most often ignored and maligned stakeholders in a project. Many organizations have planned a major system, such as a directory service, dropped it on a completely unsuspecting user com- munity, and then are invariably surprised at the complaints they receive and astounded by the fact that the users avoid the new system like the plague. Users can make or break such a project, and it does not cost much to talk to them. If the proposed directory project is supposed to solve a problem, it might be a good idea to ask the users what problems need solving.

- *Coaches.* A good coach is the most valuable person that you can find. The ideal coach knows the organization and its politics and does not have any personal stake in the outcome of the project. Coaches help you find the speed bumps and potholes in the road of progress and help you figure out how to manage the politics surrounding a project.

- *Naysayers.* Every project will include a naysayer from time to time. This person will offer a thousand reasons why a project will fail. Usu- ally, this person is ignored and avoided by all the other stakeholders. Be very careful, because there may be a grain of truth underneath all that pessimism. Your challenge will be to uncover that nugget of knowledge without stimulating even more predictions of doom and gloom. Also, your interest in finding that nugget of truth might be interpreted by the naysayer as personal interest. When this happens, the naysayer can suddenly turn into your "best buddy" (at least in his or her mind). This might sound funny, but it happens quite often.

Ridding yourself of a clinging naysayer is a very difficult and tricky task. You do not want to hurt the naysayer's feelings, and you probably do not need another blood enemy. It's sort of like pulling off a leech, without hurting the leech.

Data ownership

Data ownership is the religion upon which directory services are built. In a large organization, the directory will contain information that originates from a variety of sources. Each one of these sources believes it "owns" that information and has the right to determine how it is created, used, and destroyed. These sources are probably right, even if the people responsible for corporate information systems (and the organizational directory service) believe otherwise.

A directory service is essentially a publishing medium. It is designed to contain information that is rarely modified, but accessed frequently. There is no golden rule that states that the information contained in the directory has to be created and maintained in the directory. Earlier we discussed directory synchronization issues. One of the most powerful uses of directory synchronization is to allow the owners of data to maintain their own, local master version of that information. The owners decide how much of that information is acceptable for public use and place a subset of their information into the directory service. This leaves ownership in their hands and allows them to decide how much information to share with the world at large. This is essentially the metadirectory concept.

The biggest problem with this approach arises when the directory is to be used to aggregate information from various sources into a single, consolidated directory entry. This is the directory "join" problem discussed in Section 4.3.1. This problem of combining information from disparate sources is technically challenging. It can be quite deadly from a political standpoint. Owners of directory data may not want their information combined with other information. Also, the amount of information that is acceptable to be published can be quite different. For instance, the people responsible for telephone systems might believe that all the information about people within the organization, their locations, and their phone numbers should be publicly available. The human resources staff might want to see that information widely available within the company but restricted to a dozen or so "public" contact numbers, such as marketing, legal services, employment, and general information. Security may believe that it is dangerous to place any location information into the directory because it could be used to identify where a specific employee can be found. Sorting through these "usage" issues will consume a great deal of time and energy when designing and implementing an organizational directory service.

4.5.2 Building consensus

Yes, we have painted a pretty bleak picture with regard to the political issues surrounding your upcoming directory project; however, the following suggestions should prove fruitful as you try to manage the wind and waves of your own political maelstrom:

- *Management direction and approval.* First and foremost, you need a vision. The overall goal and direction must be clearly stated by someone who is so high in your organization that the individual stakeholders do not feel that they can argue. The vision statement does not have to be concrete. In fact, it should be fuzzy enough that the participants can all feel that they will be included. A typical vision statement might sound something like this:

  > *It has come to the attention of the Board of Directors that many of our information systems have a requirement to share information that is common between our organizational units. In the interest of gaining efficiency and better supporting each unit's information services systems and staff, we believe that this issue should be examined to determine whether a corporate directory service would cost effectively provide this type of function in light of each business unit's operational and financial goals.*

  The purpose is to set the expectation that every stakeholder will be involved and that there will be some sort of top-level evaluation of the results.

- *Create a public forum.* Working groups are great places for issues like this to be "examined." The problem with such groups is a phenomenon we like to call "analysis paralysis." The group can become so involved in surfacing and discussing problems and issues that no actual work is accomplished. A public forum is necessary to provide a level playing field where all the stakeholders can vent their grievances and concerns; however, someone has to be in charge of cutting off discussion after a reasonable length of time and bringing the group back to the topic. The working group should also be responsible for producing an issues paper and general requirements document, which provide the foundation for the directory service implementation plan.

- *The implementation plan.* The directory service implementation plan will detail how the working group's issues and requirements are addressed. The implementation plan should be developed by your own technical staff or by a hired consultant or directories expert. From experience, it is a poor idea to have the working group help with development of an implementation plan. Remember the old adage, "an elephant is a mouse designed by a committee." Also, remember to take politics into account. The working group will likely have several members whose agenda it is to make sure that the proprietary interests of their own business units are protected and served, regardless of the impact to other business units or the overall organization.

■ *Getting buy-in.* After an implementation plan is created, it will be time to reconvene the working group to review and approve the plan. The working group should review the implementation plan to ensure that each business unit are issues and concerns have been adequately addressed. At this time, do not be surprised if stakeholders try to bring additional requirements and issues to the table. Although you would think that getting approval of the implementation plan should be fairly straightforward, you may discover that it is a painful and time-consuming process.

After you (finally) achieve consensus, it is time to brief top management. Remember the vision statement noted earlier? You will want to brief top management on the implementation plan and how it addresses the concerns put forth by each business unit. You should do everything to ensure that a representative from each affected business unit is in attendance at this briefing, purportedly to answer any questions that might arise. The real reason is to ensure that they affirm their support of the plan to top management, making it much more difficult for them to raise objections after the project gets started. Good luck.

4.6   The business case for directory services

How much will it cost to implement your organizational directory service? Finding a realistic answer to this question is perhaps the most daunting task facing any organization contemplating a directory services project. The actual purchase price of the directory software components is usually only a small percentage of the overall system cost. Vendors usually ignore the other costs related to implementing directory systems. Decisions with regard to product can have significant implications for total cost of ownership. For example, the choice of one directory technology over another can have significant impacts on infrastructure, support, and maintenance costs. You must identify these costs and the potential benefits to be derived from the new directory service.

4.6.1   Potential benefits

The main purpose for an organizational directory service is the publication of various sorts of information. Anticipated benefits would include the following:

- *Availability of Information:* Users and business applications will ideally be able to go to one place in order to get the information they need. The directory is an ideal place to aggregate many different types of information into a single, easily accessible resource.

- *Accuracy of Information:* The simple act of cleansing the data will result in more accurate data, because information that is outdated and incorrect will be purged. As information is consolidated, data will be standardized as well.

- *Improved Security:* One primary use of directory services is the support of public key infrastructures used for identification and access control. When used to support a PKI, the directory service becomes an important part of your security infrastructure.

- *Customer Satisfaction:* Improved business practices lead to better customer satisfaction. In addition, the directory service can make information available to customers or can provide information to Web-based applications used by customers.

- *Account Provisioning:* The data flow for employees entering and exiting the organization will be clearly defined as a result of the consolidation process. With this process clearly defined, account provisioning will be easier, faster, and more accurate.

- *Optimized Administration:* Through the elimination or consolidation of systems, administrative resources can be optimized. Discovering that there are several organizations administering similar systems or applications can also result in knowledge sharing between administrators.

- *Position and Role Management:* Key to understanding how and when directories are updated is knowing how data flow in and around an organization, as well as the hierarchy associated with those data. By clearly defining this hierarchy as part of implementing a metadirectory, an organization will gain a detailed understanding of who "reports to" whom, which is useful for future workflow applications and targeted communications.

4.6.2   Risk analysis and mitigation

A directory service can help to solve certain problems within your organization. Problems, or risks, should be analyzed to determine whether the proposed directory service is an effective mitigation strategy or whether other solutions might be as effective. Just because a problem could be cured with a directory service does not mean that a directory service is the best solution. For instance, you could use a directory to store information about items in inventory; however, if you work for a manufacturing company, a traditional inventory control system would be a more effective solution. If you are a realty company, a directory service may be the ideal place to store information about your "inventory"—properties listed for sale.

Directory services present their own set of risks to be considered carefully. Because a directory is an information repository, the primary risks have to do with unauthorized disclosure of sensitive information, reliance upon the accuracy of that information, and the impact on business operations should the directory service become unavailable. Each of these risks should be listed and a determination made as to its effect on your business operations. This can either be stated as the severity of the impact or in monetary terms. For example, if you rely upon PKI information stored in your directory, the directory could become a mission-critical application. The loss of that information or the directory service itself could prevent users and applications from performing their normal functions.

Once the set of risks and impacts is identified, you should consider the range of possible mitigating strategies for each risk in order to determine which ones are cost effective and should be implemented as part of the directory solution. Mitigation strategies can be technical, physical, or procedural. They almost always incur costs that should be considered when planning for the directory service.

4.6.3   Total cost of ownership

A directory project is a complex system integration task, not just a simple product purchase. Directories are infrastructure components. Although they are usually implemented to support a specific application, it is not long before the directory service is seen as a means to publish other types of information or to support business applications. This tends to disperse the cost of directory implementations across multiple applications. Some organizations presume the total cost of implementation is contained within the initial applications and future applications do not share in the infrastructure costs. Other organizations prefer to amortize the infrastructure cost across both current and future applications.

Very few organizations have developed experience with the real cost of owning organization-wide directory infrastructures. A few global and Fortune 500 corporations have implemented organizational directories, but few formal analyses of life-cycle costs are available (except from consulting firms that specialize in electronic commerce). A life-cycle or Total Cost of Ownership (TCO) model may prove useful in projecting the overall cost of implementing such a system. Factors that initially seem rather small can have a major impact on the total cost of ownership.

Total cost of ownership includes the total direct, indirect, and hidden costs of the project during its lifetime. TCO is based on the concept of life-cycle cost. It acknowledges direct costs, such as products and labor, but also attempts to identify hidden and indirect costs, such as required network upgrades, reporting and management costs, and lost-opportunity costs. The financial success of a directory project may depend on your ability to identify these factors and to monitor and manage them during the life of the project.

Because of the variability of the factors affecting TCO, it is impossible to come up with a single "correct" set of assumptions. Each organization must create its own cost model, specific to its unique environment. Only then can the expected impact of product and implementation decisions be identified and measured.

Although construction of a TCO model is outside the scope of this book, here are some suggestions for approaching the problem:

- *Create a baseline.* You have to develop an understanding of your current systems and their total cost to own and operate. This becomes your cost baseline, against which any modification, enhancement, or new system can be measured.

- *Identify project phases.* The project should be subdivided into the following major work phases:

  - *Prototyping.* These are the activities that an organization will go through while learning about directories and selecting an approach that seems technically and organizationally feasible.

  - *Planning.* During this phase, the organization will lay down the implementation groundwork. Planning includes development of policy, requirements, architecture, and a security plan for the directory implementation.

- *Procurement.* This phase can be as simple as selecting products from a GSA schedule or commercial product catalog, or as complicated as conducting an open competition between multiple vendors.

- *Project review.* This phase is often overlooked but is critical to the success of the project, especially in open procurements. All plans are revisited to ensure that the project is still on track.

- *Development.* This phase contains all activities required to achieve an initial operational capability using the directory system, including network enhancements, configuring servers, directory-enabling applications, and developing training.

- *Initial operating capability.* During this phase, initial production capability will be established and tested. Typically, this involves most of the infrastructure and one or two client sites. When this phase is completed, an evaluation should be performed to ensure that the project is on track. Rollout activities will be planned, budgeted, and scheduled at the end of this phase.

- *Rollout.* Typically, directory projects are implemented in stages, bringing groups of users online by location or by major application. This phase contains the cost for bringing up a given location or application and should be repeated as required.

- *Operational capability.* The ongoing costs of operating the directory service are identified here, including administration, help-desk operations, and maintenance.

It is useful to identify these major phases and milestones in your project plan, not only as a method of categorizing costs but also as a precursor to managing the costs of the directory project once it is underway.

- *Identify tasks within each phase.* Once you have identified the major phases of your directory project, identify the individual tasks that will be required to perform that phase. Estimated costs will be applied to these tasks, so try to develop a complete set of tasks for each phase. This list can be as detailed as you feel it should be. For instance, you could have a single task to install a new server, or you could break that down into the following individual tasks:

  - Order hardware and software.
  - Arrange for power, desk space, and rack space.

- Allocate network addresses; update routers and host configuration tables.
- Install new system hardware and operating system.
- Configure and test new system.

- *Identify cost components for all tasks.* The costs associated with each task should be separated into categories, such as system costs, staff costs, outsourcing costs, and indirect costs. These categories would be totaled for each phase and for the project as a whole. This can be quite useful in determining cost differences between different approaches. For instance, having a vendor perform the directory design and implementation would drastically reduce your staff costs by shifting those costs to the outsourcing costs columns. Many organizations forget to take into account the "hidden" costs involved in a major project, such as reporting, project management, and lost-opportunity costs. These can be estimated through the indirect costs category.

4.6.4   Cost-benefit analysis

Each cost model that you create will describe a single potential implementation. As you think through your options, you will discover that simple issues such as choosing a specific vendor can have significant impact on the overall project plan and resulting costs. It is quite likely that you will be evaluating several possible options. In this case, build a cost model for each option. Once you have a valid set of models, you can perform a traditional cost-benefit analysis to determine the most cost-effective solution for your particular company.

If you have never performed a cost-benefit analysis, there are several good books on the subject and many business consultants can help you through your first one. Generally speaking, the goal is to identify the benefits of a particular situation and develop a value for those benefits. Then, you can judge whether the value derived from the benefits is worth the cost (from your TCO model).

4.6.5   Factors that can affect cost of ownership

Some of the costs attributable to the directory project are incremental in that they are required to support the project, but offer other future benefits. For instance, if network bandwidth must be improved to support an organizational directory, the users will obviously benefit in other ways. The organization must decide how to handle these costs. Are they simply sunk into the directory project, or are they apportioned in some manner?

Apportioned costs

Some costs may be attributable to the project, but receive cost recovery from other projects in the future. This is especially applicable if the business unit or department implementing the directory infrastructure works as a fee-for-service unit within the organization rather than as an overhead cost, or if the cost is shared by multiple business units or lines of business within a large corporation. Geographic considerations may also affect the apportionment of directory service costs. If the main servers exist in Chicago, but users in London and Tokyo also require access, you may have significant telecomm costs, or you may decide to replicate information to shadowed servers at those offices. These costs might be allocated to the directory project, or to the specific sites, or perhaps even recovered through fee for service.

Product pricing strategies

Vendors have four basic approaches to size-based prices, and those strategies can have a significant effect on the initial purchase cost of a directory service and on the future growth of such a system. Most directory products are priced according to volume. Therefore, the more entries you want to keep in your directory, the more you have to pay.

- *Per server.* You pay one price per server, regardless of the number of entries you put into the directory. As your directory grows, you do not incur additional expense. You should be aware that the vendor might have different pricing depending on the host system that the directory runs on. Although the directory server may be the same for a single-processor Windows NT and a multiprocessor Sun system, the Sun version may be substantially more expensive.

- *Per entry.* You pay a certain amount for each entry stored in the directory. As your directory grows, you have to add more entries to your license. There is usually a base price for the directory server itself, in addition to the per-entry license. This type of arrangement can give you fine granularity of cost control, but can create difficulties when you are adding entries and run over your license limit.

- *Per seat.* A few vendors may price their directory service according to the number of users that can use it concurrently. If you have a low-volume directory requirement, this may be a cost-effective way to go.

However, the costs can mount quickly for an organizational directory when you are required to increase your usage license to handle the load as usage increases.

- *Tiered pricing.* This is the most common directory pricing strategy. For example, if you purchased a size "range" or limit of up to 15,000 entries, you would be required to pay an upgrade fee to a higher tier, perhaps up to 50,000 entries, when you went over 15,000 entries. This is probably the simplest approach to directory pricing and is a good trade off (unless you have the misfortune to need only 16,000 entries).

- *Consulting services.* Microsoft Meta Services (formerly Zoomit Via) is not a shrink-wrapped product and can only be "purchased" by retaining Microsoft in a consulting engagement.

System costs

The cost of the directory hardware is an obvious cost of implementing a directory service. Be sure to take into account hardware requirements that come from directory survivability and security requirements, such as redundant or high-availability servers and firewalls and backup software.

Infrastructure impacts

You must understand and consider the impact of directory systems on existing network infrastructures. Not only will additional computer systems be added to support the directory service, but the use of directories can also impose new network traffic and create new security concerns. As the directory becomes more widely used, the number of directory users, the directory topology, and security issues will have substantial and possibly unexpected impacts on existing network capabilities. Along with additional systems come additional system administrator, network operation center, and help desk manpower requirements.

Security concerns

Because the information stored in your directory service will support users and business applications, that service will normally be considered mission critical to your organization. It can be an attractive target for various forms of attacks. Unauthorized disclosure of information is a primary concern. If sensitive information is to be placed in the directory, be sure that the directory can restrict access to information based on the requestor's identity. This requires that you can actually prove the identity of a directory user. Since LDAP is the most common means of directory access today, you should clearly understand the security mechanisms provided by LDAP and their limitations. Implementation of a Border, or "Sacrificial," directory server is a good way to restrict access to sensitive information. Using this approach, only a small portion of your information is available to the public. The information in your internal directory system is not visible to the outside world.

Availability of information in the directory is usually a major concern. Strategies to make this information available at all times can include redundant servers, hot-standby backups, shadowing, and high-availability servers. Each of these approaches adds costs.

In-house versus outsourcing implementation

The natural tendency is for an organization to assume full responsibility for designing and implementing the new directory service. This is fine, assuming that the organization is capable of designing complex network integration projects and is willing to learn about directory systems. Directories are complex and many of the pitfalls are not immediately obvious. Any company contemplating an organizational directory service should seriously consider using the services of an outside directory expert. This expert may, or may not, be provided by the directory vendor. Remember that the expert provided by the vendor will be working for the best interest of that vendor. An independent designer can help your project, not only by bringing his or her experience to the table but also by serving as a sanity check on the vendor and the design of your proposed directory system.

Support costs

Do not forget to include support cost in your TCO calculations. These include the maintenance costs for your directory software, directory-enabled applications, and the systems that they run on. Most vendors provide "major version upgrades" on a one- to two-year cycle. Moving from a previous version to the next major release typically involves an upgrade charge and usually requires significant effort to migrate existing services to the new version of the software. The cost to upgrade and the resources required to test and implement new versions should be considered in your overall cost of ownership. Do not forget the costs of implementing user software, training the users, training your helpdesk personnel, and handling the additional helpdesk work due to directories. If you have a network operations center, the systems in the NOC will likely require additions, upgrades, or at least reconfiguring to be able to monitor the health and performance of the directory components.

Management and administrative costs

Last, but certainly not least, do not forget to include a reasonable amount of management and administrative overhead. Planning, monitoring, progress reporting, budgeting, and project costing all take up significant amounts of management's time. It is not unrealistic to allocate 15 percent to 25 percent of a project's cost to managerial and administrative overhead. If you think this is unrealistic, just consider the cost of preparing one status report and presentation to upper management. Accumulating and checking facts, writing the report, preparing the presentation, rehearsing, and actually delivering a ten-minute presentation may require a full day of preparation. If you do not know how to develop a reasonable cost for administrative overhead, we suggest that you allocate a 25 percent cost factor (20 percent of the total). In other words, if the project is anticipated to cost $80,000, add another $20,000 to cover administrative and management overhead. Additionally, allocate contingency costs of 10 percent to 20 percent to cover any cost overlooked or unanticipated, such as training, documentation, backup and recovery hardware, software, or an end-of-project celebration.

4.7   Directory metrics: collecting useful data

Directory metrics is concerned with the monitoring and maintenance of directory performance based on critical operating requirements. This section discusses performance indicators, including fault management, and access information and storage.

4.7.1   Performance indicators

Performance management consists of observing, tracking, storing, analyzing, and controlling the following:

- Usage trends and response times;

- Threshold parameters and control features of the components.

Performance data should be automatically collected and processed. Usage trends can help determine component sizing, the off-peak time suitable for directory synchronization or replication processes, and the type of information people need. If the directory stores phone numbers and e-mail addresses, but users are only looking up e-mail addresses, either there is a user-awareness issue or a user-requirements issue. Response times are particularly useful for measuring if a directory product is meeting or exceeded the advertised capabilities. If a directory is frequently operating at threshold, that knowledge will enable the deployment of additional servers or lead to upgrades before the problem becomes chronic.

Closely related to performance measurement is fault management. Fault management is concerned with the detection and reporting of directory failures or errors. The directory should have an automated capability to detect and resolve troubles. This capability should include monitoring the performance of the service or system components, isolating faults as the service or system begins to degrade or, as it fails, directing repair activities.

4.7.2   Access information and storage

As part of the performance and fault collection process, be sure to collect and store information about who is accessing the information in the directory. An external directory available for public connectivity can provide valuable data. For example, a site may be mining your directory to build junk e-mail distribution lists or to target your employees for other job opportunities. Having the capability to discover this abuse of the directory can enable a system administrator to take remedial action. Additionally, usage trend analysis could show that certain divisions within the organization are using the directory more or less than other divisions, enabling the directory organization to target specific divisions for marketing. A distributed architecture would greatly benefit from locating servers near the high-utilization areas. Even if there is no immediate need for this information, in the event of unauthorized access, security personnel will be glad the information is available.

4.8   Case studies

The following case studies contain lessons learned from U.S. government civilian directory efforts from 1996–2000. Some efforts were pilots or experimental efforts, but some, such as the General Services Administration's internal directory, were operational programs. Additionally, the USGold program still exists as the Federal White Pages, available at http://www.directory.gov.

4.8.1   Health and Human Services (1996)

In 1996, the U.S. Department of Health and Human Services (HHS) began a pilot initiative to implement an X.500 DSA containing all of the

existing, publicly accessible information on all employees across all 12 operating divisions (OPDIVs). Its goal was to accomplish the following:

- Establish an agency-wide DSA;

- Connect to the U.S. Government On-Line Directories (USGold)
  X.500 infrastructure;

- Participate in the Electronic Messaging Association's (EMA) Directory Challenge '97.

HHS successfully achieved these goals. Although the EMA participation
was added as a goal six months into the project, it was an important one
since it established HHS as a pioneer in X.500 within the U.S. government.
HHS' directory was closely modeled after USGold. In fact, the Center for
Electronic Messaging Technologies (CEMT) both created USGold and
assisted HHS in its pilot. As a result of this collaboration and HHS's goal of
USGold interoperability, the HHS X.500 schema was the U.S. government
schema.

While X.500 succeeded in meeting the goals of HHS as a pilot effort, it
did not become an agency-wide solution. The biggest contributing factors
included the following:

- Since this initiative came out of the Office of the Secretary, it met
  resistance from the other OPDIVs, which tend to function independently.

- HHS had invested six to seven years into its current central directory
  and was hesitant to switch to a different mechanism without greater
  user demand.

- No "killer application" existed for X.500 to make it a necessity
  throughout the government.

- The users were happy with the existing mechanisms and were not
  demanding X.500.

- None of HHS's current applications used or required X.500 at the
  time.

4.8.2   EMA Directory Challenge (1997)

The Electronic Messaging Association's Challenge '97 was to bring together
1993 version X.500 directory vendors, services providers, system architects,
and users to accomplish three objectives:

1.   Facilitate the development of global, public directory services;

2.   Demonstrate directory vendor interoperability;

3.   Demonstrate the use of a directory infrastructure supporting multiple applications.

Table 4.1 lists the participants in the EMA's Challenge.

As the *Directory Challenge '97 Technical Report* (EMA, 1997) stated:

> *The Directory Challenge '97 is an unprecedented demonstration of the interconnection of electronic directories of a broad spectrum of user organizations, vendors, and government agencies located worldwide. This capability was demonstrated first at EMA'97 in Philadelphia, PA. The EMA'97 show was a successful demonstration of a global X.500 directory implementation. This initiative went beyond previous pilots and demonstrations to show a feature-rich, practical X.500 directory infrastructure implementation that supports global communications and specific networked applications. The demonstration provided a highly visible venue for X.500 technologies and provided another case for the need for and feasibility of a public directory service.*
>
> *The Challenge was a success, with perhaps the greatest outcome a collection of lessons learned during the creation of a globally connected X.500 architecture. Major lessons learned were in the extent of differences between the Lightweight Directory Access Protocol (LDAP) and the X.500 Directory Access Protocol (DAP), between different vendor implementations of X.500, and between different Directory User Agents (DUAs) used to view and search X.500 implementations. Another important lesson learned was in the performance issues involved with a global X.500 infrastructure. Many system architecture and design issues would need to be solved before a global infrastructure could become practical.*

The 1997 World EMA Directory Challenge also identified a number of technical problems that have yet to be adequately addressed:

- *Internet time-outs.* Most X.500 servers worldwide depend on the Internet for connectivity. The Internet is notoriously unpredictable, as any Web surfer has observed. One moment data are screaming down the wire, and the next, you are staring at a blank screen waiting, waiting, and waiting. Periodically, the session just hangs or goes away. The Challenge showed that X.500 was sensitive to speed (throughput) problems from the Internet. Also, the mechanism for mapping X.500 onto the Internet TCP/IP protocols (RFC 1006) cannot handle time-outs gracefully. When a time-out occurs, either because a packet of data got lost or the remote host is unavailable, the local DSA or DUA simply hangs for a minute or so, waiting for the connection to come back. This is not so bad at the user level, but when a national-level DSA hangs like this, it can wreak havoc by interrupting dozens, hundreds, or even thousands of directory operations. This

Table 4.1   *Participants in the EMA's Challenge '97*

EMA '97 Show Floor Participants*	Demo Supporters, Basic and User-Level Participants*
BT Networks & Systems	Access One
Communications by PROXY, an ARINC Co.	AOT Consulting
Control Data Systems, Inc.	Applied Information Management Services
Datacraft Australia Pty. Ltd.	Aspect Computing
EDIPORT, Inc.	AT&T
Enterprise Solutions Ltd.	BHP Information Technology
ICL Inc.	Boeing Company
ISOCOR	Boldon James Ltd.
Japanese Electronic Messaging Association	Booz·Allen & Hamilton Inc.
Lotus Development Corp.	BP Oil
MaXware	Brisbane City Council
MITRE Corp.	BT Global Communications
NEXOR	CiTR Pty Ltd.
Siemens Nixdorf Information Systems	Critical Angle Inc.
Soft-Switch Products Division, Lotus Development Corp.	Data Connection Ltd.
	Department of the Treasury
Telstra Corp. Ltd. Australia	Digital Equipment Corp.
Tradegate ECA	Directory Works, Inc.
Unisys Corp.	Entrust Technologies
VPIM Voice Messaging Committee Work Group	FTT Consultants, Inc.
Worldtalk	Getronics Network Services
Zoomit Corp.	GlobalTel Resources, Inc.
	Government of Canada GTIS
	ICI Australia
	Infonet Software Solutions
	Innosoft International
	Isode Ltd.
	New South Wales State Government
	NTT
	Optus Innovations
	Purchasing Australia
	Rapport Communication
	SITA Group
	St. Paul Software
	State of Texas
	University of Salford
	U.S. General Services Administration
	Victorian State Government
	Waterforest Consulting Services

* Participants as of 4/1/97.

was the most significant technical problem identified by the Directory Challenge.

- *Time coordination.* X.500 places a time stamp on operations and most directory servers are set to ignore queries with times that do not make sense—typically more than 15 or 30 seconds different from the DSA's local time. This means that the system clocks on the directory servers must be synchronized with each other. For a widely distributed directory system, this is a real problem. In a production global directory, all directory servers would have to be synchronized with an Internet-based time service that could receive its signal from the National Observatory or the global positioning system. This time coordination problem has not been addressed on an international level.

- *Quality of service.* Each organization participating in the global directory bears some responsibility for ensuring that minimum acceptable limits on server speed and response time, downtime, search size, and administrative limits are being met. Essentially, any X.500 service provider should have to enter into a service-level agreement with its parent DSA operator, specifying the requirements for providing a functional directory service. This is a moot point, because there are no country-level or service provider X.500 "parents."

- *Scalability.* The traditional X.500 tree structure tends to route queries between organizations upward and through the country-level DSAs. This structure places a serious traffic load on the country-level servers. The result is that a nation's interorganizational X.500 traffic in this model would be limited to the bandwidth of the country-level DSA. Originally, this traffic would have been spread across several service providers in the model proposed by the North American Directory Forum (NADF). Any sort of a cooperative service model based on currently available X.500 technology is undefined. There appear to be no economic incentives sufficient to convince the telecomm community to consider creating such a service.

- *Redundancy.* X.500 provides the DISP protocol for shadowing information, but it is unclear how redundant X.500 servers should be implemented in order to provide a survivable national directory capability. It is also unclear how LDAP-enabled products could be configured to access alternate servers should the local LDAP server be unavailable.

4.8.3   General Services Administration (1998)

In support of the government's objectives to easily identify and locate government organizations and personnel, the GSA Chief Information Officer (CIO) developed an X.500 electronic directory. The CIO's objective of having a directory of each GSA staff name, e-mail address, location, and organization on an externally and internally accessible system was achieved through GSA's X.500 directory. (USGold X.500 Case Study: X.500 in the General Services Administration).

As with HHS, the CEMT provided guidance and documentation for the GSA schema and implementation. Two GSA staff and two supporting contractors installed ISOCOR's Global Directory Server (GDS) in five months.

Information from three sources was collected and copied to the X.500 database:

- The e-mail directory provided e-mail addresses for each name.

- The Personnel Information Directory (PID) provided names and their assigned organizations, which are used to determine where in the Directory Information Tree (DIT) the entries should reside.

- The agency online phone book provided the phone number and physical location for each name.

The following important lessons were learned while deploying the X.500 directory:

- The CEMT was critical to the project's success. The CEMT provided foundation documentation and guidance that helped expedite the establishment of the X.500 directory.

- Because customization of the product was required, vendor commitment to the project was essential.

- It was essential to ensure that the data sources for the X.500 directory were accurate, well maintained, and synchronized.

GSA decided that, in the absence of specific security policy to the contrary, they would provide public access to their directory.

4.8.4   Department of Transportation (1999)

In 1995, the Department of Transportation (DOT) began an initiative to improve its e-mail infrastructure. The use of separate, proprietary e-mail systems by the 14 operating administrations under DOT had created e-mail incompatibility. The initiative had the following goals:

- Enable department-wide e-mail communications;

- Enable communication with other government agencies, businesses, industry, and the public using standard protocols (e.g., SMTP/ MIME, X.400, X.500);

- Provide effective security;

- Provide a user-friendly e-mail system;

- Retain and use currently installed e-mail systems;

- Build a highly reliable system.

The Administrative Support Center (TASC) successfully installed and integrated the Control Data Mail*Hub message switch and an X.500 corporate directory. The message switch served nearly all of DOT's e-mail users. The message switch processed mail between several proprietary e-mail systems, SMTP/MIME gateways, and X.400 gateways.

Central to DOT TASC's e-mail improvement plan was the development of a department-wide electronic directory. Nearly all DOT employee e-mail addresses were held in the Mail*Hub X.500 directory. The centralized X.500 directory synchronized e-mail directories among DOT systems. The DOT X.500 directory allowed internal DOT users to exchange messages between e-mail systems and with external Internet and X.400 addresses. As with GSA, all information in the DOT directory was initially publicly available.

DOT TASC learned from other X.500 projects in government and industry, sought advice from outside consultants, and participated in industry forums such as the Electronic Messaging Association prior to beginning this project. During its own X.500 and messaging development efforts, DOT TASC learned a number of useful lessons:

- X.500 technical capabilities are difficult to locate, even within the vendor community. Training internal personnel to augment external sources is very important.

- Because complex configuration of the product was required, vendor commitment to the project was essential.

X.500 succeeded and was accepted at DOT because of a number of important factors:

- X.500 was successful because it closely integrated a mission-critical application (e-mail) that required a department-wide directory.

- Management was committed to providing department-wide e-mail.

- The messaging/X.500 project team solicited input from and coordinated deployment with representatives from all of the DOT administrations.

- The messaging/X.500 project was fee for service, with charges to individual operating administrations based on the size of the administration's user base.

- The messaging/X.500 project used lessons learned from other government programs (e.g., USGold, the Defense Messaging Service), outside consultants, and industry forums.

In 1999, TASC looked at how to integrate the X.500 directory with three other systems to tie together personnel and telephone data with e-mail addresses. This design was also coordinated across the other operating administrations within DOT to acquire buy-in. At the time, a custom scripting solution was thought an optimal solution, since the metadirectory market was not deemed mature. The project did not advance beyond the design phase, however, as preparations for the successful rollover to the year 2000 (Y2K) consumed all available resources.

4.8.5   Federal Aviation Administration (2000)

In late 1999 and early 2000, the Federal Aviation Administration (FAA) engaged TASC, DOT, to perform an analysis of the FAA's current directory environment and make recommendations as to the potential for an FAA-wide directory service. TASC gathered and analyzed requirements, identified and analyzed implementation options, and developed recommendations and business-case data. The general recommendations to the FAA, based on the extensive work TASC had performed in directories over five years, included the following:

- Adopt directories as an agency-wide goal (mandate from the top).

- Admit that existing systems are entrenched (synchronize, do not replace).

- Adopt a long-term view (a phased approach is best).

- Establish a vision statement (need a clear goal to achieve).

- Practice controlled migration (a phased approach is really best and permits buy-in).

- Share information (once again, buy-in is important).

■ Assume ownership of critical issues (for interoperability, some decisions must be made at the top).

4.8.6   Bureau of the Public Debt (2000)

The Bureau of the Public Debt (BPD) maintains information in several internal proprietary directories. As BPD adopts new technologies for developing internal applications, there is a need to ensure that data elements are standard across the bureau. BPD decided to investigate the design and implementation of a metadirectory service to become the publishing point for all common information accessed by any of the internal proprietary directories. At the time, BPD was also in the process of planning a consolidated investor interface, which would possibly take advantage of the new directory structure. The plan included a Web-based system that would allow customers to access securities information and transaction history. The critical lesson that BPD learned is the same lesson that almost all organizations learn when they begin to address enterprise or metadirectory design. Without a common, unique key across all databases, consolidation and synchronization are difficult prospects. Another lesson learned is that vendor products tend to focus on the consolidation and synchronization of either databases or directories, but not both. This situation is now rapidly changing.

Bibliography

Achieving an Enterprise-Wide Multi-Purpose Directory Service: Evaluation of X.500 and Recommended Approach for Attribute Population by Personnel and Telephone Systems, Department of Transportation, The Administrative Services Center, 1999.

Detailed Design for a Government-wide Electronic Directory, General Services Administration, Federal Technology Service, Center for Electronic Messaging Technologies, 1996.

Directory Challenge '97 Technical Report, The Electronic Messaging Association, 1997.

Directory Services Design Project: BPD Enterprise Directory Implementation Plan, Department of the Treasury, Bureau of the Public Debt, 2000.

Directory Services Design Project: Enterprise Directory Design, Department of the Treasury, Bureau of the Public Debt, 2000.

Federal Aviation Administration: Directory Services Analysis & Recommendations, Department of Transportation, Transportation Administrative Services Center, 2000.

Federal Government Directory Initiatives, Presentation at EMA 2000 in Boston, Curt Sawyer—Booz·Allen & Hamilton and Martin Smith—U.S. International Trade Commission, 2000.

"Federal Government Directory Initiatives," *EMA Messaging Magazine*, Curt Sawyer—Booz·Allen & Hamilton and Martin Smith—U.S. International Trade Commission, January 2000.

Functional Requirements for the Government-wide Electronic Directory, General Services Administration, Federal Technology Service, Center for Electronic Messaging Technologies, 1996.

Goal Architecture for the Government-wide Electronic Directory, General Services Administration, Federal Technology Service, Center for Electronic Messaging Technologies, 1996.

Government Electronic Directory: Detailed Design, General Services Administration, Federal Technology Service, Center for Electronic Messaging Technologies, 1996.

Strategic Planning Guidance for the Government-wide Directory, General Services Administration, Federal Technology Service, Center for Electronic Messaging Technologies, 1995.

USGold X.500 Case Study: Department of Health and Human Services, General Services Administration, Federal Technology Service, Center for Electronic Messaging Technologies, 1998.

USGold X.500 Case Study: X.500 in the Department of Transportation, General Services Administration, Federal Technology Service, Center for Electronic Messaging Technologies, 1998.

USGold X.500 Case Study: X.500 in the General Services Administration, General Services Administration, Federal Technology Service, Center for Electronic Messaging Technologies, 1998.

5

Trends and Emerging Directory Technologies

by Alexis Bor

5.1 Introduction: how did we get here?

This chapter puts directory technology into a context that lets the reader appreciate the difficult path that had to be taken to get to where we are today. We will explore the current developments, many of which continue to change at a very rapid pace, and try to put them into perspective. Based on these observations, we will then make some educated predictions as to where the technology will lead us over the next decade.

5.1.1 Recent past as predictor of near future

It is important to understand the origins of directory. Early attempts focused on two primary areas: e-mail and network operating system–related information. In the early days of networking, tables were maintained manually to keep track of nodes on the network. Typically, these were in the format of a flat file and system operators were responsible for periodically picking up these files and installing them on their local systems. This was true with many different networks, including IBM's System Network Architecture (SNA), Digital Equipment's DECnet, and what has come to be known today as the Internet.

For example, in DECnet Phase II in the middle of the 1970s, you were limited to 32 nodes on your network. At the time, it was difficult to fathom a network expanding to that size. The cost of circuits was high, network interfaces were also expensive, and there were very few network-enabled applications. Managing network configurations by hand was still possible. By the late 1970s, it was becoming clear that a limit of 32 systems on a single network was inadequate and DECnet Phase III was released. It supported a whopping 255 nodes in a network. Everyone seemed content at the time. Network nodes were assigned a name and an address. System managers usually knew all of the other system managers who were connected on the network. Typically a network administrator would maintain this table, and it would be passed around to each of the systems. At first, this table would be passed around weekly or even less often. However, it was quickly getting to the point where new systems would appear on the network without the knowledge of most people. The most significant factor within corporate networks that made it easy and inexpensive to add machines to a network was the advent of network buses, such as Ethernet. All you had to do was run a cable through your office building and every machine could tap into that cable and make a connection. You no longer had to run circuits between machines. This technological advance created significant pressure on the maximum size of networks.

Digital Equipment Corporation released DECnet Phase IV in response to customer pressure to increase the size of their corporate networks. This release increased the network to 63 areas, each of which could contain 1023 nodes. To solve the table management and distribution issues, Digital built a "copy" function into its network control program that permitted the system manager to copy network tables and have them automatically update the internal configurations of the network software. This was well and good, but a problem arose. These tables were becoming very large and consuming significant amounts of expensive disk space, as well as other valuable system resources, such as memory and CPU. Other proprietary networks, such as IBM's SNA, had similar problems. At the same time, software vendors began to have success in establishing TCP/IP as a recognized protocol within corporate networks. UNIX vendors had an advantage in this area by bundling TCP/IP with the operating system. It was becoming clear to network vendors and users that they were starting to run into scalability problems in maintaining their local network tables.

Initial directories

Initial directories focused on limited areas of functionality: e-mail, network name-to-address resolution, and locating network services, such as printers and file shares. In the first half of the 1980s, e-mail directories were mainframe-based, such as PROFS/OfficeVision, or minicomputer based, such as Digital Equipment Corporation's All-In-1.

Other e-mail users were considered renegade by IT staffs, because they were outside of any corporate control. The majority of these users would communicate within their communities using the Simple Message Transfer Protocol (SMTP) transmitted over TCP/IP or use mail based on a nonsanctioned protocol developed by employees at Digital Equipment Corporation and called Mail-11. As the Digital VAX became popular, Digital made the decision to include the Mail-11 protocol with the VAX/VMS operating system; the client rapidly gained popularity and was referred to as VMSmail, VAXmail, and DECmail. Initially, Mail-11-based messages only ran over networks supporting the DECnet protocol. Eventually, gateways were established between DECnet and TCP/IP, enabling protocol converters to exchange e-mail between Mail-11 and SMTP.

A common characteristic was that these users had to remember the e-mail address of people with whom they desired to communicate. There were no directories available to simplify locating e-mail recipients. Often, people would refer to each other by their e-mail addresses instead of their name. Occasionally you would find department phone lists that contained e-mail addresses. Only the most astute would know how to weave their e-mail from one network to the next.

Mainframe- and minicomputer-based e-mail systems continued to add more and more services. For example, PROFS added a directory service with the name of CALLUP, while All-In-1 used Digital Directory Service (DDS). Most large companies had deployments of both and would levy significant per-user fees to fund the operation of their e-mail systems. These services ended up maintaining directories with current information for each environment, but users had no way of communicating with each other.

Along came a company named Soft*Switch, which built a directory service that would algorithmically convert e-mail addresses from one environment to another, then pass the messages through a gateway. Soft*Switch established an e-mail address that appeared in each of the environments, making it possible to locate someone in the local directory and send that person an e-mail message. Yet, under the covers, this message address would force the message through the gateway to the proper destination.

At the same time, another force was evolving. Many user organizations did not want to invest in the perceived high cost of centralized mainframes and their expensive value-added services, while others had major political differences with the mainframe staffs. To fill this need, LAN messaging became popular. Systems began to roll out, often at the department level, without the knowledge or coordination of other groups. Two of the most popular systems were MSmail from Microsoft and cc:Mail, which later became part of Lotus, then IBM. Each of them had local directory services. Quickly, gateway products became available that would let messages flow between vendor products. Directory information did not flow between systems, however, and remained proprietary.

Initial directory strategic vision

Early in the development of standards-based directories, a vision of a directory service that would be able to link directory objects from around the world was in place. Within a country, servers would connect to service providers or some government agency–sponsored activity that would then provide connectivity to other countries. In the early 1990s, a European research project called the Paradise Project, headed by David Goodman, pushed the technology way beyond the dreams of many. It was able to link servers, mostly located at universities, in 30 countries and provided millions of entries. All that a user application had to do was link to its local directory server, and the protocols would find the requested information, no matter where it was located in the world. The amazing part of this technology was that the user did not have to have any knowledge of the particular server where the actual data were stored.

This development of X.500 led to a vision of a globally connected directory service that would provide information between corporations and other users. In North America, an organization formed by service providers called the NADF, or North American Directory Forum, brought together many X.400 e-mail service providers in the hope of being able to link massive numbers of users together, generating pay-per-message revenue and creating a new revenue stream for directory usage. This effort eventually fell apart, primarily as a result of the massive political pressures from each company, which slowed the process to a crawl and broke all of the early financial models of rapid revenue from such a service. Several years later, I chaired an effort that attempted to revive the NADF as a working group at the Electronic Messaging Association (EMA). The timing of this effort again proved wrong. Many of the participants were visionaries who understood the value and need of such a service, but the industry was still years away from being ready for such a directory. Other efforts, such as Vector Directory Service headed by Bill Lucas, preceded the NADF and made some progress, but eventually lost momentum.

A major problem with early X.500 directories was the difficulty that developers and users had with developing and deploying directory-enabled applications. The early API of choice was XDS, and it often required an experienced programmer two weeks to write a simple directory-enabled application. To make things even worse, it also required the installation of another protocol stack on an already resource-exhausted PC or MAC. Along to the rescue came the Lightweight Directory Access Protocol. Its only requirement on the desktop was a TCP/IP protocol stack that supported a sockets interface, such as WINSOCK. The desktop application

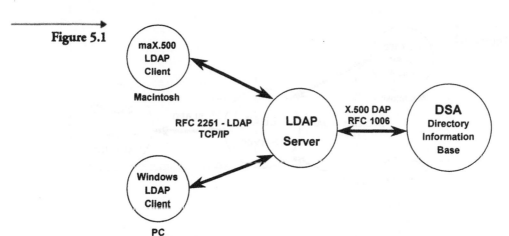

Figure 5.1

would then pass simple commands to a server that would translate the commands into X.500 DAP protocol and pass them on to an X.500 server (Figure 5.1).

The advent of the LDAP interface breathed new life into the struggling directory market. Suddenly, applications were beginning to appear; however, they typically limited themselves to a "White Pages" view. The directory market continued to struggle. With few sales, vendors needed to recoup their costs and maintain a reasonable profit margin. One company that bucked the trend was Control Data (later acquired by Syntegra), which developed a product called Mailhub—an exhaustive set of scripts that would coordinate and synchronize information between many disparate e-mail systems. The complexity of this product resulted in very significant consulting opportunities for Control Data. (In fact, this same business model appears to be currently repeating itself with metadirectories.) Users were seeing the overall price of software products come down. At the same time, many vendors were pricing their products at close to $10 per user entry. It was very difficult for user companies to justify this expense, because they also had to purchase and maintain the computers and software that the directory would run on. Even if a user company would purchase several directory servers, it was unlikely that they would be seen popping up throughout companies or at other trading partners. You rarely saw a situation in which two X.500 servers, communicating via the Directory System Protocol (DSP), were from different vendors. This simplified the interoperability requirements.

At about that time, Tim Howes at the University of Michigan, with others, released a version of an LDAP server that behaved identically to other LDAP servers, except that instead of accessing an X.500 directory using the

Figure 5.2

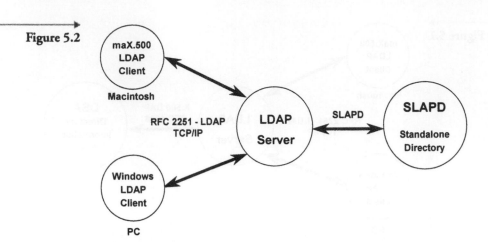

Directory Access Protocol (DAP), it made local database calls. Figure 5.2 demonstrates this new approach. It turned out to be a very simple concept, which separated the protocol from the server. Later in this chapter, we will discuss the long-term impact of the strategy of separating directory query protocol from directory servers.

Suddenly, LDAP ushered in a new era of directory servers. Users were able to develop LDAP-compliant applications and run them against freely available, standalone LDAP servers. Many user companies took the approach that if this technology became popular, they would invest in production quality products and retrofit their environment. The dream of standards-based directories becoming commonplace in enterprises had taken its first major step forward.

This vision of widespread directories worked well for Novell and its NetWare Directory Service (NDS). By the mid-1990s, the vast majority of commercial directory servers were NDS and deployed at the department level, typically bypassing the CIO and high-level budgeting and planning phases. Another phenomenon was raging at the same time. The World Wide Web (Web) had become commonplace. Users had learned how to download free copies of Web browsers from around the Internet. Probably the most popular was NCSA Mosaic. In April 1993, NCSA Mosaic, the first user-friendly Web browser, was released. It was developed at the National Center for Supercomputing Applications at the University of Illinois in Urbana-Champaign. At the time, there were about 200 Web servers in the world. By 1994 Mosaic had several million users and had effectively given birth to the dot.com industry that was projected to be worth $1 trillion by 2001. Soon, a new startup company, called Netscape Communications, hired away key people and became known as a premier Web browser company. With their early successes, Netscape understood the dream and potential of directory and decided that it should go after the directory market. Netscape hired the key people developing LDAP at the University of Michigan, headed by Tim Howes, and ported the public domain LDAP software to a commercial grade. As the product got closer to shipping, Netscape, the hottest dot.com, easily found 40 vendors to release a joint press release announcing their full support of LDAP. Finally, on April 22, 1996, the press release had given directories the jumpstart that they needed.

Unfortunately, many of the key features of X.500 were falling by the wayside as low-cost products were rushed to market. Lost in the fray were the X.500 products' strongest points: standards-based access controls and replication, as well as server-to-server protocols. Even worse, many of the X.500 vendors failed to communicate to the user community of the value of these features. In hindsight, perhaps the worst marketing flaw was not to join forces within the X.500 community to demonstrate how a single X.500 server and an LDAP server cannot be differentiated by an application. Figure 5.3 shows how applications do not have a sense of which specific product is being used.

In 1997, the EMA had a Directory Challenge where X.500 servers located all over the world connected over the Internet and demonstrated that a directory infrastructure was possible with off-the-shelf products. Many of the vendors, consultants, and users involved, however, were unable to find a place for LDAP servers in this demonstration. At the same time, quietly, in Redmond, Washington, Microsoft was busily developing Active Directory, which would offer LDAP applications a directory service incor-

Figure 5.3

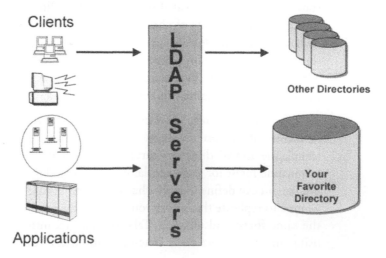

porated into the operating system, while recognizing the value of a common access control, replication, and server-to-server protocols. Microsoft gambled that it could incorporate X.500-like features in a proprietary manner and, yet, establish itself as a dominant force in the directory market. In the past, Novell was very successful with this. A similar attempt by Sun has yet to show any impact on the market, probably because often there is no pressing requirement to migrate an enterprise to a directory infrastructure. At the same time, Windows 2000 requires Active Directory, and the evolution of Microsoft Exchange 2000 requires Active Directory as well. This is enough to cause most enterprises to pursue migration from Windows NTv4 to Windows 2000 urgently. LDAP again is benefiting from vendor vision.

Current directory developments

Directory activity continues to move forward. It is now clear to most observers that directory technology is an essential infrastructure component. A number of recent directory developments have solidified this belief. The most significant development is the integration of Active Directory with Windows 2000. The impact on computing is of astronomical proportions. Practically every corporation has deployed an enterprise directory or is in the final stages of planning an enterprise-wide deployment.

Through personal experience over the past few years, it is clear to me that Active Directory is very capable of acting as a general-purpose directory for many applications. To this point, however, Microsoft has not been willing to market Active Directory as a general-purpose directory. To make things even more confusing, the normal Microsoft pundits also make strong statements against the capabilities of Active Directory, typically pointing out that their products of choice are better, in their opinion. This chapter will not make any specific comparisons between products, since product selection should take into account much more than a few technical factors. Many enterprise-specific business and technical factors need to be discussed to make such a proclamation, which would not apply to everyone.

It is worth looking, however, at a few points that would identify some situations of interest to many. Active Directory is capable of creating a standalone LDAP directory server. This would mean creating a separate standalone forest for each standalone directory. The schema is very extensible, so you can define exactly what you want to hold in the directory. If you wanted to replicate the server, you would only need another server joined in the same forest and domain. Take special precaution creating user entries using the user object class. When you add users, you end up applying security principles, and it takes some time to complete all of the security requirements that Windows 2000 places on them. Using a different object class, such as `contact`, easily solves this. This makes Active Directory a viable standalone LDAP server at a price that is hard to beat—typically pennies per entry versus dollars per entry as with most other products.

This will force a consolidation of the directory-server market over the next few years. Directory vendors will have to look at ways to play together to be able to gain market share. This should result in some interesting market opportunities that will benefit users. The first area of evolution will be a major shift in how directories are used. In the early 1990s, I headed up an industry effort with an organization called the XAPIA, which developed a data exchange format in which vendors were able to exchange data in a common format. Some vendors did some preliminary testing with it and were convinced that it was a powerful idea. With the popularity of XML, many applications developers have begun to recognize the value of a common language for exchanging information. In the directory arena, the specific XML extension is called Directory Services Markup Language, or DSML. The vast majority of directory vendors support it and are making a significant effort to make it a success. Products have begun to intermix LDAP and DSML, and this trend should continue with most directory servers.

The next area of evolution will be the coming of age of metadirectories. Initially, metadirectories were a solution to a common need for synchronizing data for different sources, such as databases and directories. However, we are now seeing vendors such as MetaMerge bring forward new concepts that will enable live connections to a wide variety of information without requiring intermediate storage. It is possible that the next generation of directory servers will be broken into two classes. The first will be focused on high-performance server engines with significant replication and access control capabilities. The second class will be metadirectory engines that perform two classes of service: traditional synchronization, which applies formatting rules and joins disparate sources of information, and high-performance DSML engines, which enable applications to do queries, as well as update information without knowing the underlying data locations and formats.

5.1.2   Components for future directories

There are a number of components that need to be looked at when assessing the future of directories. In this section, we will discuss some of them and what they mean.

First of all, the directory needs to be an enabling tool. It needs to be treated as an infrastructure component that provides the necessary day-to-day information and can be relied upon as a trusted source of information. Common interfaces to the directory must exist. Today, the most common interface to the directory is LDAP. At the same time, DSML is making a rapid rise to prominence as an XML method to access the directory. We call this directory enablement.

Directory enablement covers a number of areas, including the general area of directory-enabled applications where applications are capable of retrieving information from the infrastructure through the use of directory. This is typically done by using various software development tool kits that are available on the market. Some of these include the iPlanet Directory SDK, the Java-based JNDI, and Microsoft's ADSI. The next step is the directory-enabled enterprise. This is the recognition within the enterprise that the directory service is part of the infrastructure and contains information necessary to support a wide variety of services. Then, the next big step is directory-enabled eCommerce, where applications, typically spanning multiple enterprises, are enabled to operate as one, typically using DSML as the method of choice for exchange directory information.

Another key component of the directory framework is information. This includes the modeling of information stored in the directory, defining where the data are coming from and possibly going to. It is critical in this component to identify clearly the specific schema that defines how the information is represented in the directory.

The next component of the framework is how the directory information is distributed between servers. In an X.500 environment, protocols were established that permitted server-to-server operations, thus making the collection of servers appear as a single system to the application. In the haste of establishing LDAP as the "new" directory of choice, the IETF standards process ignored this critical component. Some vendors filled this gap with proprietary mechanisms, such as Novell's NDS or Microsoft's Active Directory, but many other vendors do not acknowledge the importance of server-to-server protocols. Some of the key reasons for server-to-server protocols include the following:

- The ability to manage and plan the response capacity of the directory service;
- A greater level of accuracy;
- A single access control structure;

- A level of trust between servers, especially when they hold different naming contexts within the enterprise;

- The ability to enforce unique distinguished names throughout the directory.

The future of directory depends on the ability to scale and support a very wide variety of information.

5.2   Prevailing directory trends

Metadirectories were first defined by the Burton Group in a paper in 1995, which has since spurred a whole industry of tools, debate, and consulting opportunities. In the late 1980s, many companies began to tackle the issue of how to populate their e-mail directories with phone numbers, mailstops, organizational information, and e-mail addresses from other e-mail systems. At that time, there were no tools available to perform such a task. Companies typically started projects that would identify sources of data and develop custom code and processes that would synchronize data between the various sources. Over time this technique was called "Directory Synchronization." It was common during meetings of the EMA that users would get together and compare notes on how they were doing this directory synchronization. A common theme at the time was that no two efforts were the same, and, thus, it would be very difficult to build a generic tool. At the time, I was chair of the EMA Directory Committee and there was an outcry for a standardized definition of an exchange format for directory information. Through an industry organization called the XAPIA, I helped start a committee that I ended up chairing (that is what happens when you volunteer a new thought and are enthusiastic about it) called the XAPIA Directory Synchronization Committee. The work tackled the thorny issues of finding common ways to represent and exchange data. The final work was adopted by a few vendors, with one actually releasing the capability in a tool kit. This work did prove, however, that it was possible to define an interchange format for directory information. Figure 5.4 shows how the vision of metadirectory will give applications a level of abstraction.

The next effort in this space was the Lightweight Directory Interchange Format (LDIF). It was first released as an Internet draft and is currently known as RFC 2849. It is widely used today as an exchange format for directory information. It is simpler in design than the XAPIA effort, but bulkier in size.

Figure 5.4

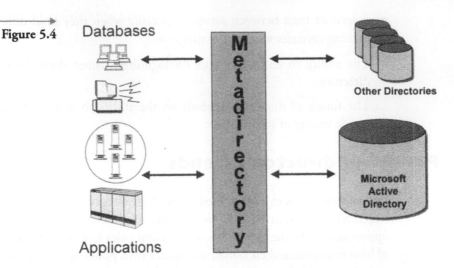

Databases

Applications

The next generation for the exchange of directory data that has started to get everyone's attention is DSML. Efforts are currently under way to standardize the exchange format. Eventually, you should see LDAP servers also accepting and returning directory data in an XML format.

After the Burton Group published their metadirectory paper, vendors began to embrace the concept as a possible way to boost sales in a slow-moving directory market. In the summer of 1997, I experienced an incredible marketing event. I was at the EMA Annual Conference in Philadelphia. On the exhibit floor, it seemed that every booth that had some flavor of directory product had focused in on the term "metadirectory." At first I was shocked that so many new products had come to market so fast in this time. I started going around the various exhibit booths and asked to see what they had in metadirectory products. One after another was quick to point out the great features of metadirectory and how their products played in this arena.

But, upon further review, I found that not a single vendor had released a new version of a product that added metadirectory functionality. No version numbers had changed. This seemed like a major fraud to me. The vendors were simply showing off their directory synchronization techniques—often nothing more than a long-existing bulkload tool. How could this be happening?

It turned out that most companies did not understand the potential of managing many disparate sources of data in a cohesive directory service. Most vendors, or at least their marketing teams, did not understand that people information was just a minor subset of the kind of information that you would want to keep in the directory. Everyone was stuck in a paradigm that should have only been a stepping stone to further and more exciting uses of the directory.

Finally, in the past few years, a number of "true" metadirectory products have hit the market. The best known as called VIA by a Toronto, Canada–based company named Zoomit. Another was developed by a company in Santa Monica, California, called ISOCOR. Just as ISOCOR started to gain momentum, it was purchased by Critical Path, and somehow it has since disappeared off of most people's radars. The importance of metadirectory, howver, has not been lost. In June 1999, Microsoft purchased Zoomit. It appeared that Microsoft understood that for Active Directory to be successful, people would want to populate it with all kinds of information. It was easier to buy a tool and repackage it than to develop one from scratch. Also, the brain trust of Zoomit had many exciting ideas that Microsoft could take advantage of in future releases of Active Directory. The current releases of the VIA product have been renamed to Microsoft Metadirectory Services (MMS). It has become a significant consulting tool for Microsoft and its partners in delivering the needed care and feeding of Active Directory.

At the same time, a number of competitors to MMS are trying to make it into the market. They include companies such as Access360, Radiant-Logic, and MetaMerge. Other, more established companies, have offerings as well, such as iPlanet, Siemens, and Syntegra (formally Control Data Systems). MetaMerge appears to have come together with a serious contender to MMS. MetaMerge performs many of the functions that MMS does, but is also much more lightweight and can be easily extended by the use of many different scripting and programming languages.

We should see a lot of jockeying for position in this marketplace over the next few years as each of the vendors tries to catch up to the others. Companies such as MetaMerge appear to be heading in a very interesting direction. It believes that it can abstract directory services up one level and, thus, provide a metadirectory bus that connects any kind of datastore with a set of standard interfaces. If MetaMerge succeeds, the boundary between databases and directories will become totally blurred. Recently, I worked on a similar strategy where a messaging middleware bus was used to queue generic operations to a back end datastore, and it successfully abstracted database and directory interfaces from the applications, making it possible to interchange and integrate whatever datastores are available in specific situations.

5.2.1 Directories and data mining

When users start to take seriously the capabilities that directories bring to the table, they start to look for information to put into them. For example, human resources has certain useful information, while missing other data such as mailstops and telephone numbers. User companies go through a process to find the information to make the directory more useful. Unfortunately, this information is often scattered across various sources and inconsistent in format.

Metadirectories often come to the user's rescue. Disparate sources of data can easily be reformatted and joined with other related information to form a consistent directory. It is important to realize, however, that there are many other sources missing some of these data and that would like to be updated. For example, it is not unusual for human resources to want to have current telephone and e-mail contact information available. A metadirectory product can easily supply this information. The actual exchange of data does not have to be a specially formatted file that is imported by the HR database. Most metadirectory products today have the ability to make direct connections to remote databases and can easily update the information automatically.

More important in the mining process is the decision making that must occur. Decisions on data sourcing for every attribute must be in place. For example, when an Exchange user changes some piece of information, such as his or her title, it may be appropriate for the metadirectory tool to restore the title field to the value that is stored in the HR database. These decisions are critical for the smooth operation of the directory service.

5.2.2 Implementing today's directories

Wireless technology for data communications is now an accepted means of connecting devices to networks. For example, wireless LANS now enjoy 11-megabit transmission rates. For all intents and purposes, devices connected with this technology are peers to tethered devices. However, owing to their mobile nature, their support environment continues to change. For example, if you move from one end of a building to the other end, it is likely that your closest printer has also changed. A directory service becomes necessary to help locate the connection information for the new printer.

Early efforts are under way to develop strategies for storing device information in the directory and, as a mobile device moves, to locate support devices based on location and other parameters. This operation must be transparent to the user.

Recently, a number of handheld devices, such as the Compaq IPAQ, support the same 11-megabit wireless standard and are appearing in many companies as organizer tools that have direct access to people's mailboxes and even give users the ability to surf the Web. Another class of devices operates in a wide area. These devices do not enjoy the 11-megabit speed offered by the wireless LAN technology and must rely on slower links. Currently, there are industry efforts underway looking at integrating directory services.

The Directory Interoperability Forum and the Mobile Task Forces of The Open Group recently met in Austin, Texas, to map out a strategy to support the directory requirements of mobile computing. As a result of this meeting, additional work will take place that will help vendors pursue a common strategy.

5.2.3   Standardizing today's directories

In this section, we will explore strategic directions in the standards-based directory arena with particular emphasis on LDAP and XML.

LDAP: a key building block

The LDAP was founded in the early 1990s to solve the problem of getting directory information to the desktop. Then, the dominant desktops were either Apple Macintosh or Microsoft Windows–based systems. Each of these operating systems had severe limitations to the amount of memory available. For example, Windows applications had to fit into 64 K of memory. This meant that if you wanted to add an X.500 directory client to your desktop, you had to fit a new protocol stack and other software into the already crowded memory. People were already struggling on trying to figure out how to put TCP/IP or DECnet on those desktops and really had no room or interest in using up any existing memory for a directory application.

Prior to LDAP, the only way that any desktop application could retrieve directory information was to use an API called XDS (X/Open Directory Service). After submitting the work to the IEEE, the documentation for it was a couple of inches thick and it often took people two weeks to figure out how to use it. Recognizing this, a group of people got together to develop a simple sockets-based interface running on TCP/IP that would support a very limited set of operations. This interface on the desktop was very lightweight. It would typically communicate with a server that ran on a UNIX system. The server would receive requests from the desktop and translate them into X.500 operations and issue the X.500 call on behalf of the desktop user. This worked very smoothly and was surprisingly very fast.

While I was doing research and development work at Boeing with directory in 1991, I configured a Sun Sparcstation II to run an LDAP server. The Sun then passed the LDAP request to the X.500 server that was holding up to 100,000 entries and hosted a MicroVAX 3800, which then performed the X.500 operation and returned the results back to the Intel 386–based desktop via the LDAP server on the Sun. The entire operation typically took 20 milliseconds, which was incredibly fast considering the systems used.

This was a major milestone in my directory efforts. For the first time, I was able to demonstrate that any desktop throughout the Boeing Company could have access to a directory that contained employee information for everyone in the company. This eliminated the need for someone to connect to PROFS or All-In-1 to find an e-mail address or phone number. This effort helped remove one of the obstacles to deploying LAN-based e-mail solutions. More importantly, it started a movement of placing information in a central repository that any desktop could access with very minimal effort and cost. Applications started to consider using directory instead of negotiating exports from various data sources. The LDAP interface had proven to be incredibly simple to program. We were typically able to build prototypes in two to four hours using this simple interface. This was a major paradigm shift. LDAP continued to evolve.

The next step was to put other types of objects into the directory. As part of the research and development directory project, I added many different types of information, such as glossaries, project management tools support, catalogs, application support, and business processes. The business process object became very interesting to a wide audience and is described in the next few paragraphs.

101 processes

In response to a request from organizations involved with projects that were government sponsored, I was approached with a problem. The government had defined a set of processes for review of the various programs. They consisted of approximately 101 different processes. The management offices maintained a binder listing all of these processes and the focal points for technical, business, and auditing functions. These processes had contacts at various locations across the company, with larger processes having support organizations in nine separate locations. These binders were issued periodically to all of the staff involved in these processes, as well as to the government representatives. I designed a technique to store and retrieve this information and extended the directory schema to support it. This was at a time when the Web was still in its infancy, but I had long since realized the value of a common interface so that I could avoid writing, installing, and maintaining separate desktops. We developed a Web-based interface to the directory that provided custom forms and tables that would display the 101 processes. A user could search on various pieces of information, such as the name of the process, description, location, or members.

It turned out that the processes themselves were very static, but information about people kept changing. Everything from phone numbers, locations, or e-mail addresses would change. This application took advantage of the automated update process in place that maintained people information. Thus, if someone had changed his or her name, phone number, or other information, the change would automatically appear in this application as well. This entire application was specified, designed, implemented, demonstrated, and released in a period of two weeks. The biggest challenge was locating and transferring the process definition data from the PC database that it was located in to the directory. Once again, the simplicity of the Web interface, as well as the simple LDAP interface, made it possible to replace a process that was perceived as flawed with an easy-to-use and accurate tool.

LDAP's deficiencies

LDAP is a wonderful access protocol for directory. Many products have placed an LDAP interface in front of their products. Even Exchange 5.5 had an LDAP interface. A major shortcoming to LDAP, however, is the lack of distribution protocols. If information is not found in an LDAP-based directory, the application is typically returned a referral if the server knows where the data are. The application is then responsible for binding to the other directory to get the data. This is fine if you can get the data that you need via an anonymous authentication. However, if you must authenticate, then you most likely do not have credentials in this directory to get to the data. In addition, access controls are based on user identification, and without this authentication, access controls become useless. Even worse, most vendors have implemented proprietary access controls, which makes replication between vendor products useless.

XML and directories

The eXtensible Markup Language (XML) has gained widespread acceptance as a common method for representing and exchanging information within applications. XML enjoys the notoriety of having many hundreds of extensions. One such extension is the Directory Services Markup Language (DSML). It was developed under the auspices of OASIS (http://www.oasis-open.org). The initial version of DSML, version 1.0, was very limited in functionality but initiated discussions within the directory and Web-based applications communities. With prodding from the Directory Interoperability Forum (DIF) at the Open Group Conference in July of 2001, major momentum for continued extensions was generated. In a joint meeting between the OASIS DSML working group and the DIF, close to 30 industry experts began the review process and development of DSML 2.0. This included five separate proposals for the next version of DSML from Novell, Microsoft, iPlanet, Verisign, and Access360.

The industry experts displayed exceptional levels of cooperation and, as a result, DSMLv2 was put on a fast track with a very aggressive ten-week schedule for completion, adding the majority of LDAP operations as defined in RFC 2251. This will now make it possible to perform all LDAP operations (search, add, modify, delete) using XML. Perhaps the most significant result of this effort is the recognition of the importance of not modifying or creating new protocol requirements in the existing series of LDAP RFCs. Instead, the DSML effort will identify any protocol issues and let the LDAP expert group at the IETF facilitate changes, as appropriate. As a result, vendors will be able to develop the necessary code to support DSML rapidly, since it is fundamentally a straightforward mapping to their existing LDAP operations and will result in very rapid release of DSML versions, as more features are added.

The impact of this is tremendous. Web-based applications will be able to leverage LDAP-enabled directories. With the help of the DIF, interoperability tests will provide a vehicle for LDAP servers to verify their ability to execute XML-based operations, while applications will be able to validate their applications as capable of successfully operating against any LDAP certified directory. Also, XML could become the format and method of choice for loading and unloading information from directories, as well as exchanging information with metadirectory servers.

Additional directory standards

The Lightweight Directory Interchange Format (LDIF) as defined by RFC 2849 is the current format of choice for the import and export of directory data. Unfortunately, it suffers from inconsistencies of implementation between directory vendors and often presents challenges for users who try to move directory data in this format from one vendor to another vendor. The recent developments with DSML are expected to replace the use of LDIF. This evolution will be accelerated by the rapid emergence of metadirectories as a tool for the synchronization and exchange of information between data sources, such as databases and directories.

5.3   Today's directory deficiencies

There are numerous reasons why directories have not been deployed as rapidly as many anticipated, despite the availability of directory products for over ten years. This section will explore some of the obstacles and what is being done about them.

The evolution of directory had specific focuses by the various directory vendors. Some vendors focused on building general-purpose directories. X.500 directories focused on servers that needed to cooperate with each other. This required cooperation between vendors in developing communication protocol standards that allowed the servers to communicate with each other, manage access control between each other, and replicate information between servers, easily intermixing vendor products while assuring transparency to the end user. In addition, vendors needed to develop common interpretations of those standards to assure interoperability. This was done primarily through work hosted at the National Institute of Standards and Technology (NIST), an organization that is part of the U. S. Department of Commerce. This effort was called the OSI Implementers Workshop (OIW).

In the early 1990s, a new access method to X.500 was defined, called the LDAP, which made it possible for applications to communicate with directory servers without the need for adding an additional protocol stack, OSI, or having to program a very complex set of APIs called XDS. Over time, people began to realize that it was not necessary to put an X.500 server behind the LDAP server. As long as the client application could issue LDAP commands and get the responses that it expected, it would not be able to tell the difference between an X.500 server or some other datastore, such as a database. The first implementation of this was spearheaded by Tim Howes at the University of Michigan and the backed server was called Stand-Alone LDAP server (SLAPD). Most early LDAP-based servers were focused on single-server solutions that did not require any communication with other servers. From a technical perspective, this freed the implementation from worry about the many issues of distributed servers. From a marketing standpoint, it made it possible to sell many copies of the software to various departments at a company without the involvement of the senior IT management or the CIO. The price was typically low enough that a department manager had signature authority and could easily find ways to get around any procurement requirements. This method of establishing market share had already proved very successful for Novell. In fact, Novell's directory product was able to dominate the directory market strongly with NDS with estimates of over 85 percent of deployed directory servers being supplied by Novell. Now LDAP vendors were on the same path. Netscape, seeing an opportunity there, was able to hire some of the key developers of LDAP from the University of Michigan.—namely, Tim Howes, who became the chief architect at Netscape. Other members of the team, including Mark Smith, also joined Netscape. Suddenly, Netscape had a well-known and respected directory team. They took the publicly available source code from the University of Michigan, as well as the knowledge of the developers, and produced the Netscape Directory Server. This made it possible for corporations to purchase a supportable LDAP product, while helping establish Netscape as much more than a browser company.

Then, on April 22, 1996, flying high and appearing to be making significant market inroads into Microsoft's traditional customer base, Netscape signed up 40 companies to issue a joint press release declaring that they would fully support LDAP and integrate it into their products. In the subsequent weeks and months, many more vendors stepped up and announced their support for LDAP. In fact, Microsoft announced that it was adding LDAP access to Exchange, and Novell announced that it would release an LDAP interface to NDS. At this point it became clear that LDAP was becoming a force to reckon with in the marketplace. A number of Internet LDAP directories came online, and e-mail clients started to support accessing address books using LDAP optionally. Many e-mail vendors were concerned that users would first migrate to an LDAP address book directory from a competitor and eventually continue that migration away from their messaging product. Vendors ended up building clients that were LDAP capable, but at the same time increased the address book performance and features within their messaging products to avoid erosion of their market share. These LDAP directories were special-purpose directories typically incapable of extending their schemas to support additional customer needs or of supporting the various syntaxes that were generally available with general-purpose directories.

Microsoft Exchange 2000 has taken the step to break away from a proprietary e-mail directory to using Active Directory, which is shared by other applications. Other e-mail systems, such as iPlanet's messaging product, have always relied on an LDAP server for their directory store. The implications of this are significant. The same directory is providing e-mail services and network operating system services, such as login, print, and file sharing, and serving as a source of data for white pages and other directory applications.

Directories can be broken down into several categories:

- General purpose;
- Specific purpose;
- Hybrid of both.

A general-purpose directory is not focused on any specific application. It provides general-purpose capabilities. A specific-purpose directory is focused on a specific technology or vendor product. Examples of these are e-mail servers. They typically have a very specific database engine underneath the covers. During the last period of development, vendors typically expend a significant amount of energy improving the underlying database performance. This results in much better performance of the messaging product, but typically at the price of degrading general-purpose performance or functionality. Another example of a specific-purpose directory is one used in support of a network operating system. This directory would provide good performance for functions such as locating printers or file shares but would be very limited in providing general-purpose services. Finally, a hybrid directory has its origins in the network or application environment but over time extends itself to support all applications. Two examples of this are Novell's NDS and Microsoft's Active Directory. Both have evolved from very special-purpose directories to ones that provide reasonable performance as general-purpose directories.

5.4 Directory incompatibility

Many of the directories currently on the market have evolved in the era after the Netscape joint press release that announced 40 vendors working toward a common goal. The good news was that there was sudden competition between vendors to develop great products and directory-enabled applications. The bad news was that this competition forced vendors to get to market quickly, which in turn forced each vendor to select protocol features that are included in their products while not coordinating the interpretations of the specifications in a joint fashion. Applications depending on these directories had to decide which vendor's product to choose as a reference. These applications would typically work very well with the chosen product but fail when used against a different vendor.

The Directory Interoperability Forum was created to address this issue. Vendors, often with pressure from their customer bases, have brought together a set of experts that have developed a suite of tests to validate basic operational capabilities. Periodically, a call to all vendors is issued for running these tests. Typically, most of the vendors bring their technical teams together for a common few days of testing, resulting in a certification issued by the Open Group. Directory servers receive a certificate called LDAP 2000, while applications receive certification called Works with LDAP 2000. See http://www.wwldap.org for more information.

Ongoing issues will continue to plague users and vendors. For example, vendors may be defining custom schema definitions that are in direct conflict with each other. One such conflict is the definition of inetOrgPerson, which was developed by Netscape to define a common set of user attributes. The original Internet draft for this definition came out many years before being adopted as an informational Internet RFC. During this time period, most vendors, except for Netscape and a very few others, did not believe that this schema definition would go any further than with Netscape products and it was ignored. Unfortunately, Netscape was very slow in moving it forward. During that time, other vendors have developed similar schema in direct conflict with this schema. It is now very difficult for many vendors to deploy inetOrgPerson, because numerous attributes have similar names with different definitions, including different object identifiers.

In reality, inetOrgPerson object class is inadequate for most user companies and companies still require custom schema extensions to support attributes not covered by this RFC. Unsuspecting companies are often finding themselves fanning the flames of internal differences by mandating this object class within their enterprise directory architecture.

5.5   Directory interoperability

There continues to be significant interest and demand from users for directories that can grow in number, including the number of servers and the number of disparate vendor products.

5.5.1   Interoperability obstacles

It is important to understand the potential roadblocks to deploying directory services. They range from technical issues, design considerations, corporate cultural issues, to the lack of well-established data-management processes within the enterprise.

Technical issues

A number of technical obstacles exist for the successful deployment of directory services. The vision of directory is to be able to retrieve objects of interest without any consideration of who the vendor of the target server is, the location of the directory, or the ownership or management of the server. To achieve this, the following key features are missing from the LDAP technical specifications as defined in the various IETF RFCs:

- A common access control mechanism;

- Distributed operations;

- A replication protocol;

- Knowledge.

A common access control mechanism is needed for numerous reasons. Applications need consistent operation and implementation of rules for vendor-neutral development of code. It is currently very difficult or impossible to have a set of credentials behave the same way from one vendor's directory server to another vendor's directory. In addition, it is impossible to predict behavior when you are replicating from one directory product to another, because the access control rules are not consistent, and the implementations do not understand the foreign specified access control rules. In a large-scale deployment, it is much more efficient to have servers perform referrals to other servers on behalf of the client. This is called chaining. With chaining, you can establish a level of trust between the servers and maintain consistent behavior. In addition, by trusting adjacent servers, it becomes possible to use the same user credentials on each server.

The following technical issues also need to be addressed with the deployment of this technology:

- *Naming.* Every entry in the directory has a unique pointer or name called the distinguished name. For the directory to succeed over the long run, you must iron out your naming design to eliminate duplicate names for entries. With a single directory service, this is avoided by protocol enforcement. With the proliferation of many standalone directory servers within a company, however, it is very likely that multiple servers will have naming contexts with the same name. The implication of this is extreme when there is a lack of protocol between servers. You can expect to receive a referral to another branch of the directory tree and your application will not know which server to locate, which will cause unpredictable results. Except for the simplest case of anonymous access, it is most likely that the user will not have the proper credentials to access the referred directory.

- *Schema.* Schema design is also a significant technical barrier to long-term success. Multiple factors play a role in this. The first is the definition of a common name and format for a specific piece of enterprise-wide information that all line-of-business applications can depend on. This requires coordination and the establishment of an enterprise-wide role of schema czar. The next is the need for data management, including keeping information current and accurate within the directory. This typically involves the deployment of a metadirectory product that enforces a set of rules. In the longer term, the biggest issue becomes the impact of mergers and acquisitions. In this situation, you have two schemas that will most likely have discrepancies and inconsistencies that have to be rapidly resolved.

- *Access control.* For long-term success, a directory must be able to establish a single access control policy for the enterprise and extend it beyond the enterprise. Without this, it becomes very difficult or impossible to establish reliable and secure replication between directory servers. This is especially true when the directory servers are from different vendors and their access control policies do not interoperate. For the long term, the standards bodies need to address this again and the results will most likely be very similar to what X.500 defined many years ago.

- *Interoperability.* A key area for long-term success is the interoperability of applications with directory servers. Any application using standards-based interfaces, such as LDAP or DSML, should expect identical results no matter which vendor product it is accessing. In fact, the application should not even know which product it is using. To achieve this, a voluntary labeling program has been established by the Directory Interoperability Forum (DIF). It consists of holding events where all interested vendors get together and run interoperability test suites. Vendors are able to correct discrepancies and deliver assurances to their customers that they have conformed to the directory specifications.

Nontechnical obstacles

There are also many nontechnical issues in deploying this technology. They are often rooted in the lack of business processes conducive to developing a common data-management strategy. Often, as companies look seriously into deploying directories, they find themselves also experiencing a major culture change. Suddenly they find the excitement of improved business processes moving from just talk to reality.

5.5.2   Metadirectories: panacea or pothole?

One of the questions that we all face when a new technology is rolled out is how long it will be relevant. This especially applies to metadirectories. Many companies have already invested millions of dollars in the synchronization and coordination of data between e-mail systems and various corporate support systems, such as human resources. Much of this has been done using in-house resources and custom code and scripts.

Now companies are faced with migrating their existing processes to a new technology that often requires significant commitments in consulting expenditures to achieve a seemingly similar functionality. The issues that they are facing are legacy systems that have lost their developers while new messaging and directory technologies continue to evolve.

5.5.3   Future directory products: Will the operating systems eliminate the standalone marketplace?

A very provocative question to ponder is where standalone products will go in the future. Many have argued that if directories become embedded within operating systems, standalone products will disappear over time. A parallel to this happened with TCP/IP over the past decade. In the early 1990s, TCP/IP had become a mainstream technology. Most systems would deploy TCP/IP as part of the available communications protocols on the system. The trend to incorporate TCP/IP started with the UNIX operating system. Most vendors offering a flavor of UNIX included a TCP/IP protocol stack as part of the operating system. Companies sprung up that offered TCP/IP stacks for the same UNIX systems but with significant performance improvements. One such company, The Wollongong Group, offered versions of its products for practically every platform, including systems from Digital. It successfully staged an attack on Digital's DECnet protocol. With the help of others, such as TGV (Two Guys and a VAX), TCP/IP became more popular on a Digital VAX system than its proprietary DEC-net protocol stack. In the Windows space, there were three leading TCP/IP implementations. Owing to many factors, each of the implementations suffered various setup and compatibility problems. Many customers began to pressure Microsoft to solve this problem. Eventually, Microsoft decided that TCP/IP should be embedded into the operating system. Even though this impacted a number of vendors, the users were the strong beneficiaries of having TCP/IP work out of the box.

Now, the same question appears to be facing directory vendors. Will the inclusion of standards-based directory protocols reduce the market for standalone directory vendors? With the release of Active Directory by Microsoft and the integration of iPlanet directory technology into Sun operating systems, users have begun to ask this question. Many user companies are just beginning to explore the vast capabilities of a directory. Investigations into the viability of storing objects of all types and sizes are underway. Recently, I developed a prototype of a directory service that enabled thin clients to establish their entire operating environment based on authentication to the directory. Everything from initialization parameters to run-time executables used the directory. Due to the exceptional abilities of these directory servers to maintain caches, actual performance exceeded the use of local disks and provided the ability to centralize system management. If these directory servers are close enough to provide the needed performance and capabilities, then the secondary market for directory servers will have to stay ahead of the feature curve in order to survive. This means that everything from supporting DSML to easily integrating into metadirectory products is essential. These products must exist within an enterprise with total transparency.

It will be some time before operating system vendors will get to the point where the complete variety of directory-enabled applications will be satisfied with operating system–integrated directory servers. In the mean time, standalone directory vendors should be safe for quite some time, but they will have to rapidly embrace metadirectories, so that they can play effectively with operating system–based directories.

About the authors

Nancy Cox is a consultant and author specializing in the field of collaborative computing applications such as directory services, electronic messaging, groupware, workflow, and enterprise resource planning for large organizations. She is the author of over two dozen articles on computer applications in publications such as *Information Week, Network Computing*, and *Network Administrator. Directory Services* is her seventh book. She coauthored the *LAN Times Guide to Multimedia Networking* (Osborne McGraw-Hill, 1995) and the *LAN Times E-Mail Resource Guide* (Osborne McGraw-Hill, 1994). She authored *Building and Managing a Web Services Team* (Van Nostrand Reinhold, 1997) and was the editor of Auerbach's *Handbook of Electronic Messaging* (1998 and 1999 editions) and *Electronic Messaging—Best Practices* (2000 edition). She also served as a board member of the Electronic Messaging Association (1995–1996). She holds a B.S. from the University of Georgia (magna cum laude) and an M.B.A. from the Florida Institute of Technology. Nancy can be reached at NACox@aol.com.

Jan De Clercq is a senior consultant in Compaq's Technology Leadership Group (TLG), focusing on security for Microsoft platforms. Jan has written several Compaq white papers, Windows 2000 magazine articles, and columns for the *Duke Press Security Administrator* monthly newsletter. He's coauthor of the book *Mission-Critical Active Directory* (Digital Press). He has been a speaker at Microsoft conferences, the RSA conference, the ISSE conference, the EMA conference, and the Compaq Technology Symposium. Jan has been involved in several Windows-, security-, and PKI-related projects for large Compaq accounts. Over the last year he has been a trusted advisor on security topics for several large Windows 2000 designs and deployments and large PKI designs. He holds a master's degree in criminology (RUG-Gent) and I. T. (VUB-Brussels), as well as a special degree in telecommunications (ULB-Brussels). Jan is based in Belgium and can be reached at Jan.DeClercq@compaq.com.

Micky Balladelli is a fellow at Avanade Inc., based in France, focusing on Windows 2000 services. He is a speaker at various Microsoft and Windows 2000–related conferences and has worked with several companies on the design of their Windows 2000 infrastructures. He is coauthor of *Building Enterprise Active Directory Services: Notes from the Field* (Microsoft Corporation) and *Mission-Critical Active Directory* (Digital Press). Prior to joining Avanade, Micky spent 16 years at Digital and then Compaq. Micky Balladelli can be reached at mickyb@avanade.com.

Mark W. Foust is an independent consultant. He worked for Novell on some of their largest and most visible accounts, including Wal-Mart, Andersen Consulting, and the Weather Channel. Mark has been privy to one of the NDS source coders for tuning and optimization information. He began his NetWare experience working for Novell's largest customer, SABRE Computer Services (a subsidiary of American Airlines). He has published an AppNote on NetWare 5 security available both in print and on Novell's Web site. He is a Master CNE as well as a Microsoft Certified Engineer. He is the author of *NetWare Administration: NetWare 4.0–6.0*, published by Digital Press. Mark can be reached at mfoust@microsoft.com.

Curtis M. Sawyer has worked in directories at Booz Allen Hamilton for five years. He currently leads support to the Information Dissemination Management project for the Defense Information Systems Agency. Before joining Booz Allen, Curtis was employed for four years by the Defense Intelligence Agency, where he performed UNIX systems administration and integration. He holds a B.S. in computer science from Virginia Tech and an M.S. in computer science from American University. Curt can be reached at curts@acm.org.

Bob Johnson is an associate with the international consulting firm of Booz Allen Hamilton and specializes in electronic directory services and public key infrastructures. He has been involved with several very large directory service implementations within the U.S. government and the private sector, including the Department of Transportation, NASA, IRS, Department of Defense, and others. Before joining Booz Allen, he served as NEXOR's Business Development Manager for North America for three years and was a consultant with Control Data Systems, specializing in electronic messaging, directory systems, and security for several years. Bob can be reached at johnson_robert@bah.com.

Alexis Bor is president and CEO of Directory Works (http://www.directoryworks.com), a consulting firm specializing in directories and related technologies, including architecture, design, deployment, and training. Involved in directory technologies since the 1980s, Alexis is recognized as an industry expert. He has deployed enterprise-wide X.500 directories and has delivered directory consulting to major corporations, including AT&T, Bank of America, Boeing, Charles Schwab, Disney, Dow Chemical, Ford, Hitachi, Intel, Kodak, KPMG, Microsoft, Pfizer, Qualcomm, TRW, University of Iowa, and Virginia Power. He is currently vice-chair of the Directory Interoperability Forum. In the past he has been president of the Business Quality Messaging Forum and chair of the Directories Committee at the Electronic Messaging Association. He has a B.S. in information and computer sciences from the University of California and an M.B.A. in telecommunications management from City University.

Index

Printed and bound by CPI Group (UK) Ltd, Croydon, CR0 4YY

03/10/2024

01040342-0018